Secrets of the world's inspirational women

Zerbanoo Gifford

westland books pvt. ltd.

571 Poonamallee High Road, Kamaraj Bhavan, Aminjikarai, Chennai - 600 029.
I Floor, Praja Bhavan, 53/2 Bull Temple Road, Basavangudi, Bangalore - 560 019.
I Floor, 3-5-1108 Maruthi Complex, Narayanaguda, Hyderabad - 500 029.
Plot No.102, Marol Coop Ind Estate, Marol, Andheri East, Mumbai - 400 059.
F-5 Okhla Industrial Area, Phase-1, Mezzanine Floor, New Delhi - 110 020.

Copyright © text Zerbanoo Gifford 2007

westland edition 2007

All rights reserved. Without limiting the rights under copyright reserved above, no part of this text may be reproduced, stored in or introduced into a retrieval system, or transmitted, in any form or by any means (electronic, mechanical, photocopyint, recording or otherwise), without the prior written permission of the author.

First Published 2007 by Blacker Limited in
conjunction with Phact Publishing.

Blacker Limited, Hillcroft Barn, Coombe Hill Road,
East Grinstead, West Sussex RH19 4LY
www.blackerdesign.co.uk

Design Consultant: Rosalyn Dexter
Design and production: Blacker Limited

Photographs have been supplied by the individual subjects and are reproduced with their kind permission.

ISBN : 978-81-89975-27-2

Cover design: Rubicon

Printed at
Saibonds Print Systems Pvt. Ltd., Chennai 600 094.
e.mail : saiprints@saimail.com

Published by
westland books pvt. ltd.
571, Poonamallee High Road, Aminjikarai, Chennai - 600 029.
e-mail : ewb@ewbpl.com

For my darling Map

I am sorry I never learnt to spell your beautiful Persian name Maperviz. Of course, the meaning 'first star of the night' is very poetic and worthy of one as heavenly as you, but Map too has a practical ring. In fact my inability to spell your name beyond MAP when I was young led to your name change. When people change their names, they take on a new life. I don't know whether I changed your life but you have always been at the heart of mine.

Thank you for being Mummy's best friend.

Thank you for being with us when Daddy died and for reciting our beautiful Zoroastrian prayers to ease his passage into the next life.

Thank you for helping to bring me up. I know I was naughty but it was fun. I love you so much. This book is for you, a little thank you for being my Map.

contents

Thank you — 8

Today's heroines — 10

Just like mother? — 30

Her heart belongs to daddy — 72

Meeting the family — 88

Life's lessons — 106

Men: the surprising secret to a happy life — 148

Pillow talk	178
Answers to their prayers	216
What's love got to do with it?	238
Working girls	262
The f-word	316
The secrets of success	338
Sisters are doing it for each other	378
A galaxy of stars	392

Thank you

To everyone who plays the National Lottery. Thank you for transforming my life. This book was made possible by a NESTA (National Endowment for Science, Technology and the Arts) Fellowship, and for those who don't know, NESTA receives its funding from the National Lottery Good Causes. I hope you will buy, borrow and not steal this book, and enjoy reading about the lives and the secrets of the World's Inspirational Women.

Loving thanks to Venu Dhupa whom I first met a lifetime ago when she was working at the National Theatre in London. Venu came to see me while I was helping to set up Charities Aid Foundation India. I gave Venu advice on fundraising and some practical help. Who would have thought that years later our lives would be reconnected at NESTA. Venu has now advised me and been more than helpful. She made my Fellowship an extraordinary experience. There is no doubt that 'gratitude is a memory of the heart'.

To Richard for the British title of this book, *Confessions to a Serial Womaniser*, and for staying happily married to a 'serial womaniser'. To quote Dame Marjorie Scardino, when talking about her own partner, *'What more can I say, than you are an absolutely perfect husband'*.

Thank you to Mark for patiently explaining to his mother that we have to learn to trust in the higher direction as only God sees the bigger picture.

To Alex for encouraging his Mum and his continued interest in, what he calls, the 'Extraordinary League of Women'.

Thanks to Mummy for being there for me. Thanks to Genie for being a super sister and Rustom and Naswan for being great brothers.

Thanks to Marie and Louise for feeding me with Italian delicacies and telling me to relax when I was writing these 'Confessions' in Menton.

Thanks to Yasy for loving me and taking care of me always.

To Patsy Robertson for her guidance and to Carole Stone for her support and to GK Noon for his generosity. To Owen for masterminding a world-wide-web-of-women – **www.asha-foundation.org/women**.

Alison, Daisy, Jeroo, Jessica, Mitra, Ruth and Shireen for their advice and practical help. Special thanks to Rosalyn Dexter for using her creative gifts to lay out the book and a thank you to Simon Blacker for translating her genius and adding his with good humour.

Thank you to Kusoom for keeping me focused and for all her kindness, and to Elwyn for eating, shooting and leaving, long before it became fashionable.

To Jonathan Kestenbaum for his and NESTA's support.

To Jeroo for the beautiful portraits that graced the National Portrait Gallery in London and the cover of this book.

To Air Chief Marshal Suri for introducing me to some fascinating women, but more for his great sense of humour and to Asha, his better half.

To Roxna Swamy for being my secret heroine.

To Owen Pearson and Khushroo Daruwalla for creating a world-wide web of women

Finally to all the women I met and to everyone who helped make this book possible. Without them the world and especially my life would not be such fun.

Les héroïnes d'aujourd'hui
Сёстры работают ради друг друга
Las heroínas de hoy

Today's heroines

A bird in the hand

There is a Persian story about an arrogant man who called a large crowd to witness his ability to belittle a Sufi Master. He asked the wise man whether a bird in his hand was dead or alive. He thought that if the Sufi says it is alive I will squeeze the life out of the bird and the bird will be dead. If he says it is dead I will release the bird and it will fly away. Cringingly, he said 'Master please tell us all whether the bird I hold in my hand is dead or alive as you know the answer to everything'. The great Sufi Master looked at him and said 'Dead or alive it is in your hands to decide'.

All great souls know that whatever one does in life is ultimately in our own hands. God has given us free will. For those who do not believe in God they still have the individual choice to think good thoughts, speak good words and act with kindness. They also have the choice to be completely stupid and unpleasant.

In the same way, it is in your own hands how you use this book. It can be read from cover to cover, it can be dipped into or it can be used as a self-help manual or even a book of ancient and modern wisdom. It is the collective biography of hundreds of inspirational women throughout the world at the beginning of the new millennium. It is their lives that you hold in your hands.

Today's heroines

This is a book about women who have taken the world on, and made things happen; women who have that captivating beauty and strength of personality that embraces life in all its endless variety; women who have transformed their own lives and the lives of others by their hard work, guts and acts of compassion. This book offers a snapshot of the beginning of a new era, when attitudes and behaviour towards women have changed, thanks to the struggles of suffragettes, feminists and enlightened men. This is not to deny that there are still women all over the world in rich and poor countries who have difficult lives and have to struggle for survival. But this is not a book about anger; it is a book about admiration. It is a celebration of women's achievements and their wisdom. It tells of inspirational women, their experiences and views on their formative years, their strategies for tackling life's obstacles, and their noble ideals. The pages of this book reveal their secrets on how to advance in the workplace, maintain a loving relationship, and develop a contented outlook on life.

My listening gave me insight into a quiet revolution that is helping to transform women's lives globally. It is true that gender equality remains a distant dream and women's participation and representation still clearly lags behind men. Despite years of resolutions, revolutions and revelations, women are behind men in every sphere of policy-making, particularly in global forums. Their voice is seldom heard but this does not mean they are silent.

I shared so many remarkable stories that have shaped women's lives and was spellbound by their amazing courage and zeal for life. These are today's heroines. They come from every part of the world. They have different names for God, they speak different languages, they live their lives by different rules, but they are all truly great women.

Collective sensibility

This book tells of my encounters with remarkable women from all walks of life and all parts of the globe. It gathers together the life experiences, reflections and hopes of almost 300 women with whom I was lucky enough to engage during the two years I spent researching the achievements and attitudes of women at the beginning of the new millennium. It offers insights into the individual lives of these women and demonstrates how the qualities that made them admirable are often surprising. They were not selfish; rather, it was their sweetness of being, their ability to understand their duties to others and to act responsibly that made them so attractive and inspiring. They shared their blessings of knowledge, skills, resources and love. I met women who had opened the doors to the arts, sciences, spirituality, the professions, and the worlds of commerce and industry, during the last century and many who have walked confidently through those doors more recently.

I was interested to know whether women doctors and directors, politicians and poets, scientists and heads of corporations and charities, could come together to make a positive impact in the twenty-first century. I was pleasantly surprised. Many women were already actively involved in making the world a fairer and kinder place. Their collective power is testimony to their warmth, their worth and their wisdom. It has not been possible to represent hundreds of women's lives fully or equally. Rather, these pages give a flavour of their personalities, ideas and achievements. The quotations that I have chosen from individuals are those that echo the collective sensibility.

During my odyssey I realized there is an urgency to hurry history; there needs to be more investment in women's skills and more opportunities for leadership especially among the young. More women must be elected at every level of public participation, in their neighbourhoods, schools, and workplaces. Today women have economic power as consumers, political power as voters, cultural power as tolerant citizens, ecological power as conservationists, as well as social power as mothers and workers. Collectively, they can shift the balance of representation and bring forward a new agenda of true equality.

The wisdom of the universe

There are over six billion human beings in the world, and yet, however widely you travel, you meet just a few special people.

It became clear why I met each woman. This fact reminded me of a story told by a dear friend, Princess **Usha Devi Rathore** of the royal family of Burdwan. The story was about a Maharaja who might have even been a relative. This particular Maharaja was very irritated with his clever chief minister who always said 'everything was for the best'. One day the Maharaja cut his hand and when the chief minister said, 'It was fine,' the Maharaja had him thrown into the dungeon. The Maharaja then went hunting. In the jungles he was captured by a gang of thugs who took him to be sacrificed to the Goddess Kali. The leader of the thugs examined the Maharaja and when he discovered the cut on his hand he was rejected for sacrifice as damaged goods. When the relieved monarch returned to his palace he released the chief minister. He agreed that the latter had been right about the cut on his hand, but asked how his own stay in the dungeon could be something to be thankful for. The chief minister laughed. He pointed out that if he had accompanied his master on the hunt, he would have been the one sacrificed as he was unblemished. So everything that happened in life was always for the best.

So it was for me, it seemed I met no one by accident and everything was for the best. I was introduced to the former Australian television star and charismatic founder of the Interfaith Seminary, the Reverend **Miranda Macpherson**. She looked into my eyes and told me to trust in the wisdom of the universe and I simply did that. I came to appreciate the great sense of philosophical and spiritual acceptance that many of the women were blessed with, whether they handed over to God, the unity of all things or their own passions. I was destined to meet all the women in this book, and you were meant to read about them. Everything they spoke about was to be shared and cherished.

Another encounter I shall never forget is with the artist **Jeroo Roy**. As I walked into her flat I found myself face to face with one of the most arresting paintings I had ever seen; a Botticelli Venus, rising from her shell. This Venus was young, beautiful and wearing a sari, complete with a nasty black eye. I assumed her injury was a result of a punch-up. Apparently not. Jeroo explained that it was a real woman who had been made to swim in the River Ganges by her in-laws in order to purify herself before marriage. The pollution from the sacred river left her blind in one eye and subsequently she was abandoned by her husband and family. Jeroo's painting captured both the social tragedy of the young woman's life and her eternal beauty. Jeroo's social conscience and eye for inner life was a remarkable combination. I knew I had to persuade her to paint a portrait of every woman that I met, to be exhibited around the world, as a visual reminder of the beauty and vitality of all the women I had encountered.

The birth of a womaniser

One evening my true love declared that I must be exhausted meeting so many 'inspirational women'. I had met over three hundred, a different one each day of the year, excluding public holidays. I was cautioned. I would become a serial womaniser if I did not call a halt. It was already too late. *Secrets of the World's Inspirational Women* was conceived that day.

The UK title had the word 'womaniser' in it because throughout history womanisers have been admired for their roguish charm. Casanova, Don Juan and even James Bond never encountered the quality or quantity of talent, from so many countries, cultures and backgrounds that I was blessed to have experienced. I know no man who has encountered a self-confessed goddess, a hugging saint, a scientist who took on the multinationals, a French Resistance heroine who took on the Gestapo, a judge who took on Saddam Hussein, a high flier who was educated by an elephant, a spiritual giantess who danced with Fred Astaire, the original Cosmopolitan Girl, a politician who lives with two Oscars and a princess who is able to touch her nose with her toes.

I became a new kind of womaniser. My pleasures weren't short lived; they were to be savoured for generations to come. It was **Antonia Byatt**, the Director of the Women's Library in London, who had the wisdom and foresight to insist I record my womanising. She realized that in today's 'fast world' people did not write *billets-doux*, in fact they did not write anything apart from text messages. How were future historians ever to know what people really felt? Fortunately all the women I met were generous enough to be honest with their emotions and let me tape our encounters. I was able to receive their precious gifts of candour and time with empathy and respect. I recognized that each woman had a distinct and unique way of seeing and knowing the world and I wanted their words to speak their truth. I did not censor what they told me.

Like so many people these days I did 'google' some of the women I was to meet. On the few occasions I could not find anything, I felt I was going on a true blind date. To make it easier for everyone, there is now a website dedicated to the world's inspirational women. Please do browse **www.asha-foundation.org/women.**

To follow my quest

The astonishing adventure that led to this book began when I was awarded a fellowship by NESTA – the National Endowment for Science, Technology and the Arts. The fellowship programme operates through talent-spotting rather than open application. The exceptional potential of a NESTA Fellowship is the emphasis on self-development and creativity. You are encouraged and trusted to do the right thing for yourself. You are given the time to explore the most productive ways to work. Most importantly you can take risks and try new ways of thinking and being.

Most fellowships demand that you state the outcome before you begin. This immediately curbs creativity and limits the possibilities for finding new ways of working. NESTA is different. It demands you to challenge yourself and expose yourself to the fear of failure. You must learn to be daring and use your imagination in a new context.

I was clear how I wanted to use my Fellowship although I was unclear what the results would be. I wanted to test the idea that the 21st century was to be a women's century, that there was a new enlightenment and confidence amongst women that might change the old dynamics of negative power in the workplace, the family, the nation and even the world. I knew so many thoughtful and magnanimous women throughout the world who craved real change for everyone. I felt that this historical moment was a timely opportunity for women to work together for something kinder and more just. The NESTA Fellowship afforded me the time to spend with women from very many backgrounds, and over sixty countries, to see if there really was a climate of selflessness for courageous and intelligent action.

Given the emphasis NESTA placed on self-development, it may seem strange that I spent so much time with women, trying to analyse and discuss their ideas about life, love and unique legacy. In fact, I allowed the whole process to take over my life. I began by taking comfort in the fact that I would be spending my time talking and writing, two activities I enjoy. However, I soon realized that my role was to develop as a listener and a reader of people. I had mistakenly focused on the outcomes and yet it was the freedom to suspend the result in favour of the process that proved so illuminating. I started to feel more at ease with myself and was able to begin to observe the little things, to understand the subtleties of personalities and make the connections between people and the issues that mattered most to them.

The women I met came from such different walks of life and backgrounds that it gave me a context for understanding myself and the time I had spent in media, politics, and the charity sector. The project made sense of all the contacts and friendships I had cherished and built up over the years. It pulled together all the threads of my life.

My past had certainly been varied and full. I had been engaged in pioneering politics. I had written books and drawn attention to forgotten heroes who had campaigned against the slave trade, and Asian luminaries whose lives were an example of excellence and selfless devotion to others. I had founded a multi-million pound charitable foundation, ASHA, to help engender a climate of social equality and community understanding. I was certainly adaptable and enjoyed new working methods and environments, but the whole point of being daring was to move into the unknown. Few people can do that without some trepidation.

When I started my project in 2004 so many things began to go wrong in my personal life. My father was diagnosed with cancer and I felt powerless to ease his pain. He had always been extremely big hearted; the life and soul of every party. When he was at the last stages of cancer at St Mary's Hospital in London I wanted to be with him to ease his passage into the next world. The evening he died I had a pre-arranged speaking engagement. No one would have thought badly of me if I had cancelled, but even in all his pain my father insisted that, 'the show must go on'. When I returned very late at night, he held my hand and then died. Even on his deathbed, he saw my need to be alive as more important than his death. The most important lesson that I have learnt from this experience was that life should be lived and never postponed. It was a lesson spoken by my dying father and echoed by the remarkable women I met who all cherished life, and refused to be victims.

Rules of attraction

What attracts you to somebody? I really don't know. Maybe the other person makes you feel alive.

I was attracted to those who lived life in the fast lane on full throttle and who had a passion for something greater than themselves which they pursued often at their own expense but for the greater good. They were basically disillusioned with the status quo and wanted to change the guidelines, not just for themselves but for everyone. They loved being women and had no hang-ups about men. They had no fear of life; in fact they embraced it with an unbelievable fervour. I had always been fascinated by people who have overcome and endured hardships, physical disabilities, suffered depressions, lost parents, partners, children, elections, fortunes, homelands, and missed an education. And yet, as the Scottish ballad declares: 'I am hurt, but I am not slain; I'll lay me down and bleed a while. Then I'll rise and fight again'. I love fighters. People who live life brilliantly, who are intelligent, idealistic and independent, have helped shape the world and understand 'the laws of karma', that you reap what you sow and that every thought, word and deed has repercussions for good or evil. Most importantly, they were women who had a magical presence and their lives were memorable and vital.

I too wanted to be alive when I undertook this great adventure. The inimitable American award-winning film producer **Elaine Attias** confided that in Hollywood if someone showed passion the others who had little of that commodity were drawn to them. We both agreed that passion to a cause greater than oneself was captivating. More importantly, passion accompanied by commitment to a grand vision that encountered failures and still never faltered, gripped the imagination. My quest was to meet women of these qualities whose legacy would be timeless but whose impact was timely.

It was unusual, distinctive women who became my inspiration. Chief Executive of India's *Afternoon* newspaper, the discerning and elegant **Farzana Contractor** penetratingly observed that the *'new celebrities'* were often overplayed. She asked *'What are these new celebrities famous for? Isn't it time we rediscovered old values, to be honest with ourselves and set standards to gauge real worth. For God's sake, shouldn't they achieve something in life before they aspire to be famous? It's time to bring back subtlety, class. Time to show reserve, restraint, and time to let someone else praise you'.* I agreed with Farzana. Too many people were trying to promote their 'nothingness'. I wanted to engage with women who made my heart sing and whose lives had made a difference to the world. The groundbreaking scientist **Mae-Wan Ho** also felt that *'the real doers were not very good at promoting themselves because they have more important things to do'.* I had always been fascinated with the valiant 'grassroots warriors', the peace women at Greenham Common, the mothers who had campaigned in Chernobyl, the tribal women who had protected their trees. They were the unsung heroines. I wanted to meet them too.

Elaine Attias

Farzana Contractor

'an inspirational person was somebody you wanted to spend time with, who had a couple of dents and a lot of juice.'

Beverly Payeff-Masey

Beverly Payeff-Masey

Maeve Sherlock

Coomi Kapoor

Mae-Wan Ho

The best chat-up line ever...

I had the best chat-up line ever. 'I would love to put you in my book of the world's inspirational women.' It worked a treat. I charmed my way into chief executives' offices, the United Nations, high security residences, five-star hotel rooms, film sets, editors' newsrooms, the House of Lords, cricket matches and even a palace. I breakfasted with the most amazing women; I dined with them at swanky restaurants, took tea with them, partied with them. They shared their many secrets with me. They did not try to give me a PR 'spin' version of themselves. They were always honest. They understood that the spirit of the project was not to praise or damn individual women, but to consider what women as a whole have experienced, learnt, and tried to change over the last ninety years. In return they gained my respect and gratitude for participation in this unique study of women's experiences, aspirations and insights from around the world.

I sought out the good, the great and the grassroots across disciplines, communities and faiths. From academics to actresses, entrepreneurs to environmentalists, politicians to philanthropists, spiritual giantesses to spirited sportswomen, chairwomen of media empires to directors of international charities and corporations. I had no agenda in mind. I didn't have a single thesis about women that I wanted to prove or a political agenda to follow. I was open to meeting any inspirational woman that caught my fancy along the way. Over a late night dinner in Manhattan, pioneering design architect **Beverly Payeff-Masey** observed that *'an inspirational person was somebody you wanted to spend time with, who had a couple of dents and a lot of juice'.* That sounded perfect!

Throughout my journey I was determined to be open to surprises, to the unexpected, and I was not disappointed. I learnt so much about myself through my interaction with women from so many cultures and countries. I realized that if one is observant everything gives people away. From where they choose to be met, to the clothes they wear, their answer-phone messages, the information and photographs they offer and what makes them laugh.

The former President of the Indian Women's Press Association, the insightful and intellectually honest **Coomi Kapoor**, commented, *'If you have power, fame and money, you've got it made'*. I certainly met many great women who had it made. I also fell for others, like **Maeve Sherlock**, the indomitable Director of The Refugee Council, who observed, *'Success is making a difference to many people's lives, and it's a passionate commitment to something bigger than you, a noble endeavour'*. Certainly changing lives of others, whether through campaigning or just individual compassion is captivating. You may forget what a person looks like and what they have said but you never forget how they made you feel and their kindness. Without exception they all made me feel special.

Connie Jackson, strategy consultant, remembered the words of her African American pastor in Chicago who told his congregation, *'It's important to be successful but more important to be significant'*. Often one doesn't realize how central one is in other people's lives, until it is too late. As **Esther Rantzen**, TV presenter and founder of Childline, so poignantly said, *'Success is how many lives you have impacted on and how many people love you'*.

Today fame is fleeting and particular to a place and time. I have been privileged to spend time with a galaxy of stars, but how many of us can name the world's stars on a clear night? **Kirsten Rausing** is one of the richest and most gutsy women in the world and yet do people in Brazil know she is a renowned horse breeder as well as on the board of Tetra Pak, the Swedish multi-national food packaging company? **Yue-Sai Kan** is considered one of the most influential women in China and her popularity is such that her face is even on a Chinese postage stamp. Yet do Iranians know what she looks like? In England everyone knows the Oscar-winning actress, **Glenda Jackson**, but how many people around the world know she's a British Member of Parliament? If you know anything about the Kurds, you'll have heard of **Zakia Hakki**, but few know that she was the first woman judge in the Middle East and is now a Member of the Iraqi government. The iconic beauty **Madhuri Dixit** is adored by the millions who watch Bollywood movies, but how many Hollywood fans would recognize her? People know about artists, politicians, industrialists and celebrities in their own country, but only a real megastar can cross every boundary. You can count on your fingers the number of women that are known by everyone throughout the world. The Queen of England is a true exception. Mrs Thatcher is still an inspiration to many. The other modern icons, Marilyn Monroe, Princess Diana, and Mother Teresa are dead, but alive in the hearts and minds of millions around the world.

Go with the flow

How did I decide on my inspirational women? The criteria for selection were haphazard, as is life. I was attracted to different aspects of different people.

For me, some women were like magnets, I was drawn to them. I remember being in the United Nations building in New York and going straight up to the German champion of the disabled **Dinah Radtke**, who was sitting in her wheelchair. Something drew me to her. Not everything in life is explainable.

On another occasion I was in a hotel in Hardwar, on the banks of the River Ganges. Suddenly a glorious figure in orange robes walked into the hotel restaurant, followed by an entourage. I had to find out who this woman was and what on earth she was doing surrounded by these happy devotees. I walked straight over to her and said, *'You've caught my eye, I have to go with the flow, are you able to spare an hour for me before I catch the night train to Delhi?'* She looked me straight in the eye and said *'How did you know that my slogan is 'go with the flow?'* One of her disciples jumped up, giving me a seat, and there I was, in a hotel on the other side of the world sitting next to the great **Swamini Kaliji**, the original Californian yogini, founder of TriYoga – an arm of the ancient tradition which integrates Eastern thought and Western tradition and now flourishes across the globe.

She spoke to me with her fingers, which were spontaneously linking, interlinking, and generally mesmerizing me. Having only a limited finger vocabulary, normally reserved for irritating individuals, I was at first confused but I learnt that before language, feelings formed into finger gestures called 'Mudras', an important part in the religious practices of Buddhist and Hindu rituals. The Prayer Mudra, with hands together at the heart, symbolizes worship for the Christians.

Neither Swamini nor Dinah spoke in just conventional ways. Dinah needed a voice amplifier and Swamini spoke with her hands as well as her eyes and mouth. The spiritual giantess **Phyllis Krystal** had explained that one of the secrets of life is to listen to others with 'loving ears'. Of course it was fortunate that I was an English speaker as, wherever I went, nearly everyone spoke in English, even if it was faltering. It was only in France that English was still resisted.

In Paris, I had a springtime date with the late French Resistance heroine, **Lucie Aubrac**. *'Great women are physically compelling,'* she said in French, and in her mid-nineties Lucie was formidable in both languages — the slightly intimidated English version and the truly fantastic French one! It soon became clear how Lucie was able to persuade the chief Nazi officer to agree to her request to marry her lover who was being tortured at Gestapo headquarters. She convinced the officer of the importance of her marriage so that the child she was carrying would have a named father on the birth certificate. It was during the marriage registration that others in the French Resistance were able to organize an escape for Raymond, her Jewish husband. Her exploits have been made into an award-winning film, simply called *Lucie Aubrac*.

As my travels continued around the world, I realized I had reached my peak in the town of my birth, Kolkata, formerly Calcutta, which I had not visited since my youth. It was here that I became the object of fascination. Word had circulated that someone was arriving who was seeking out the world's most bewitching women. I landed exhausted at the airport and was whisked through the traffic to a press conference at the family mansion of the art collector and philanthropist **Rekha Mody**. On the front lawn, under the cover of a Rajasthani tent with television cameras rolling, I spoke about my quest to the assembled media. Suddenly a ripple went through the audience as an elegant sari-clad figure approached the tent. The press conference was over and my first Indian encounter began. The mystery lady was none other than the **Maharani of Tripura**, the last reigning queen of India's northern-most state, near Assam, where tea is grown. As she walked towards me, our eyes met and I knew instantly that here was my 'warrior queen'. She requested I join her immediately for tea at her palace.

The Tripura family seat in Kolkata was a marble art deco palace. As the Maharani led me into one of the sitting rooms, I felt I might just bump into Agatha Christie's' Belgian detective, Hercule Poirot, and an assortment of glamorous suspects away for a murder weekend. I started as the bell rang and, without a hint of irony, a tray of thinly-sliced cucumber sandwiches appeared. What was so attractive about the Maharani was her graciousness. We spoke about her time in politics and how she had championed the cause of the tribal peoples. She was a true queen of her people. After tea I was given a tour of the Palace. In one of the rooms time had stood still since the death of the former Maharaja, her father-in-law. My eyes fell upon a table of neatly arranged silver framed photographs, signed by nearly all of the twentieth-century world leaders. Amongst them was the only non-politician, Nobel Prize winning poet and Indian nationalist, Rabindranath Tagore. It was Tagore's poem, contrasting the butterfly to the humble bee, that had originally inspired me on my quest. I had given myself the challenge to see whether I could be like the useful bee that spontaneously carried pollen from flower to flower, thereby setting the whole landscape alight with colour and fragrance – rather than the vain butterfly that fluttered around thinking she was beautiful but actually doing nothing. Could I be a catalyst for great and good change? Could I bring these twenty-first century daughters of history together and be part of a great collective noble endeavour to transform others' lives?

What a wonderful world

The world has been good to me. My life has been a magical mystery tour, a madcap adventure, and a series of unexplainable coincidences. Wherever I go, I somehow sit next to a friend of a friend, or I end up as life-long buddies with a stranger. As they say, 'strangers are friends waiting to be met', and I met extraordinary people in unexpected circumstances and have made many true friends. It is said that we are connected to everyone through six degrees of separation. I have now met so many women from all over the world, from Hong Kong to Hampstead, Port Louis to Paris, New York to New Delhi, that there are only two degrees of separation between me and the rest of the world's women. In fact, I probably know you through an organization that you belong to or a contact in common! And if we don't, I am sure the world will conspire to make it happen.

tale madre tale figlia

تماما مثل امها!

precis som mamma?

有其母, 必有其女?

Just like mother?

First love

The first and most intimate relationship is with your mother. The love starts in the womb. Everything she eats and drinks sustains you. Everything she feels is transmitted to you. Even before birth there is 'womb talk'. Babies are aware of the mother's voice, as well as their odour and are programmed to recognize the person to whom they should turn for nurture and protection from the moment of birth.

All human life begins with a separation from the mother that is usually never complete. The intimacy and intensity of this bond is often unrivalled in life. Prophet Muhammad was once asked to whom one should show the most kindness. He replied: *'Your mother, next your mother, next your mother, and then your father'*. All cultures and religions insist on the protection and reverence of the mother. No wonder 'mother' is the most emotive word in the world.

Whoever I met – however rich, powerful or successful and no matter where they lived in the world – spoke about the influence of their mother, whether positive or negative. Few relationships between mothers and daughters are consistently easy but it was fascinating to hear women reflecting on this fierce bond. I am no exception. Indeed, when I returned from meeting all the extraordinary women within this book, it was usually my mother I phoned first. I wanted to share my excitement with her and to check my own feelings against hers. As my closest adviser, I trust my mother completely. She doesn't need to flatter me, she doesn't take vacations and she has no agenda to push. In the pages of this book, as in my life, I turn to my mother for the honest and generous advice that I have come to rely upon. Many of the women I met also shared this strong and unconditional relationship with their mothers and treasured it as much as I do.

Many women stressed a collective understanding that if you have a strong relationship with your mother it gives you enormous confidence, the bedrock for any successful woman. Oxfam trustee **Gillian Clarke** spoke for many with her simple assertion *'there is no substitute for mother'.*

Sixties icon, the captivating actress **Sarah Miles,** observed that *'we are always closest to those who know us best, and Mother knew me better than anyone'.* National Theatre producer **Thelma Holt** recognized that her mother was 'a real rock of support throughout her life'. Editor **Sarida Brown's** mother was totally dedicated to her. When she left her life in Egypt to move to England she was happy to live in a little caravan in Cambridge so that Sarida could benefit from a grammar school education. **Holly Sargent**, Senior Associate Dean at Harvard University, never lost sight of the fact that her mother dedicated her life to her. When she was dreadfully ill as a baby, her mother had prayed and made all kinds of promises that she should live. It is no exaggeration to say that so many women spoke lovingly about their mothers that I could have written a book on mother-love alone.

Sarida Brown

Thelma Holt

'We are always closest to those who know us best, and Mother knew me better than anyone.'

Sarah Miles

Sarah Miles

'Mother made me house-proud. I learnt from her to keep your man happy you have to look after him (cooking, shirts pressed and no nagging).'

Clare Beckwith

Clare Beckwith

Holly Sargent

Gillian Clarke

Home makers

Many of the women described the difference between their mother's life and their own in quite straightforward terms. *'She was a stay-at-home mum, a housewife, a homemaker.'* It might be easy to assume that for women who are more comfortable with their legs under the executive desk than the kitchen table, their mother's life as housewife and carer did not appear as exciting or important as their own career choice. In actual fact, many thoughtful daughters looked back with affection and some pride on their mothers' lives.

Some realized that their mothers' domestic and family-centred lives brought accomplishments and fulfilments that were not easily dismissed. More than just respecting her mother's life, editor and social commentator the glamorous **Shernaaz Engineer** appreciated that her own path may not be more fulfilling in all respects. *'My mother has been a stay-at-home mum for most of our growing-up years, working as a nursery teacher much later. She married at eighteen and had both her children by twenty-one. She never had a career or financial independence. I am single in my thirties. I have both. But I think hers was a more fulfilled life overall, although mine is more exciting!'*

Although TV presenter **Clare Beckwith** also has an exciting life, she spoke about valuing the traditional mother and housewife role most strongly. *'Mother made me house-proud. I learnt from her to keep your man happy you have to look after him (cooking, shirts pressed and no nagging).'* She confesses her family is her career! As Clare was aware, such a confession may seem controversial in an age when women are encouraged to prove their rights and achievements in the workplace. For Clare, who is content to follow her mother's path and plan her work commitments around the demands of motherhood, the drive towards the workplace may not always be a freedom. *'Women have the opportunity to create and follow careers, but for many this has become a trap. Some women would love spending more time bringing up their children. Unfortunately that is looked down on these days. It shouldn't be considered inferior, because bringing up a happy family is tremendously important as well as the basis of a strong and secure society.'*

Elaine Attias

Shernaaz Engineer

'Mummy was a product of the generation that raised children and supported their husbands. She was a very beautiful woman who gave all her children a tremendous sense of security. We didn't have to do anything, be anything to be loved and that was a source of strength.'

Elaine Attias

Kusoom Vadgama

'The main difference between my life and my mother's life is that whereas her life was dominated by circumstance, I dominate the circumstances.'

Kusoom Vadgama

Eve Pollard

Elaine Attias is widely admired for her prize-winning career that spans film writing, producing, and a life-long commitment to political activism. Like everyone, her success is partly attributable to her education, character and opportunities, but she is also adamant that being able to rely on the unconditional love of her mother played a crucial role. *'Mummy was a product of the generation that raised children and supported their husbands. She was a very beautiful woman who gave all her children a tremendous sense of security. We didn't have to do anything, be anything, to be loved and that was a source of strength. That is actually one of the problems in the world today. Nobody gets that kind of security.'*

It is certainly not the case that unconditional love creates a complacent child. Indeed, many of those who emphasized the imprint of this love were dynamos and risk-takers. Perhaps knowing that they would never endanger being adored, they were able to step beyond the expected life. Fleet Street editor and broadcaster **Eve Pollard**, whose journalistic success has proven her guts as well as her talent, acknowledged that *'her strength and humour to deal with life came from the love she had from her mother'*.

Breaking with tradition

Despite the fondness and gratitude that was expressed towards mothers, there was also realism. Many women had a strong sense that their mothers had far more restricted lives then their own. Their mothers were more accepting and responded to decisions and situations dominated by other people, generally men, and some were clearly restless, if not desperate, housewives.

Historian and Doctor of Optometry **Kusoom Vadgama** admitted that *'the main difference between my life and my mother's life is that whereas her life was dominated by circumstance, I dominate the circumstances. She often lived with in-laws or with an extended family*

Maja Daruwala

'Mother was a creature obedient to the mores of the time and did not feel impelled to achieve in her own right as an individual or to become a career woman with money of her own. She was content to be the army wife, the lady of the house and the stimulating mother.'

Maja Daruwala

Margaret Owen

'My mother died frustrated that she had not done all she wanted to.'

Margaret Owen

Tamsin Larby

'The main differences between my life and my mother's life are expectations and economics.'

Tamsin Larby

where subservience ruled. I chose to do as I feel right in my mind and not fear what others might say. My mother spent her life pleasing others, as demanded by the Indian way of life. I spend my life to please myself and those I love'.

Director of the Commonwealth Human Rights Initiative, **Maja Daruwala**, also mused that *'Mother was a creature obedient to the mores of the time and did not feel impelled to achieve in her own right as an individual or to become a career woman with money of her own. She was content to be the army wife, the lady of the house and the stimulating mother. Later in life when I dinned feminism into her she would talk about things she should have done'.* Maja's story of women looking back on a life unlived is a familiar one as many energetic and talented women of earlier generations simply did not have the opportunities or resources to fulfil their potential against the fixed grain of gendered expectations.

The life half-lived is perhaps more difficult to accept. **Margaret Owen**, lawyer and founder of 'Widows for Peace and Democracy', spoke about her mother's frustrated resentfulness. She was the daughter of a Lithuanian refugee who grew up in a poor immigrant home but won a scholarship to Cambridge and qualified as a doctor. Despite such early promise, she eventually shaped herself as the wife of an eminent lawyer and silenced her own potential. *'My mother died frustrated that she had not done all she wanted to; she had been submerged by her ascending status to the employer of nannies, gardeners, maids, someone who oversaw starched table napkins, doilies, finger-bowls, polished silver and cut glass. She felt I had more freedom and was even jealous that I had four children and still could work.'*

Importantly, many mothers who missed out on their own career fulfilment, passed down a real yearning for their children to succeed. They wanted their daughters to have more choice and more opportunity to exercise that choice. Actress and director of V-Day, Until the Violence Stops campaign, **Tamsin Larby**, summed it up: *'The main differences between my life and my mother's life are expectations and economics'*. Often mothers had clear expectations of better things for their daughters.

'Mother taught me what unconditional love was. She is the thread that keeps all our lives together.'

Shakira Caine

'My mother was a dominating and exotic force. She was very artistic and taught sewing and draping ... I am the product of my mother's ambition.'

Zandra Rhodes

'I still think, "What would Mama have said?" She would have taken life by the scruff of the neck, knowing one way or another that you will cope.'

Carole Stone

'Mother was highly intelligent but was never allowed to explore her mind or creativity until we were all grown up.'

Margaret Lobo

Clothed in Mother's love

Shakira Caine spoke about how her mother was forward thinking and wanted the world for her. *'Mother taught me what unconditional love was. She is the thread that keeps all our lives together.'* Working as a dress-maker, Shakira's mother had the strength of character to bring up her young family single-handedly after the early death of her husband. When Shakira travelled to London as Miss Guyana for the Miss World contest, it was the evening gown that her mother had designed and made for her that she wore. Clothed in her mother's love and protection, Shakira was able to fulfil both their wishes.

Clothed in Mother's ambition

Fashion designer **Zandra Rhodes**' mother also exerted a direct influence. Known internationally as a one-off, a creative genius, Zandra assured me that she was very much her mother's daughter. *'I could have been named Sandra but mother needed something more out of the ordinary and so the Z.'* Her mother was a fitter for the Paris fashion house of Worth and later a lecturer at Medway College of Art. *'My mother was a dominating and exotic force. She was very artistic and taught sewing and draping.'* Zandra began her studies at the art school where her mother taught before moving to the Royal College of Art in London to study printed textile design. Although her own achievements in the fashion world have taken the artistic gift of her mother in new and adventurous directions, she sees her own success, including the setting up of London's Fashion & Textile Museum, as completely linked to her mother's hopes for her. *'I am the product of my mother's ambition.'* Zandra's dramatic fabrics and designs were favoured by Diana, Princess of Wales, Jackie Onassis, screen diva Elizabeth Taylor, as well as modern idols such as Kylie Minogue, Sarah Jessica Parker, Joan Rivers and Anastasia. Her mother's aspirations were fulfilled to the full in her Zandra.

Mama mia!

Broadcaster **Carole Stone** spoke lovingly about her mother who was a powerful and enduring influence on her life. 'She was an enlightened woman, born wise. Mama used to run a corner shop and when people stole from the shop, she used to make them sign a book. She would make sure they came and saw her every week and told her how they were getting on. She made friends with everyone. She had a bartering system for people who didn't have any money, as the shop was situated in a poor council estate. People used to bring in something and she'd say "Well I will keep it here and if I've got someone who wants it, I'll swap it for you". Mama was central to everything I did, she was my guiding force.' It was evident that Carole had not just inherited her sweet nature but her strength of character from her mother.

Carole produced the BBC's Any Questions political debate programme, for ten years, building up a reputation as the most influential networker in Britain, bringing together top names from politics, science, business, media and the arts. Her own prowess as the 'queen of networking' is based on her mother's 'shop-style' of friendship without prejudice, only in her case it is skills and charms that are bartered rather than goods. 'I still think, "What would Mama have said?" She would have taken life by the scruff of the neck, knowing one way or another that you will cope.'

Mother courage

Margaret Lobo, Director of the Otakar Kraus Music Trust, spoke movingly about her mother and the hard life endured in Canada. 'Mother was born in Scotland to a Canadian Air Force man and a Scottish lady who met during the First World War. Her mother died in the severe influenza outbreak when she was one year old. Her father took her back to Canada and soon remarried a woman who had four children of her own. Mother was very neglected and made to feel an outsider through her whole childhood, but she continued to show respect to her stepmother and ensured we all knew her as a good grandmother.

Mother met my father in the factory where they both worked. When she became pregnant he was obliged to marry her. She produced eight children, one of whom died at birth. She was the most loving, devoted mother one could have wished for. She struggled all her life to ensure we studied, ate well and had a loving, caring home.

She endured over 40 years of my father's attitude, and was never allowed friends or to partake in outside activities. Due to the economic circumstances she was forced to work in a bakery and as a waitress. All her money went towards feeding us children and my father would put the rest towards drinking. She was highly intelligent but was never allowed to explore her mind or creativity until we were all grown up and she began to attend some evening classes in physical fitness and cake decorating. My father would wait for her to come home and, in his jealousy, would accuse her of being out with other men. In the end she felt it easier to just give in.

Never once did she criticize our father. My father's mother had also died of influenza when he was three so he was left to bring himself up and received little love, support or education, in spite of being a very intelligent man. My mother recognized these qualities in him and we know she loved him and did all she could to ensure he had a family life.

Mother was 69 when she died of a massive stroke, it devastated the whole family.'

Losing mother

Those who had lost their mothers could barely articulate their grief, and the imprinted pain of that loss always remained vivid.

Venu Dhupa, Director of Creative Innovation at the South Bank Centre, and a former actress and theatre director, spoke about her exceptional mother and how close they were. The shock of her death literally turned Venu's hair white. For another actress and theatre executive, **Sanjna Kapoor**, who comes from the dual theatre dynasties of the Kapoors and Kendals, losing her mother Jennifer at the tender age of sixteen was a similar blow. *'My grandfather took it horribly. My grandmother took it worse. It was a huge blow to everyone. My life went for a toss.'*

Losing a mother at a young age is clearly more difficult and unresolved feelings are not always channelled positively. Building design guru and author **Rosalyn Dexter's** mother died when she was young, but the nature of her death was particularly significant. Her mother had been recovering from an operation in a hospital in Sydney – where the family had arrived only weeks before – when her father decided to put Rosalyn with just her four older siblings on a plane to return to the family in England. Her plane crashed in Singapore. Rosalyn returned to Sydney, but in her absence her mother had died. Rosalyn remembers how she and her elder siblings were greeted in Sydney by the most disturbing sight. *'I saw everybody in black and my father was crying. I never asked him and they never told me.'* As Rosalyn explained, she always felt responsible in some way for the unspoken fact of her mother's death because of her failure to say goodbye. Time did not heal this wound and she was left with a *'hairline crack in my whole system, my whole life'*, that needed to be healed. At the age of thirty-four, Rosalyn sought therapy and was able to break the cycle of sabotaging herself which had taken her from millionaire to broke three times. She was finally able to come to terms with her mother's early death and learnt to channel her extraordinary spirit into her books and creative work.

Single mothers

Although, until recently, being a single parent was to endure social stigma, it is fascinating that the daughters of single mothers were actually given a greater sense of purpose and direction as a result of the intense closeness that developed between parent and child. A mother's anxieties and ambitions often shape her children's lives but this is particularly strong in the case of single mothers.

Professor Dame **Gillian Beer**, King Edward VII Professor of English Literature and President of Clare Hall, Cambridge, was raised single-handedly by her headmistress mother and recognizes that it was because of the close connection to her mother that she grew up wanting to achieve. '*I wanted to succeed in life for my mother who raised me single-handedly.*' During the war, Gillian felt tremendously lucky that they were evacuated together from London to Somerset. '*As mother was divorced, she was able to continue in her work as a primary school teacher. In those days married teachers and civil servants were made to retire, as their husbands were supposed to be the breadwinners. Mother became the headmistress of the local village school and we passed the war in the countryside together.*' When Gillian won a scholarship to attend a boarding school, she missed the companionship of her mother and the stimulation of adult conversation. '*I think there were periods when I was reasonably happy but I found it quite oppressive being only with children my own age, because I was used to living alongside my mother and having conversations of different kinds. I kept my suitcase under my bed in case I ever had to escape school.*'

Designer **Han Feng** was brought up single-handedly by her mother in Nanjing, China. They lived in poverty, with the two of them sharing a single room. Like so many single parents, Han's mother concentrated on her only child. As Han said '*I had little opportunity for creative expression when young, but I did develop an eye for spatial patterns and learnt to seek out the beauty next to me*'. Inspired by her mother's resilience, Han left China with nothing and started a new life in America.

Han Feng

Venu Dhupa

'I had little opportunity for creative expression when young, but I did develop an eye for spatial patterns and learnt to seek out the beauty next to me.'

Han Feng

Sanjna Kapoor

Gillian Beer

Rosalyn Dexter

Phyllis Krystal

She describes herself as a 'fish in water' in New York. Today Han's designs are worn by the glitterati from Gwyneth Paltrow to Blythe Danner, Jessye Norman and Amy Tan. **Han Feng's** home is a work of art. A bath graced her sitting room and could have doubled as a sofa, light bulbs had feathers stuck on to make them look like glowing birds and her bed was draped in mosquito nets, recalling Imperial extravagance. I gained an added sense of her creative genius when I saw the costumes that she had designed for Anthony Minghella's adaptation of the opera *Madame Butterfly*, as the arrangement of colours, drapes and lights truly brought to life the tragic drama of a single mother in Japan.

Keeping mum

For just a few women, the relationship with their mother was not a positive one. All the same, each one of these women had managed to work through these difficulties in their adult life and transform early misfortune into mature strengths. The self-awareness, understanding and forgiveness that these women showed to their mothers had enriched their lives at all levels and made them more able to analyse their own attachments to others.

Author **Phyllis Krystal**, who wrote the landmark text *Cutting the Ties That Bind*, was brought up by a controlling Edwardian mother. The effect of this upbringing was profound. '*I used to be extremely retiring and very shy. I was not to be seen or heard and so I was never seen or heard until fairly recently in my life.*' She described her mother as '*the most dominating women I have ever known in my entire life*' and explained how '*she was terrified to spoil me so she became extremely severe*'. In the 1950s Phyllis studied the work of American psychic Edgar Cayce and eventually developed her own method for contacting the inner source of wisdom which she calls the Hi C (for Higher Consciousness). The touchstone of her therapy is being able to release oneself from attachment to, or reliance on, outer security or control. This was clearly a process that Phyllis herself had to work through, given her mother's fierce grip.

When Phyllis spoke about her understanding of childhood and her insistence on approaching others with loving ears, it was obvious that she had an understanding of the positive relationship between parent and child even though she never enjoyed this with her own mother. '*I think it is the most important thing to be there for your children but most of all to love them and to be strictly honest with them. The majority of children say that they don't want a doctor for a daddy or a secretary for a mummy, or whatever. They want a real father and a real mother, human beings. The second thing they always tell me is that if either or both of their parents would give them their undivided attention for even five minutes a day they would feel validated.*'

Campaigner for widows' rights **Margaret Owen** also confided her experience of a domineering mother. '*My mother was on the outside highly confident, my father thought her the most brilliant woman he had ever met. But she did not achieve as she wished to and was ambitious for me, pushing me, wanting me to gain a place at Cambridge, but also domineering and belittling me within the family.*'

The Reverend **Leonora van Gils**, founder of the Human Dolphin Institute, who spent her formative years in Denmark where her stepfather was physician to the Royal Court, was also deeply affected by her mother's negative attitude. '*She was a difficult person to please and often sarcastic and hurtful, quite materialistic.*' For Leonora, these shortcomings have proved a valuable, if difficult, lesson to learn. '*Through my mother's difficult and diverse personality I learnt an awful lot about how not to be. I also learnt tolerance, compassion and forgiveness at the deepest level.*' After a career in acting and selling properties, Leonora changed direction to work on health and healing, building up a VIP client list which included British royalty. Later she moved to Florida and established a 'Healing Retreat Center', where people could come to swim with dolphins. All the same, she sold her retreat and returned to Europe to look after her dying mother and heal their relationship, which she never regretted.

Motherhood and apple pie

For many educated and economically secure women, motherhood is now a choice. Women's control over their own fertility has been a major goal of the global women's movement. Women have been able to plan and manage their experience of motherhood, as well as their decisions not to become mothers, in a way their own mothers usually could not. As a whole, the women spoke of mothering as a deeply rewarding relationship, although they acknowledged that the joys of being a mother are often put under pressure by the demands of a career and the myth of the superwoman.

Marchioness **Tracy Worcester** was absolutely clear about wanting to devote herself to her children. As a former actress, she did not strive to achieve the career or public recognition that many women of her own generation often prized over and above motherhood for a very good reason, her own childhood. *'My parents were away most of the time so I was brought up by a Scottish nanny, Sheila. She had good strong Scottish values of justice, kindness and truth. It was customary in my mother's time to give her life to her man. Children therefore had to come second.'* Tracy's own experience of being denied her mother's total love provoked a keen understanding of the long-term impact: *'The degree of closeness with parents as a child will define the closeness in later life'*. It was vital to Tracy to be able to offer that time, care and unconditional love to her children. *'I married a man who could support me and I moved out of the commercial world. I was free to climb down from the ladder of self-promotion, and care about my children and the well-being of others.'*

For Tracy the myth of the super-mum pushed by the media actually made motherhood more difficult to embrace because it represented an impossible ideal of the high-flyer, big-earner who still created a perfect family. She felt: *'Being a mother is the most rewarding experience. Sadly it is undermined in a culture driven by an economy that needs every hand to be part of the economic growth paradigm. Super-mums are what we have been programmed to desire to emulate. They are mothers who are too stressed and busy to concentrate on their children but they bring the material wealth into the family'*.

Alpana Kirloskar

Tracy Worcester

Sue Stapely

Rachel Oliver

'Being a mother is the most rewarding experience. Sadly it is undermined in a culture driven by an economy that needs every hand to be part of the economic growth paradigm. Super-mums are what we have been programmed to desire to emulate. They are mothers who are too stressed and busy to concentrate on their children but they bring the material wealth into the family.'

Tracy Worcester

Growing up

Yoga teacher Princess **Usha Devi Rathore** confessed that she had always been rebellious and that it was only when she became a parent that she finally shifted up a generational gear and stopped imagining she could be a super-mum. *'Being a mother made me grow up, and having responsibility for another being that I loved more than myself changed my whole attitude to life. I often wonder how people who don't have children mature.'* Usha was fortunate in being able to plan her teaching around motherhood *'so that I was always primarily a mother'.*

The architect **Alpana Kirloskar** also spoke about the adjustments of bring up her children, and working around their needs. As she said, *'I was always there at meals, bathtime and holidays. It's a mother's joy to always be there for their children'.*

This desire to strike a happy balance between the demands of motherhood and the workplace was discussed by almost all working mothers, although very few felt that they had achieved perfection, and the sense of being torn remained a daily dilemma for many.

Adopting a new role

Bangladeshi-born organizational consultant **Rifat Wahhab** was the only woman to have spoken about adopting a child. *'I wanted to adopt a child; we were not fussy about the gender or Bangladeshi factor. The roles that are most important to me are that of being a wife and I wanted to be a mother. To bring children up so that they are happy, secure and fit to meet the challenges of the world is the greatest task a parent faces.'* She echoed most mothers when she confessed that *'work is a doddle compared to this task'.*

Beyond the myth of the super-mother

It would be disingenuous to praise motherhood and its emotional riches so highly without also speaking of the sheer hard work, time and energy that mothering demands. Motherhood was seen as a lifelong commitment. For many, bringing up children was an important spiritual responsibility as well as a joy. It brought forward wisdom, compassion and other feminine qualities and taught women to focus and not waste time.

Before lawyer and communications consultant **Sue Stapely's** mother died, she confided in Sue that she couldn't imagine how a modern woman coped with multiple roles. Sue's own mother had always been financially dependent on her husband and saw her role as providing a happy, beautifully managed home and parenting her only child. In contrast Sue worked, studied, mothered and is a recognized champion of many causes. She has used her legal skills and inside knowledge of the media and politics to change the way the law treats the disadvantaged. Sue has been at the forefront of the women's campaign, and has helped families with disabled children, and mothers wrongly imprisoned, having lost their babies to cot death. Little wonder her mother was in awe of her!

Rachel Oliver of the Farmers Union was very articulate about the way in which the pressure for women to work may have actually reduced rather than increased their choices. '*I think that my generation has had a harder time than the previous ones, because in my mother's generation it was okay if you wanted to be a housewife, have children and not work. What makes it difficult for my generation is that we were expected to want to do, and to be able to do, both.*'

In today's busy world nearly every mother I met had commitments outside their home. There were few super-mothers who kept the technicolor uniform of a super-hero beneath the stained apron and the creased work suit. No single woman had a magic formula for making motherhood less arduous or emotionally demanding, although the benefits of flexible working and an extended family were clear. Equally, no mother felt that the rewards of motherhood were inadequate.

Working mothers

There are now hugely increased expectations of what women can achieve and the positive spin on 'having it all' meant that women were often unprepared for the reality of life as working mothers. **Antonia Byatt**, who runs the prestigious Women's Library, London Metropolitan University, gave a very honest account. *'When I had my first child I couldn't imagine not putting my career first and I assured my employer I would be back in three months. I did go back but I now realize this was a painful mistake. Work could have waited but I will never have the time with that small baby again. Interestingly I've been looking at the lives of some of the women campaigners whose collections we hold in our library, who also have regrets about the time the women's movement took from their personal lives. But perhaps that had to happen for women to prove they could get to the top, and we should be grateful for their incredible energy and commitment to women. It is just that the top for a lot of women isn't always straightforward; if children are involved it is still an issue for most of us.'*

The women's liberation movement was directed at giving women more choice and control in relation to both work and family obligations. Most women might now have the right to choose both a career and a family, but they are not always adequately supported in that choice. Governments are increasingly seeking measures to help working mothers, but all the emphasis is on childcare provision, as if women can just go on working more hours as long as they don't have to look after their children! As the very low birth rate in Continental Europe shows, for young women who are yet to become mothers themselves, the demands of working on dual-control are understandably daunting.

Women from different ages and varied cultures revealed pressure points for working mothers, as well as some strategies for easing these. Britain's first black woman MP, **Diane Abbott**, spoke for many working mothers. *'My son has made an enormous difference in my life. Of course it makes your life more complex and you do more running around and sometimes*

Diane Abbott

Leila Seth

Rifat Wahhab

Padma Bandhopadya

'… you have low moments, worrying that you are not a very good politician and not a very good mother. You are trying to do two things at once and you feel you are not doing either very well.'

Diane Abbott

'Don't ignore your friends, family and especially your children, in order to get on in your career – you must build them into your lives because they are the only ones who will give you the solace that you need. Nobody goes to their deathbed wishing they had spent more hours in the office!'

Rifat Wahhab

you have low moments, worrying that you are not a very good politician and not a very good mother. You are trying to do two things at once and you feel you are not doing either very well.'

The extraordinarily high standards that women set themselves make such feelings of doubt almost inevitable, but one is consoled by **Rifat Wahhab's** wise words on the subject. *'Don't accept the second best. Ask for everything: time to look after your children, time to care for those who have cared for you. Don't ignore your friends, family and especially your children, in order to get on in your career – you must build them into your lives because they are the only ones who will give you the solace that you need. Nobody goes to their deathbed wishing they had spent more hours in the office!'*

One positive way forward that several women followed was to make their children feel part of their working life. **Padma Bandhopadya**, India's first Air Marshal, described how her children *'never complained about their mother never being there to cuddle them. They were very self-sufficient and confident about handling themselves. At times they used to help us so much that I could study well and pass my exams with good grades. Without their support, I could never dream of reaching the heights'*. Similarly **Leila Seth**, India's first woman High Court judge, remembers her son Vikram, the famous novelist, telling her *'Mum I am so happy you work, you talk to us about so many interesting things'*.

For others, taking a slower but steady path to the top of their fields may have been frustrating but it did not prevent them from achieving proper recognition in the long term. Professor Dame **Gillian Beer** looked back on her own career at Cambridge University. *'I slowly accumulated my professional work which was appreciated by my peers. I became a professor in my fifties, which was much later than a lot of men. How things have changed! There is now a female vice-chancellor at Cambridge and a new energy to promote women. It has become a matter of policy but provoked by women themselves.'*

Devaki Jain

Uta Frith

'I wanted to be a good mother. Of course it is not easy to combine this with a career in a competitive profession. I believe I was delayed in my career by about ten years through having two children. I think that this is generally true for other women scientists I know. But what is ten years?'

Uta Frith

Elizabeth Diggory

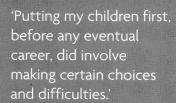

'Putting my children first, before any eventual career, did involve making certain choices and difficulties.'

Shireen Isal

Shireen Isal

There is also the option of staggering work and motherhood rather than trying to balance both simultaneously. Economist **Devaki Jain** compromised in the short-term but also reached professional heights once her family had grown up. *'The children simply could not be palmed off on anyone and it was creating tremendous family stress, as my husband was also at the peak of his public life, and therefore with one stroke I resigned my lectureship and spent five years completely domesticated. I lost the opportunity of running with the hares, so to speak, finishing a Ph.D., publishing a research paper that I had prepared on India's river disputes and gaining fame and name as an economist.'*

The pioneering German-born scientist and Professor of Cognitive Development, **Uta Frith**, passes her own life lessons on to her students. *'I have always tried to tell them that they don't have to make a choice between a tough career and being a woman, but they can actually have both. I wanted to be a good mother. Of course it is not easy to combine this with a career in a competitive profession. I believe I was delayed in my career by about ten years through having two children. I think that this is generally true for other women scientists I know. But what is ten years?'*

Elizabeth Diggory, the late Highmistress of St Paul's Girls' School, explained that many of the mothers of her pupils also advocated this possibility. *'My generation almost pretended they did not have children to enable them to go back to a career. Now a lot more mothers urge me to ensure that girls know they have to make choices. There is a generational shift. Women can do things in stages; you don't have to have it all at once.'*

Impresario **Shireen Isal**, admired for her dedication to the performing arts, was clear that her life balance was always dictated by the needs of her children. *'Being a mother and consciously trying to be a successful one has been of overriding importance to me. It has been an all-important factor in the decisions I have made, both professional and personal. Putting my children first, before any eventual career, did involve making certain choices and difficulties. But my goal was clear.'*

Nafis Sadik

'working life made me a better mother.'

Nafis Sadik

Wendy Savage

'I don't think I'd have been any good as a mother if I hadn't had my career as well. I enjoyed my children, but I couldn't have been a full-time wife and mother.'

Wendy Savage

Lynne Franks

'not seeing enough of my children when they were small was a great disadvantage for me and them.'

Lynne Franks

Anu Aga

'I am a great believer that success at work should not take a toll on family life. Then success is a failure.'

Anu Aga

Less conventionally, Director of the UN Population Fund, the trailblazer and champion of women, Doctor **Nafis Sadik,** made the point that: *'working life made me a better mother'*. Professor of Gynaecology **Wendy Savage**, who courageously took on the British medical establishment on the issue of home births, also endorsed this view. *'I don't think I'd have been any good as a mother if I hadn't had my career as well. I enjoyed my children, but I couldn't have been a full-time wife and mother.'*

However, while the rewards of having a family and a career may eventually be reaped double-fold, it would be wrong to suggest that there was not a price to be paid. PR guru, **Lynne Franks,** the inspiration for the comedy series *Absolutely Fabulous,* acknowledged that *'not seeing enough of my children when they were small was a great disadvantage for me and them'*. Her candid feelings were shared by many who said that the cost of success was often losing out on their children's growing years and they wished they had spent more time with their children and been home for them when they were young.

In the long term, if a happier and easier balance is to be struck for working mothers, it is necessary to revise the basic assumption that women with children simply need reliable childcare. Attention also needs to be paid to the impact of separation and long working hours on mothers as well as children. While it was apparent that a proportion of the high-achievers really did live to work, many women at the top of their fields stressed the importance of a balanced life and the need to value personal and family relationships. A high-flying career woman by anybody's standards, **Anu Aga**, former Chairperson of the Thermax Group, and one of India's most respected industrialists, expressed the danger of imbalance beautifully. *'I am a great believer that success at work should not take a toll on family life. Then success is a failure.'*

Simone Tata

Dorothy Dalton

'As you grow older, the joy of children is more accentuated. You rise from a stage where the child is dependent on you to a stage where you become dependent on your child. I am not talking of financially dependent, but affectionately dependent. Your child becomes a companion; a friend, a councillor.'

Simone Tata

Martina Milburn

Frances Cairncross

Lisette Talate

Barbara Rogers

Companions

It is easy to think of motherhood as the defining period when children are young and dependent on their parents for daily care and protection, but for several women motherhood was most fulfilling when their children had grown up and the relationship became more one of companionship.

A former headmistress and founder of the charity JOLT (Journey of a Lifetime), **Dorothy Dalton** admitted, '*I enjoyed my two sons much, much more as they grew older and became people*'.

For **Frances Cairncross**, the company of her two daughters has added a new dimension to the masculine world she inhabits through her work as Rector of Exeter College, Oxford, and in the world of science and economics. '*I have had the most immense pleasure from having two daughters and because I have always lived in a world dominated by men their female companionship has been marvellous for me. They have taught me to buy more interesting clothes and put my make-up on properly!*'

Martina Milburn, Chief Executive of the Prince's Trust, confided that '*One of the best things about getting older is watching your children grow and develop. Seeing them leave the muddle and confusion of adolescence and emerge as confident, interesting people is a huge privilege*'.

Similarly, the dignified and intelligent Swiss-born **Simone Tata**, Director of the multi-national Tata Industries – that encompasses steel to scientific and social research, clothes to cars, hotels to Tetley tea – spoke with an authentic understanding that '*as you grow older, the joy of children is more accentuated. You rise from a stage where the child is dependent on you to a stage where you become dependent on your child. I am not talking of financially dependent, but affectionately dependent. Your child becomes a companion; a friend, a councillor*'.

Another fine mess?

Clearly, not all relationships between parents and their children were easy or harmonious. Actress **Sarah Miles** admitted, somewhat disarmingly: *'I wasn't a very good mother and my son wasn't a very good son. I'm sure between us we made a right mess of it. He was expelled from kindergarten and kicked out of tennis school, and so it went on and on. He was a nightmare all through his upbringing. Then, of course, I found God and went into three years of silence so that wasn't the greatest time for my son. I was completely alone listening to the word of God. We didn't have a usual relationship and yet I just adore him'.*

Exes and extras

Conventionally we tend to think of divorce as breaking up families but **Barbara Rogers**, the founder editor of *Everywoman* magazine, made me realize that re-marriage and step-parenting can be an important part of an extended family structure that is seldom acknowledged or discussed. Given how many 'exes and extras,' as she called them, are now combining to make new families, her story is very relevant. Barbara admitted that being a stepmother was an extremely difficult task and not only because you tend to experience more of the bad times and less of the good times with your step children. Even if you are able to form a good bond and spend a great deal of time with them, you are always viewed in a different light and receive less support than other carers or family members. Perhaps there is still a slight hangover from the wicked stepmothers in the fairy stories we all grew up with. Although it is hard to imagine Cinderella with a kind stepmother, many real families do now thrive on positive extended family arrangements and caring stepmothers play a crucial role.

Certain sorrow, uncertain joy

If the rewards of motherhood can be priceless, then it follows that the pain of losing a child can also be without measure. The honesty of the women who spoke about these experiences of loss was moving. Not only did their stories confirm that nothing could prevent a mother from loving her child, but they also spoke of the realities of a painful motherhood in a world where mental and physical disabilities and the cruelties leading to death often go unspoken and can therefore become almost unspeakable.

Lisette Talate was nominated for the 2006 Nobel Peace Prize for her work helping to empower the women of her Chagossian community. She spoke about how her people were displaced from their homeland by the British government in the 1960s, to make way for an American military base on the island of Diego Garcia. The cruelty of wanton colonialism. Along with her people, Lisette was rounded up and put on a boat to faraway Mauritius. During the boat trip, the Chagossians were forced to sleep on the lower deck and remained unfed while the horses, which enjoyed the upper deck, were well-fed. For her the consequences were tragic. '*I lost two of my children on the voyage to Mauritius in the space of eight days.*' Her people's experiences were a terrifying echo of the grotesque and inhuman trafficking, over two centuries ago, of slaves across the Atlantic from Africa, for the demands of colonial expansion and imperial greed. Now, in our lifetime, a settled and peaceful black community in the Indian Ocean was being subjected to the same barbarity. Lisette has dedicated her life to ensuring that her people return to their island in the Chagos Archipelago and live there in peace. But she feels her own life can never be restored to wholeness. '*There is no comparison that can be drawn between the life led by my parents and my destitute life. Not only was I not able to give my children my time and attention but I was unable to give them as much food as they wanted and I was unable to fulfil all their basic needs, let alone their wants.*'

Dorothy Boux

Lakshmi Shankar

Joan Davies

Pheroza Godrej

'the sadness of seeing one's own child, ill and locked into a situation they can't get out of … Suffering from schizophrenia … underneath there is a self and the self is not touched. You have to understand the situation and cope with it. I have learnt patience and to control my tongue. My daughter has learnt to accept the limitations of her illness and to give generously when she can.'

Dorothy Boux

'In those days you married because you wanted children together.'

Pheroza Godrej

The loss of a child also devastated **Lakshmi Shankar**, one of the world's most acclaimed singers. When her daughter first fell ill, Lakshmi prayed to God, shaved her head, and would have done anything to have saved her daughter's life. Eventually she accepted that she would see her child die before her, the cruellest fate for any parent. For **Joan Davies**, the first woman to teach at Sandhurst Military Academy, death through war was not unfamiliar but she was devastated by the loss of her second child, a daughter, to cancer: *'The grief is inarticulable. You just never get over it.'*

Having married one of India's most illustrious industrialists, art historian and gallery owner **Pheroza Godrej** was keen to have children. As she says, *'In those days you married because you wanted children together'*. Pheroza became pregnant with her first child at the age of twenty-eight, but was involved in a horrific stabbing incident when she tried to protect her father-in-law from an angry worker who turned up at their home during an industrial dispute. Tragically, her baby was lost and Pheroza naturally suffered a dreadful trauma. Nursed back to health by her own mother, Pheroza went on to have a daughter and a son whom she *'can't do without'*.

A love less ordinary

Mothers whose children have disabilities also carry certain sorrow but sometimes experience uncertain joy as well. Author and calligrapher **Dorothy Boux** explained *'the sadness of seeing one's own child, ill and locked into a situation they can't get out of ... Suffering from schizophrenia ... underneath there is a self and the self is not touched. You have to understand the situation and cope with it. I have learnt patience and to control my tongue. My daughter has learnt to accept the limitations of her illness and to give generously when she can.'*

Usha Prashar

'I never regretted not having children.'

Usha Prashar

Meher Master Moos

'I never had a desire to have children … I was destined to do other things in the world.'

Meher Master Moos

Dana Gillespie

'I could never be as good as my own mother. I would be dabbling at being second best and it would be unfair on any child.'

Dana Gillespie

Tricia Sibbons

'It's a very personal thing. Children are a great commitment and I personally did not have the resources for both the world and children.'

Tricia Sibbons

A leading light in the Baha'i religious community, the wonderful **Zena Sorabjee** similarly spoke movingly of her unconditional love for her son. 'When my third child was born, I felt that it was God's will that he was not like other children. I should not feel embarrassed in taking him around. He has always been included in everything the family does and is part of our celebrations. I tell his brothers and sisters, who are high achievers, that they must be kind, patient and always look after their brother. He will get to heaven before them and be there to welcome them.'

Not to be a mother

It is increasingly common for women to make the choice not to have children and yet there is still an awkwardness around this issue. Several women set the record straight on this account.

Baroness **Usha Prashar** stood out as absolutely confident and refreshingly straightforward in her decision not to have children. 'When I married in 1973 I said to my husband that I would not give up my name, no dowry, no children and that my career was important. I never regretted not having children.' Usha's work has been all-fulfilling and her contribution to public policy has impacted on the worlds of race relations, charity, the Civil Service and judiciary – and all achieved in a single lifetime.

Professor Dame **Meher Master Moos** also confessed, 'I never had a desire to have children. It was never in my horoscope to bring up children. I was destined to do other things in the world'.

International Jazz singer **Dana Gillespie** explained that she did not have children because 'I could never be as good as my own mother. I would be dabbling at being second best and it would be unfair on any child. Every child deserves a mother that had maternal instincts'.

Responsibility

Founder of *Cosmopolitan*, and one of America's most influential women, **Helen Gurley Brown** made her decision not to have children at a very early age. When Helen's father was killed in a lift accident she took responsibility for her disabled sister who had contracted polio, and her widowed mother, even though she was only fifteen. '*It was quite a challenging childhood. We were only two girls and we didn't have any money and my sister was in a wheelchair. I was her little nursemaid and I had to start working when I was eighteen and I couldn't then go to college.*' Having acted as a surrogate mother for her sister, Helen grew up realizing that she '*didn't want the responsibility of children, of their health, their well-being and education and clothes. I think I understand what children are and what they mean, and that is no regret of mine*'.

Freedom

For other women work was their priority and being able to choose not to have children had enabled them to focus on their professional success without regrets. As **Maggie Bellis**, Director for Transport for London, explained, '*In my life I have the freedom to pursue my own interests and career because I never had children*'.

Pragmatism

Reverend Canon **Vivienne Faull** spoke of the decision as one based on pragmatism. '*When my husband actually did start living in closer proximity, we had to make the hard decision of whether to start a family or not. We would have both enjoyed having children but at that time were caught up in our jobs and realized that the children would have suffered. We found it hard enough juggling two careers and a home.*'

African perceptions

Claire Bertschinger always wanted *'to work in Africa as a nurse and never expected to marry and have her own children'*. It was through her work as a Red Cross nurse and, later, muse for the Live Aid Campaign, that she changed the lives of millions of children. Social and charitable entrepreneur **Tricia Sibbons,** whose trailblazing work has transformed the lives of many young people in Southern Africa, admitted: *'When I was working in Africa they could not understand why I didn't have children, they found it very strange. It's a very personal thing. Children are a great commitment and I personally did not have the resources for both the world and children. I admire women who can do both and do them well. It's to do with inner energy'.*

Altering one's perceptions

Gwyneth Lewis, Wales' first national poet, spoke in more detail about this difficult emotional decision. *'The decision not to have children with my husband, who's twenty-three years older than me, was not an easy one, and required clarity of thought and emotion. It was not taken on the basis that being childless would make me a better writer (a sentiment with which I profoundly disagree), but because I believed that it was the right thing for our marriage. Being childless necessarily alters a woman's perception of time in relation to her body. While writing poetry and publishing are no substitute for this, they are a second body which is not confined to my own in time and space.'*

'I never married and so I never had children. Children are a reward. You have to earn the right to have children.'

Kirsten Rausing

'It is more wonderful than anyone can imagine and makes us both feel complete. It is like falling in love, but less complicated. And it is guaranteed to last for ever.'

Clare Short

Children a reward?

Although **Kirsten Rausing** is one of the world's most accomplished women, she does not have children of her own. Yet she had the wisdom and humility to say, '*I never married and so I never had children. Children are a reward. You have to earn the right to have children*'.

Never too late

Clare Short is best known as one of Britain's most famous and fiery woman politicians. She has always staked her political career and reputation on making a difference to the lives of others and even left her position in the British Government over the Iraq war. However, Clare's most surprising announcement came in 2003 when she was reunited with her son, given up for adoption thirty-one years earlier. Married, but only eighteen and still a student, Clare had become pregnant in 1964 and decided it would be best to have her baby adopted. Despite all her political success, the reunion with her son Toby, a city lawyer, proved to be Clare's most significant life moment. Her story confirms the almost indescribable bond between mother and child that can bring unrivalled joy and fulfilment. In a joint statement issued at the time, Clare and Toby declared: '*We are at the moment happier than we have been in our lives. It is more wonderful than anyone can imagine and makes us both feel complete. It is like falling in love, but less complicated. And it is guaranteed to last for ever*'.

Di papà ce n'è uno solo

قلب او متعلق به پدرشه

Ihr Herz gehört Papa

Isin tyttö

Her heart belongs to daddy

Daddy's girl?

Educationalist **Patricia Licuanan**, who chaired the historic United Nations Beijing Conference for Women, told me the moving story of her birth. Her father, the Filipino hero, General Francisco Licuanan, was a prisoner of war at the time and had described what happened.

'It is a strange feeling to be a prisoner of war in one's own country; to see your countrymen going about their everyday business while you are confined within the walls of a prison compound; to spot a familiar face in a passing crowd and not dare show any signs of recognition; to be close to your family and yet to be isolated from all contact with them. Our prison routine varied very little. Every morning we were awakened at five o'clock and assigned to various work details: cleaning the buildings and the surrounding grounds, burying garbage, loading trucks. I was assigned to clean the area in front of the buildings, including the front sidewalk that ran alongside Taft Avenue. As I swept, under the eye of an armed guard, people would go by on their way to work. Sometimes a friendly look or sympathetic smile would be cast in my direction and I would be tempted to whisper my name and say "Call my wife. Tell her I'm alive". But remembering the beating that one fellow prisoner took for just such an infraction of the rules, I would keep silent.

In the early morning of May 15, 1942, I was sweeping the sidewalk under the watchful eye of a Japanese private when a newsboy came walking by. Hunger for news of the world outside our prison was to us prisoners even stronger than hunger for food. As the newsboy came opposite me, I threw a quick glance at my Japanese guard. He was leaning on his rifle looking into the distance, idly pulling hairs out of a week's growth of beard. With a whisper I called the newsboy to me, thrust a coin that I had hidden in the inner pocket of my pants into his grubby hand and got one of the newspapers. I turned my back to the guard and hurriedly looked through the four-page newspaper. I scanned the column devoted to personals. One item leaped out as if it had been printed in capital letters. It was a small inconspicuous paragraph that simply said "A baby girl was born to Jeanie Benitez at the Philippine General Hospital". Somehow I knew that my wife had chosen not to use her married name and had used her nickname to conceal from the Japanese that she was married to an army officer. But it was a useless precaution – I let out an exuberant yell that startled my guard who came running towards me with his rifle cocked. But joy and excitement made me forget all my prisoner's fears. I rushed towards him waving the newspaper, gasping almost incoherently – "I'm a father! I'm a father!" pointing with an eager finger … "see here – it says I have a baby". And resorting to my meagre Japanese "a baby – kodomo, my kodomo!!"

The guard grabbed the newspaper from me and approached the officer who was on duty that day. It was only then that I realized what I had done. As the officer, whom I knew as Captain Watanabe, strode towards me, samurai sword swinging from his belt, I braced myself for the expected punishment. "Where is your house?" he said to me gruffly. "In San Juan", I answered, purposely vague, fearful that my indiscretion would lead to some harm to my wife and baby. Then he said "This afternoon when truck go to Camp Murphy (now Camp Aguinaldo) – I tell driver take you to see baby". I could not believe what I had heard. I looked at Watanabe's face. It was the same inscrutable, almost expressionless, Japanese face we prisoners had learned to hate. I blurted out "No, my wife is in the Philippine General Hospital – near here".

There was a slight pause, then he said, "I take you there", waving his hand as he called for an army staff car. In a few minutes we were walking up the hospital steps. At the desk I asked the nurse for my wife's room. She gave me the number but eyeing me warily added "it's not visiting hours – it is too early". "I know" I told her, "but I'm a prisoner of war. This is my only chance to see my wife and baby".

Patricia Licuanan

Elaine Attias

'Paternal love creates in a child a need to perform. The child needs the security of being loved but also needs the discipline, ambition, and the creative energy which comes from wanting to perform, wanting to explore, wanting to do.'

Elaine Attias

Simone Poonawalla

Jo-Anne Nadler

Ignoring the nurse completely, Watanabe interrupted saying – "we go" and headed for the second floor where my wife's room was located. And such was the authority of the Japanese military at the time that nobody dared protest further. We found the room. "You go in" Watanabe said, "I wait here". Pretending not to notice my surprise (prisoners of war were never left unguarded), he pointed at his watch "twenty minutes".

That is how I saw my wife again and my oldest child, Patricia, when she was only two days old. I lost track of time and was reminded only by a soft knock at the door. I came out of the room. Without a word, Watanabe set the pace, walking briskly down the corridor. As I kept step with him, I felt I had to say something. "I want to thank you", I said "I want to thank you for what you did for me".

Barely turning his face he replied briefly, "No, do not thank – feeling of fathers all the same". I saw his small eyes brighten with sudden tears. Quickly he turned his face away and walked faster towards the door.

And so Captain Watanabe and I left the hospital, not as we appeared to the nervous but curious nurses who stared at us as we went by, not a Japanese officer and a Filipino prisoner of war, but as men who had suddenly rediscovered that the bonds of higher human feeling transcend the baseness and hatred engendered by war.'

Patricia Licuanan's father was clearly thrilled at the arrival of his daughter and there is a love that runs between father and child for many women I met. However, unlike the unconditional love that the women so valued in their mothers, the love of the father was often more directly connected to particular expectations of what the child might become. As film producer **Elaine Attias** explained, *'Paternal love creates in a child a need to perform. The child needs the security of being loved but also needs the discipline, ambition, and the creative energy which comes from wanting to perform, wanting to explore, wanting to do'*. Indeed, from the women's perspective, either they hero-worshipped daddy, who was principled, patient and a pillar of wisdom, or they found his presence a difficulty in their lives.

Bronwen Astor

Sathya Saran

'In the past, during census time in India, when a man was asked how many children he had, he would say six, even though he had eight children. He didn't count the girls.'

Sathya Saran

Meher Heroyce Moos

Rakhi Sarkar

Judith Chomsky

Julia Middleton

Daddy cool

Many women spoke with great love and gratitude about their fathers. The elegant and soft spoken magazine editor **Sathya Saran** set the scene by saying '*In the past, during census time in India, when a man was asked how many children he had, he would say six, even though he had eight children. He didn't count the girls*'. Sathya's father waited fourteen years for a son and heir and '*when I arrived it didn't matter to him if I was a boy or girl*'.

Like the beautiful **Bronwen Astor**, many others saw their fathers as their hero. Horse breeder **Simone Poonawalla** lovingly described her father as '*the renowned entrepreneur, hugely kind and intelligent. If people treat him badly, he still turns round and does them good. He is my hero*'. **Julia Middleton**, the founder of Common Purpose, an international organization that aims to bring leaders from diverse backgrounds together to create new networks for senior decision-makers, also adored her dad and attributed everything she knew to him. For Julia he was the font of all wisdom, true and good. Actress **Sarah Miles** idolized her father who was '*cuddly and accessible, yet all-knowing, perfect in every way. But then aren't all heroes perfect?*'

Political author **Jo-Anne Nadler** grew up in the 1970s. She became fascinated with politics because of the vivid story her father told her about his own refugee childhood as a Jewish Pole escaping the Nazis. That such big sweeps of history had shaped her own family made politics seem real and compelling and inspired her both in her academic studies and to pursue a career as a journalist with the BBC and as a writer.

Meher Heroyce Moos, the renowned travel writer, spoke about the inspiration she took from her father. '*A good many years prior to his marriage my father worked in Kabul, where his maternal uncle was the then King's closest friend. They were the sole importers into the kingdom of Afghanistan. I hero-worshipped my father. He influenced my extrovert nature and my passion for travel.*'

Unconditional confidence

And, just as daughters adored their fathers, many fathers doted on their daughters. **Dorothy Dalton** was the youngest of three daughters and was her father's baby who '*could do no wrong*'. Human rights lawyer **Judith Chomsky** was also very close to her father and he encouraged her to '*read widely and brought me up thinking I could do anything. I could even do things that people considered boyish. I was a tomboy and it was not at all discouraged*'. The unconditional love of the mother was matched by the unconditional confidence of the father.

Master teacher

Several fathers were central in securing their daughters access to a first-class education. Acclaimed champion of women **Nafis Sadik**, whose father, the Vice-President of the World Bank, insisted that his sons and daughters had equal rights to education, explained that in those days many of her girl cousins were never sent for a higher education. She was fortunate to have a supportive father and later an understanding husband. Throughout her illustrious and trailblazing career she has dedicated herself to ensuring every woman deserves that right automatically and does not have to be thought lucky. Nafis commands respect in the international arena, not only because of her huge presence, but because she is one of those exceptional women who demands respect for every other woman, no matter how powerless she is.

Rakhi Sarkar, the sophisticated and influential founder of the International Centre for Modern Art, is one of India's trusted opinion formers in the field of art and culture. She is now leading the creation of the premier institute of modern and contemporary art in Asia. Rakhi spoke of her gratitude to her distinguished father AK Basu, an expert in banking at the International Monetary Fund, who equally '*had a tremendous thing for education and ensured all his daughters completed their graduate studies at a time when the first agenda in a girl's life was to get married*'.

Difficult dads

Difficult relationships with fathers were more common than with mothers and often centred on the fathers' inability to make a positive connection with their daughters.

For the Reverend **Miranda Macpherson**, founder of the Inter-Faith seminary, her father's lesson was a valuable one, although not easy to learn. *'My father taught me the meaning of forgiveness which is just the hugest gift I could have imagined being given. I can't say that that was easy. He was such a tricky character; he was so difficult to deal with. It was so traumatic just to be in a relationship with him as a child that I had a breakdown at the age of thirteen.'*

Dame **Kate Harcourt** recalls how her father *'was a remote figure to me, as I spent most of my life at boarding school in New Zealand and I only ever saw him during the holidays so was never able to develop any sort of relationship. He died six months after I left school, when I was seventeen. I never really knew him or was able to recognize his quality. I remember his propensity for sarcasm and not much else'*.

Marian Rivman also remembered her father's *'hair-trigger temper'*. *'When all my friends were learning how to drive, which I also wanted to do, my father told me I could drive "over his dead body", a tempting idea at times! He valued my education and I was expected to excel at school, which I did. He made it perfectly clear that I was expected to go to college and that I would have to pay for it, which I did. I was expected to live a carbon copy life of my parents, a close-knit Jewish family in the Bronx neighbourhood of New York. Their greatest hope for me was that I would become a school teacher, get married and have children. He never understood I wanted more. My musings about the future were always greeted by remarks like "be realistic", "who do you think you are?" "don't be so full of yourself" I had no idea how I could possibly escape my seemingly mundane destiny.'* Marian created her own destiny and today is a successful New York PR consultant.

Miranda Macpherson

Kate Harcourt

'My father taught me the meaning of forgiveness which is just the hugest gift I could have imagined being given.'

Miranda Macpherson

Marian Rivman

Eve Pollard

Nadya

Barbara Follett

Eve Pollard, one of the stars of British journalism, remembers that her father was *'unappeasable'*. Even when she was the editor of one of Britain's national newspapers, her father thought she should be working on The Times. *'He was a bombastic, very charming, typical Hungarian.'* Eve clearly had affection for her father that came through everything she said about their relationship. *'I insist that my parents met because of Hitler; they both fled the Holocaust but they wouldn't talk about it until my father was very old. It was a combination of pain and guilt; "Why did I survive and not them?" My father was a mad inventor of different things, some good and some bad, so some worked and some didn't. One thing he invented was a thing called the tentomatic, which was a tent where the arms and legs came out of the car rack – you pushed it on top of your car and then filled the tent round it. When I see films of daughters who have wonderful relationships with their fathers, I get very emotional.'*

Designer **Nadya** had a difficult time communicating with her father. *'Although I never doubted his conceptual love for me, I felt he wasn't able to understand me. He was very relieved when I married. He thought I'd finally be the normal daughter he could welcome. So, the first night I was cooking dinner as a married woman, he called and asked what I was making. It was the rabbit and snails I'd learned to love in France. He actually never asked again. I noticed that whenever he came over for dinner, he ate first.'*

The father of 'folletting'

Politician and human rights activist **Barbara Follett's** father was difficult because of his alcoholism. *'I was born in Jamaica because my father, Vernon Hubbard, had gone there to set up the local branch of a British insurance company. After the war he returned to Britain and settled in Billericay in Essex. In 1952 we moved again to Ethiopia where my father set up the first insurance company, in partnership with Emperor Haile Selassie. It was in 1957, at a banquet given by the Emperor for Yugoslavia's*

President Tito, Daddy fell into a drinks trolley during the royal toast. This was deemed an insult to the Emperor and again we all had to move, this time to Cape Town. He continued to drink and we all suffered the consequences.' Barbara learnt from her father's life that it is possible to make a fresh start, however unfortunate the past has been. Barbara was herself able to make a new beginning when she escaped apartheid South Africa for Britain. Today she is one of the driving forces of the British Labour Party and with her husband, the writer Ken Follett, has given practical help to many aspiring women politicians. In fact Barbara was largely responsible for helping the British Labour Party redefine its image and for adding a new word to the dictionary 'folletting'.

Single fathers

Unlike the exceptionally intense bond that normally characterized the relationship between single mothers and their children, many single fathers were strict or detached in their approach. This was the case for the beautiful and talented linguist **Anna-Liisa Fazer**, whose father was a distinguished colonel in the Finnish Army. Although he loved her dearly, she missed not having a mother she could talk to while she was growing into a young woman. Air Marshal **Padma Bandhopadya** remembers her father disciplining his children and expecting the highest standards from them. Design guru **Rosalyn Dexter's** father was very handsome and charismatic and when her mother died he was left with five children to bring up. *'My father was an eccentric. He'd gone into medicine as a sensible option in life but at heart he really was an artist, a dreamer. He was a good father, he loved us, but he was not suited to the role of fatherhood. Father would always make sure that we had food on the table and make sure that we went to the best schools, but too many of them. I went to about thirty schools, lived in forty homes, and I suppose that laid the ground for me being a very good designer, because I had to make every place feel like home.'*

Girls will be boys

Throughout history men have always wanted a son and heir. For the Hindus it was the son who lights the funeral pyre for his departed father. That was the job for a son not a daughter. It may take decades for these kinds of cultural prohibitions to be finally broken but there is no doubt that in most cases the emotional bonds between father and daughter did not correspond to cultural restrictions.

Commonwealth human rights lawyer **Maja Daruwala's** own story is a delightful illustration of this point. *'There's a family story that when I was born in Quetta, my father, who was in the Army, was correcting his papers when his batman ran in saying "another baby", meaning a girl-child, had been born. I should say my father always tells this story with a rider that he never wanted a son.'*

It is also a significant thought that fathers of girl-only families wanted to make their daughters independent and self-sufficient. Not having the son to socialize into this role seems to have been an advantage for the daughters. **Esther Rantzen**, the TV presenter and founder of Childline, described how she and her sister were *'brought up as if we were sons, because father didn't have any sons'*. Similarly, **Sue Douglas**, who has had an outstanding career as a Fleet Street editor, studied physiology and biochemistry at university, partly to fulfil her father's expectations: *'I started learning physics and chemistry and wanting to be the boy for my father. I also played with trains!'*

Dame **Jo Williams**, Chief Executive of Mencap, felt she was the wrong gender for her father and it made her want to prove herself as a girl. This feeling was exacerbated when her brother was sent to a private school and she was sent to the local school. *'I think it had a huge impact on me because I was just determined that I could do as well. So I became Head Girl. I just wanted to prove myself really.'* Like Jo Williams, the author and agony aunt **Katherine Whitehorn** always felt her brother received favourable treatment, even though she too was given a first class education. Maybe at least part of their drive and vision to be

Anna-Liisa Fazer

Rosalyn Dexter

'Father would always make sure that we had food on the table and make sure that we went to the best schools, but too many of them. I went to about thirty schools, lived in forty homes, and I suppose that laid the ground for me being a very good designer, because I had to make every place feel like home.'

Rosalyn Dexter

Katherine Whitehorn

Mithali Raj

Esther Rantzen

Jo Williams

recognized as equal to anyone came from this early desire to prove their worth. In Jo's case she was able to take her father to Buckingham Palace and he was overwhelmed with pride for her when she received the Queen's recognition of her selfless devotion to others.

Captain of the Indian women's cricket team, **Mithali Raj,** explained that her father played cricket for the Forces and it was her entry into this man's world that allowed Mithali to discover her own talent and ambition for the sport. *'I used to go with my elder brother to the cricket nets and started to play cricket at the Boys Camp. I trained as a classical dancer and that really helped me with my footwork. Being the only girl in a boy's team I got a lot of support and motivation and my hobby turned into my profession. My father was so proud of me when I became Captain of the Indian women's cricket team, even though women are still not given the top ranking, backing, or the recognition that men cricketers receive.'*

In a story that seems to break all the expectations of the patriarchal family, Professor Dame **Meher Master Moos,** the youngest law professor in North America and one of the few women among the world religions, respected for their scholarly knowledge, explained how her arrival was the source of great joy. *'My horoscope foretold that I was destined to become a leader, so my parents gave me the best of everything. Father built this beautiful house in East Africa overlooking the sea, as he wanted me to be in an inspiring environment. We had a library full of books where I could read peacefully and prepare myself for my higher education and future life. I was taken on a world tour of Europe before settling down to study law. In 1957, when there was a Girl Guide's camp in Windsor, my mother was the Deputy Commissioner, and saw to it that I attended and represented Tanganyika. I was always put in the lead.'*

Perhettä tapaamassa

Встреча с семьёй

Träffa familjen

七大姑，八大姨

Meeting the family

We are family

No honest womaniser will admit to having a 100% success rate. Often one finds oneself alone in a hotel room with just the Gideon's Bible for company! Fortunately I feel quite comfortable in hotel rooms as I grew up in a hotel.

One of the delights of living in the hotel that my parents owned was growing up aware of the extended family, both the blood family of grandparents, aunts, uncles, cousins, godmothers, and also the surrogate family of long-term hotel guests who became family. The fact that everyone around me brought me up also meant that everyone had a stake in me. I learnt so many different lessons from different people.

I remember Dr Palmerfield, the original grumpy old man, who spent some time at the hotel. A medic, whose lack of bedside manner was notable, he travelled the world, including the Falkland Islands, considered extremely remote in the 1950s. As a result, during the 1982 local elections in Britain when the only topic of conversation was the war in the Falkland Islands, I was one of the few people who knew where the islands were! When I was introduced to **Sukey Cameron**, the Representative of the Falkland Islands, at the 100th birthday bash of Foyles, the world's most famous bookshop, I could not stop chatting to her. It brought back all the memories of my childhood and all the characters that came to our family hotel in central London. It also reminded me that no knowledge, however random, is ever wasted.

Extended family, extended strength

Many successful women grew up in extended families. Women, who were distinguished, dignified, and were seen across the world as symbolizing strong womanhood. Many spoke with warmth about their childhoods that helped to shape their strong personalities and determination to make a difference in the world. Her Excellency **Lindiwe Mabuza** is the South African High Commissioner to the United Kingdom. Her whole being changed when she spoke about being brought up in an extended family and how she benefited from a childhood shared with her father's other wives' children and her beloved grandmother. **Lyutha Al-Mughairy**, Chief of the Information Centres Service for the United Nations, enjoyed a similarly supportive environment in her home in Oman and remembers an aunt who loved her like a mother.

Judge **Zakia Hakki**, member of the Iraqi Parliament and the first female judge in the Middle East, was made to realize from a very young age that, as a Kurd, she was from the 'wrong race' and, as a Shia, from the wrong branch of the Muslim faith. All the same Zakia took strength from her home environment, her grandfather's house where the extended family lived. Her aunt, as well as her mother, breast fed her and that strengthened her bond to her cousins who were like her brothers and sisters. The women looked after the family and the men made the money. It was a very traditional Muslim family but it gave Zakia the tremendous strength to break with unjust traditions outside the home.

Not only did classical vocalist **Lakshmi Shankar** live with her extended family in India, but she also went on tour with the whole Shankar tribe. Organizational consultant **Rifat Wahhab** had also drawn strength from the extended family. *'I am so grateful to have been born in Bangladesh; the powerful memory and experience of being looked after by so many people, I am sure this shaped me.'*

Lindiwe Mabuza

Shakira Caine

Sukey Cameron

Lyutha Al-Mughairy

'We lived in an extended Muslim family in Guyana and although we weren't financially well off we were rich in every other way … We were brought up with immense love and generosity. That kind of upbringing gives you great security. You never feel lonely and what you don't have, you never miss. The only thing a child ever misses is not being loved and we were surrounded by love.'

Shakira Caine

Shakira Caine recalled how, even though life was difficult when her widowed mother was bringing up her three younger brothers and her, her grandmother and extended family were always there for them. '*We lived in an extended Muslim family in Guyana and although we weren't financially well off we were rich in every other way. There was never this idea that if someone came to our home they were just given a cup of tea; there would always be a huge meal. We were brought up with immense love and generosity. That kind of upbringing gives you great security. You never feel lonely and what you don't have, you never miss. The only thing a child ever misses is not being loved and we were surrounded by love.*'

There is often an assumption that the extended family is an Eastern structure but a significant number of women living in the West also praised its securities. Indeed, given the pressure on working mothers and the increased numbers of step-families, the concept of an extended family in which all members can be trusted and relied upon to care for each other's children is understandably appealing.

Political campaigner for women's rights **Lesley Abdela**, who was an only child, remembered the sociability of her extended family and how she was brought up with '*a whole tribe of boy cousins and from the age of six we went for weekends and holidays with them*'.

When the formidable Baroness **Usha Prashar** came to school in England from her home in Kenya she was able to enjoy the continuity and security of living with an elder brother and sister-in-law in Leeds.

Lesley Abdela

Martina Milburn

Mae-Wan Ho

Harriet Crabtree

'Auntie was like a goddess. She always wore trendy clothes and was so sophisticated. She allowed me lots of freedom. She was always in the background for me.'

Martina Milburn

'Grandmother would look at you and you would just melt because there was so much love. She wouldn't condemn anyone; she was a true Buddhist.'

Mae-Wan Ho

Family favourites

Many women spoke about how close family members shaped their lives, especially aunts and grandparents. Dame **Jo Williams** of Mencap recalls how *'the most significant thing that happened in my life was the affection given by one of my aunts, who married late in life. She was my role model. She encouraged my gift of being able to communicate with anyone, no matter what their role in life or status. She also gave me the confidence to believe in myself'*. **Martina Milburn**, Chief Executive of the Prince's Trust, similarly remembers the formative influence of her Aunty Bernadette *'who was a very clever woman and the youngest in my father's family. Auntie was like a goddess. She always wore trendy clothes and was so sophisticated. She allowed me lots of freedom. She was always in the background for me'*.

For scientist **Mae-Wan Ho** her grandmother was simply her favourite person. *'Grandmother would look at you and you would just melt because there was so much love. She wouldn't condemn anyone; she was a true Buddhist.'*

Director of the Interfaith Network **Harriet Crabtree** also adored her grandmother, who used to correspond with her every week; *'She was a constant source of strength to me'*.

It is also significant that grandmothers could be progressive figures too. **Rifat Wahhab** remembers her remarkable grandmother in Bangladesh, who insisted that none of her five daughters should leave home and get married without first earning their degree and thereby being able to stand on their own feet. *'That was over 70 years ago, revolutionary by universal standards. Her wish was fulfilled. My mother and my aunts all got their degrees and went on to marry wonderful men.'*

Patricia Licuanan, President of Miriam College in the Philippines, had a similar memory of her grandmother, a Filipino short story writer in English. She influenced generations of writers and was a professor at the University of the Philippines. *'Grandmother was quite extraordinary for her generation. She drove and was always ahead of her time.'*

Swedish saga

As an active board member of the Tetra Laval Group, and successful international horse breeder, **Kirsten Rausing** is one of the world's strategic doers. She is the model of a woman of substance. Modern and adventurous in her outlook, great fun to be with and with a quiet understated kindness, Kirsten draws inspiration from her past. She told me about her Viking ancestors in Sweden. *'They started off as seafarers. Often the men went on voyages for six to seven years. The women ran the farms, organized society and gave birth to children infrequently, usually with seven-year gaps. The women were strong and were great storytellers. The sun set early and that was their only entertainment.'*

In traditional Swedish storytelling fashion Kirsten bewitched me with her scene-setting. *'In 1912, grandmother left her small fishing village in Sweden and arrived in London in search of work. By enormous good chance a female Salvation Army officer who spoke Swedish helped find her a job as a lady's companion in Hampstead. She was clever and learnt English quickly. One Sunday, lying in bed, she was woken with a fright because all the church bells were tolling. She thought there was a terrible fire. In fact it was the declaration of the First World War. She witnessed the soldiers and volunteers marching in the street and singing "It's a long way to Tipperary". In 1915 she returned to Sweden by trawler, which survived an attack by German warships. She arrived a smart cosmopolitan lady, and soon married a captain in the Merchant Navy. She had a home with two maids of her own, and wore beautiful dresses. But, as they say, "a sailor has a girl in every port". Her captain was no different. After their divorce in 1922, my grandmother took all she could carry and travelled back to her parents. She was only twenty-five. They sent her away saying "Don't darken our doors – you're now his wife, not our daughter".'*

As I pondered the hardships of women during the centuries when only men could offer them protection and respectability, Kirsten continued with her compelling tale. *'What could granny do? In those days, if you were destitute you sold your body. She refused to do that and decided to drown herself. As she was walking into the sea, a family neighbour, a barber, saw her and rushed to save her. He and his wife gave my grand-*

mother their front room and lent her fifty pounds, which was a lot of money in those days. Grandmother started a millinery business. She used to order hats, felt and straw from places like Liberty's in London and create beautiful bonnets for her society clientele. She did fantastically well. She was very exotic and had many admirers. Then in 1924 a Mr Henry Mayne, an artist on a bike with his palette underarm, turned up and fell in love with her. He made her pregnant and they married. This was my grandfather and he didn't give up his cycling. He cycled on to the Riviera and lived in a painter's colony there. He would cable grandmother, who was by then a successful businesswoman: "Having a lovely time, send more money". My grandmother was a gutsy woman and used to say, "You don't have to play by the rules". She created her own rules.'

Bollywood blockbuster

Bollywood actress **Amisha Patel** is almost as famous for having taken legal action against her own parents as she is for her prettiness and acting skill. She has been able to draw on the strength of the extended family when her immediate family failed her. She comes from a distinguished Indian family. Her paternal grandfather was known as the uncrowned king of Bombay. Given the public profile of her family, her decision to claim her income back from her parents through legal process has been seen by some as a very public betrayal, going against the idea of a close family that draws strength from its shared resources. Yet Amisha's action helped to expose inequalities and exploitation. Fortunately, her paternal grandmother, Sheila Patel Gokhale, has been a vital source of emotional strength. *'She is my main idol because she is my sole support and completely urges me on.'* Like Amisha, her grandmother was also left alone within the traditional family structure. *'She has experienced a divorce and had an older son – my hopeless father – who didn't stand by her. She is my model of independence and success, despite the inevitable disappointment and hurt of being let down by those seemingly closest to you, Grandmother has stood by me.'*

'He would tell us fantastic stories about his adventures and how his travelling company performed Shakespeare throughout India.' Sanjna Kapoor

'My grandfather's love for me included respect and patience for a young, curious and inquiring mind.'

Jeroo Roy

'We two had a great thing going. He taught me so much. He would say "Ma petite Anne – heureux l'homme qui peut dire avant de dormer – Je n'ai pas perdu ma journée".'

Anne Perchard

'Grandfather involved me in every aspect of his business, including wrapping the chocolates in foil and even brushing up wrappers on the floor.'

Zeba Kohli

From mon grand père to Willy Wonka

Grandfathers were adored figures and their loving influence was cherished. Actress and theatre director **Sanjna Kapoor** spent her formative years with her Shakespeare-walla grandfather, the thespian Geoffrey Kendal. *'He would tell us fantastic stories about his adventures and how his travelling company performed Shakespeare throughout India. He would make the most mundane hamburgers sound like the most delicious exotic delicacy.'* Artist **Jeroo Roy** remembers being sent to live with her grandparents in Simla, where her grandfather owned a hotel. *'I went to school there and I was free to climb trees and mountains, to go horse riding. My grandfather's love for me included respect and patience for a young, curious and inquiring mind. He treated me as almost an equal and I can't recall any instance when I had displeased him, except once. Some neighbours who were painting their nails painted mine too. I remember vividly waiting for grandfather to come home, hiding my hands behind my back and then happily and proudly presenting the painted nails to him. All hell broke loose, not with me but the ladies who painted them. They were severely chastised. To this day I have never worn make-up.'*

The first woman President of The World Jersey Cattle Bureau, **Anne Perchard** also adored her Grandpa *'We two had a great thing going. He taught me so much. He would say "Ma petite Anne – heureux l'homme qui peut dire avant de dormer – Je n'ai pas perdu ma journée".'*

Zeba Kohli's grandfather really was every girl's dream, a real-life Mr Willy Wonka, Ahmed Fazelbhoy, the founder of India's Fantasia chocolate empire. *'He was a wonderful man and was respected by everybody in our Bohra Muslim community, as well as the business world. He was a philanthropist and he also represented over forty-one American international companies. He used to take me abroad when I was a teenager and introduce me to his business contacts. Grandfather involved me in every aspect of his business, including wrapping the chocolates in foil and even brushing up wrappers on the floor. He insisted I studied in Switzerland at the top European chocolate houses. He prepared me to take over the family business.'*

Family orders

Most people agree that a child's position in the family often has a determining effect on their character. Eldest children are socialized to be responsible, organized, and ambitious. Not only do the eldest and only children experience the undivided and anxious attention of their parents, but many also carry the burden of their parents' high expectations. It is no wonder that they often inherit a strong sense of responsibility. Certainly many of the 'natural leaders' I met did turn out to be eldest daughters, including **Dawn Airey, Indu Jain, Marjorie Scardino, Diane Abbott, Barbara Stocking, Sue Douglas, Wendy Somes, Kirsten Rausing** and **Yue-Sai Kan** – and the list goes on.

Interestingly, the youngest children fell into two categories, those who were spoilt and those who had to fight for attention. Those who were made to feel special had a strong emotional link to their families. They did not have the urgent need to succeed on society's terms and were often more imaginative and creative. The last of six children, Baroness **Usha Prashar** came into the family 'late' and was much younger than her siblings. *'I was a very happy child. My sisters would spoil me and a lot of care was taken about my education. My father was a very liberal father. He did not have any distinction between a boy and a girl.'*

In contrast, the youngest children who had to struggle for their place within the family were often ingrained with an acute sense of injustice that remained a motivating factor in life. Hollywood doyenne, film-maker and political activist **Elaine Attias** was the youngest of four children. She always enjoyed her mother's unconditional love but had to struggle to be noticed within the family: *'I had to really fight to get attention. I did fight like mad and developed the aggressive qualities in me and also a sense of justice. I don't know whether that is the source of my continuing passion for social justice, but it is certainly one of them. I wanted to right a wrong'.* Another early motivation may well have been Elaine's father's extraordinary resourcefulness. When his business failed, he simply put the family into the car and drove to Hollywood where he managed to build up one of America's most successful insurance business. In her own life and career,

Elaine has drawn on both the strong sense of wanting to fight injustice and the colossal optimism of her father. Both qualities can be found in her documentary work which has focused on the lives of immigrants opening up the West in America. Elaine is a woman of vision and vivacity.

A very similar family story was related by **Hilary Blume**, founder and Director of the Charities Advisory Trust, who was the youngest of three daughters: *'My childhood was a struggle against the lack of justice and the power play. My older sister was given greater rights and I could see no reason for it. I think I spent my whole childhood saying "It's not fair!" And I think I did get an absolute passion for what I see as justice. Also, being the last of three girls, you learn how to fight. We never fought physically, but I had to fight for my rights'*. Like Elaine, Hilary was inspired to take on larger battles against injustice in her adult life. She is known for seeking practical and realizable ways to make life more fair. Her creative solutions to both green tourism and charitable giving are also tell-tale signs of a younger sibling who is freer to think outside the family box.

I've got all my sisters with me

Women from girl-only families seemed to have a confidence in themselves and a real sense of companionship among their sisters. They spoke the most about their siblings and seemed to realize that sisters play was a very important part in balancing an individual, especially by criticizing them in an honest way. Some of their stories reminded me of Jane Austin's Mr Bennett syndrome in Jane Austin's classic book *Pride and Prejudice* in which sisters became a small society with their individual identities and fierce bonds.

Successful sisters included **Ana Lucia, Martina Milburn, Rakhi Sarkar, Patricia Bardon, Isabel Morgan, Wendy Fortescue-Hubbard**, and Baroness **Helena Kennedy** QC – and there are many more.

Double the pleasure

It's every womaniser's dream to date twins and have one on each arm. As they say double the pleasure, double the fun and sometimes double the trouble!

Life-long friends

Charity consultant **Ruth Powys** and her twin sister Mary felt doubly confident, even invincible. *'Having someone to play with and back you up against your parents and the world from the minute you're born imbues you with an enormous confidence in life. Comparisons between us made us obsessed with fairness. We would compensate each other for everything, right down to illnesses and infections. We are a corrupting influence on each other, prone to recklessness and giddy antics when together.'*

President of the North American Pakistani Women's Association **Arnaz Marker** is very close to her twin sister Aban, who is the President of the Handicapped Children's Association in Pakistan. Their devotion to each other has survived every separation. Professor **Zenobia Nadirshaw** is similarly close to her twin sister Zarine, even though they live on different continents. *'As I was growing up I considered Zarine my better half. She made me realize my personal achievements and that I was an individual, yet we are twinned together in friendship and love.'*

Double the fun

Push-pull

Jan Morgan remembers asking her mother who was the elder twin, Robert or herself. *'Don't you remember? Robert pushed you out and then you turned round and pulled him out!'*

You first?

Simone Poonawalla was told that she was actually the elder twin, even though she was born second, as the last to come out is the first to be conceived. *'I don't know if I believe it. My sister Delna was born nine minutes before me and we're very close. She is an extraordinary fashion designer. In twins you can feel the same pain and she often rings me as she knows how I'm feeling. She's very spiritual. I love her.'*

Spot the difference

Editor and founder of *Everywoman* magazine **Barbara Rogers**, herself a twin, felt that non-twins didn't appreciate that twins are two individuals and need to be treated differently. *'A lot of the problems twins experience could be avoided if parents simply ignored the fact that both children were exactly the same age and just treated them as two children within the family.'*

V-Day

For a significant number of women, the family and its values were a framework that they needed to rebel against in order to find their own way.

The acclaimed playwright **Eve Ensler** had a childhood riddled with conflict. She was the apple of her father's eye but also experienced his violence and her mother's inability to protect her children. Later in life she also experienced sexual violation. Aware that she was living in terror, Eve decided to use her experience to spearhead a worldwide campaign and bring the issue of violence to the forefront of people's consciousness. She drew on her conviction to involve high-profile celebrities in her concept of 'V-Day', a global movement that supports anti-violence movements around the world and seeks to end violence against women and girls, including rape, battery, incest, female genital mutilation and sexual slavery. Her defiance has certainly paid dividends. V-Day has raised over $25 million in seven years and her ground-breaking play *The Vagina Monologues* has changed attitudes to female sexuality right across the world.

Happy birthday!

Rekha Mody was the eleventh and last child of the famous Indian industrialist, Rai Bahadur Gujarmal Modi. Although she says that her family did support women's empowerment, there was also a demonstrable difference between the way boys and girls were treated. *'My brothers' birthdays were celebrated, but we girls never had a birthday celebration. It was so culturally embedded that the boys knew they were going to inherit everything and we knew we were not going to inherit anything.'* After she became financially independent, through the success of her publishing house and fine art business, she set up a number of social and charitable projects to improve the lot of women and children. These include the founding of Stree Shakti, a dynamic networking forum that provides a platform for joint actions on women's issues on the Indian sub-continent and now globally. In her own life too, Rekha has made changes in order to avoid passing traditional prejudices down the generations. She made a point of celebrating her own daughters' presence in the world: *'I celebrated the birth of my second daughter Isha with a champagne dinner for a hundred people, much to the amusement of my family and friends who did not understand the celebration of the birth of a second daughter!'*

No sexism please, we're British!

Ruth Powys also has a loving relationship to her family but needed to challenge some of their most fundamental beliefs. Born to evangelical parents in Britain, at the age of ten Ruth, along with her twin sister Mary, began to question the systems and beliefs that had structured their lives up to that point. Both directed their energies at a passionate interest in women's rights. *'I can remember ripping up my Enid Blyton books in sheer frustration because the girls didn't get to be part of the action! At the age of ten Mary and I campaigned for equal playground space for girls and in 1997, when we were nineteen, we were arrested for leading a feminist campaign against the sexist Virgin Cola launch.'* Ruth has now developed this focus on human rights in her public relations work for the charity sector. Although she rejected the lifestyle of her parents, her outspoken advocacy of freedom and rights for women and other oppressed groups may have been a positive parental lesson. As Ruth told me, *'They had strong values and were prepared to stand up for them, even if it made life difficult'*.

درس زندگی
Lecciones de Vida
Уроки Жизни
Schule des Lebens

Life's lessons

Beauty, brains and boldness

Womanisers are always attracted by a challenge. It was good fortune for me to mix with a whole variety of challenges from Bohemians to baronesses and blue-stockings! Of course there were those who had everything – the fine and captivating balance of beauty, brains and boldness.

My adoration for them was complete but I was not the first to recognize their worth. Many were the first women to achieve particular awards and some had the whole alphabet before and after their names! Society had rightly recognized them for taking their opportunities and excelling. They were Presidents and CEOs, MPs and Cabinet Ministers, High Commissioners and Ambassadors, Lord Lieutenants and High Court Judges. They were Professors, Vice-Chancellors, Canons, Ministers and Rabbis. Some were Fulbright Scholars, Ashoka Fellows, and holders of honorary doctorates. They carried the titles of Dame, Viscountess, Marchioness, Baroness, Countess, Rajmata, Maharani, and Princess. They had been awarded MBEs, OBEs, CBEs, Oscars, Lifetime Achievement Awards, and named TV Personalities of the Year. One had been nominated for the Nobel Peace Prize and another dreamed of sainthood.

All the same, few of them had the trophies of success handed to them on a silver salver. They had all worked hard and with vision to achieve their goals and had turned their aspirations into accomplishments. They possessed a strong sense of destiny from an early age, even when they had to battle against distractions, and disadvantages, to carve their place in the world. Many were given new insights and opportunities through education while others benefited from an education learnt through living. They were persistent, patient, pragmatic, and had no self-pity. They were virtuous, vivacious and very much worth meeting.

Formative years

It was fascinating to hear how childhood feelings and thoughts created an adult consciousness that was sensitized to particular ideals, and how early events powerfully informed future choices.

Barbara Stocking, Director of Oxfam, related her strong sense of wanting to strive for equality of opportunity to the inequalities that she witnessed. *'I suspect the reason I wanted to make a difference actually came from an understanding of the class background in Britain. My father was a postman, I was brought up in a town called Rugby with a famous boys' public school. They had so many more resources than we did, and seemed to have so many more opportunities. I could never understand why what seemed to be equally intelligent people in the same community had such different life chances. I'm not sure when this thinking about real class differences turned into an international outlook, but by the time I was sixteen I really wanted to make a difference in the wider world.'*

Judge **Zakia Hakki** was also motivated by her early understanding of injustice in her classroom in Baghdad. As a Kurd, she was seen as a despised minority. She was an exceptionally bright child but her achievements were constantly used against her. The teacher would provoke the other children by pointing at Zakia's work and saying that if a Kurd could do so well why couldn't they do better? She was made to feel an outsider and no pleasure was taken in her success. This only made Zakia even more determined to succeed. *'I struggled as a Kurd to have the best scores among all my classmates, just to let them know that I am not less than them; it was a struggle for equality'*. When she entered Baghdad law school, Zakia was the first student with an honours degree and achieved extraordinarily high scores of 97% for every branch of the law.

Zakia's personal achievements have been immense. She was appointed Iraq and the Middle East's first woman judge in 1959. In 1996 she fled to the US after both her husband and brother were killed for speaking out against the oppressive regime of Saddam Hussein. In 2003, Zakia became an adviser to the Ministry of Justice from the Iraqi Reconstruction Development Council, and was part of the team redrafting the judicial

'I could never understand why what seemed to be equally intelligent people in the same community had such different life chances. I'm not sure when this thinking about real class differences turned into an international outlook, but by the time I was sixteen I really wanted to make a difference in the wider world.'

Barbara Stocking

'I struggled as a Kurd to have the best scores among all my classmates, just to let them know that I am not less than them; it was a struggle for equality.'

Zakia Hakki

and political system of her country. As founder of the Kurdish Women's Federation and a member of 'Women for a Free Iraq', Zakia's campaigning on behalf of women continues to be central to her work. Despite an assassination attempt, she has continued to fight for minorities who, like her, have been made to feel that they are of less value to society. Her passion and endurance are an inspiration.

Joan Davies made history by becoming the first woman Chair of the Electoral Reform Society. The impetus for Joan to champion social inclusion also came at an early age when she saw a newspaper cutting about small children being bombed in the Spanish Civil War. Unlike Zakia's amazing academic career Joan, due to family circumstances, was only able to return to higher education after she had a family of her own. But, like Zakia, she used her education to empower not just herself but others. In her work, both in politics and teaching she has tried to represent the interests of women and children who are the often-silenced victims of futile violence and discrimination. It was not surprising that Joan's favourite childhood story was 'The Emperor's New Clothes' because she has always exposed dishonesty, whether it is the dishonesty of an unfair electoral system or the moral dishonesty of not taking action against the barbaric practice inflicted on women through genital mutilation. As the first woman lecturer employed at the Sandhurst Military Academy, she has been able to inspire young men destined to become the world's military leaders with her focused energy and common sense.

A positive early influence was formative to Human Rights Attorney **Judith Chomsky** when she experienced active involvement in community life. *'Through my fourth grade teacher I became involved in a socialist Zionist youth movement which provided me with many opportunities to experiment, explore a variety of talents from running a dance troupe to writing and leading discussion groups. When I was ten I met my husband who was also in the group. Through him I met Milton Krauss, his uncle, who was to be the single most influential person in my life. Milton, like the rest of my husband's New York family, had little formal education but their lives were filled with passionate intellectual activity. In 1967 I became active in* Vietnam Summer, *a project started by Martin Luther King. This was a turning point in my life. I became a*

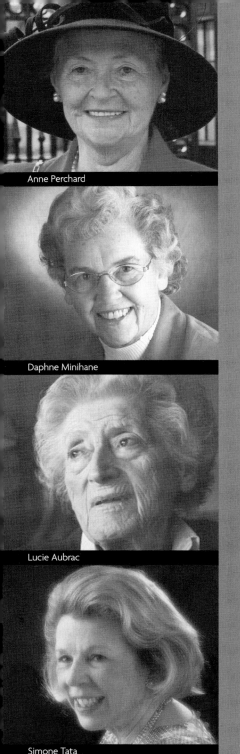

Anne Perchard

Daphne Minihane

Lucie Aubrac

Simone Tata

'The Germans took away everything: cars, cameras, radios, but more importantly our educational prospects and freedom. We were always hungry and cold, we had no heating at all so we'd go to the nearest Bake House to cook our potatoes. We worked together closely and learnt how to be economical. We learnt how to make a blanket into a coat. Those years of deprivation taught us to be resourceful and think of other people.'

Daphne Minihane

full-time organizer for the 'Resistance', an anti-war group. I was involved in various aspects of the movement for peace and justice.' From this grounding in the grassroots, Judith went on to law school and after graduation she helped found the Juvenile Law Centre of Philadelphia and began her life's work fighting for others' human rights.

Irish opera singer **Patricia Bardon** also attributes her life's path to a significant meeting. 'As a teenager I loved rock music, dancing, singing in choirs and potato crisps! My life was turned on its head at the age of fifteen when I was given the opportunity to have a consultation lesson with Ireland's most eminent singing teacher, Dr Veronica Dunne. Although I only had aspirations to be Ireland's Tina Turner at that point, she told me that if I was dedicated I could become a famous opera singer. As soon as I started singing classical music, I was hooked. At the age of eighteen, I became the youngest ever prize-winner in the history of the Cardiff Singer of the World competition and as a result my life changed overnight.'

Memories of World War II 1939–1945

Those women who had experienced the Second World War had vivid memories. The war had simply changed their lives. No matter where they had been, in occupied Europe and the Channel Islands, in neutral Switzerland, in England or Germany itself, they all mentioned the dreadful lack of food, the cold, disruption of their education and life, as well as fear of what might happen next. They also spoke about their defiance and how comradeship and community spirit gave them strength.

Lucie Aubrac worked as a spy in the strategic and dangerous underground resistance movement, Liberation Sud, during the German occupation of France in the 1940s. Like many women secretly involved in the resistance, Lucie assumed a normal life as a teacher at a lycée. Her clandestine activities were bold and revolutionary and many of her comrades were caught by Germans and executed or tortured to death. Her husband, Raymond, a French Jew, was captured, tortured and sentenced to death, but rescued at the last moment by Lucie and other resistance members. Both were vehemently pursued by the Germans until the end of the war but continued to fight for France's freedom: 'My roots were in France. This land, with its past, its traditions, its inhabitants who work on it and afterwards sleep below it, is something I don't want to lose. Our gaiety, our freedom, our pleasures, our way of life, the welcome of my uncles, wine-tasting cups in hand, extended to passers-by from the doorway to their cellar. And the pilfering conquerors, full of arrogance, who load freight trains with human beings of all ages, of all races, in addition to the Communist workers and the priests who hid Jewish children – they will never be our allies, and we refuse to let them be our masters.' After the war, Lucie resumed teaching and continued her impassioned struggle for justice through her involvement in anti-racism struggles. Her book, Outwitting the Gestapo, highlights the role of women in the resistance struggle and celebrates the bravery of those who died fighting for freedom.

A less well-known story is the occupation of the Channel Islands. Jurist Mazel Le Ruez, **Anne Perchard**, President of the World Jersey Cattle Bureau, and **Daphne Minihane**, all spoke about the dreadful cold and lack of food that they experienced during those miserable years. Charity doyenne, Daphne remembers the fear that everybody had that they would be deported for the slightest reason. 'The Germans took away everything: cars, cameras, radios, but more importantly, our educational prospects and freedom. We were always hungry and cold, we had no heating at all so we'd go to the nearest Bake House to cook our potatoes. We worked together closely and learnt how to be economical. We learnt how to make a blanket into a coat. Those years of deprivation taught us to be resourceful and think of other people.'

Even though she was brought up in Switzerland, a neutral country, industrialist **Simone Tata** spoke about the disruption of the war. 'My schooling was very much interrupted and influenced by the Second World War. There were lots of hardships, restrictions on food, on clothing, on eating. I remember it was the coldest winter I had ever seen. It was a period of real anxiety, never knowing whether we would be invaded, never knowing how things would end up.'

May the force be with you

A surprising number of the women had been brought up in an armed forces environment and recognized that the discipline of this lifestyle and its demands for self-reliance shaped their personalities. It instilled an ability to welcome new surroundings and a confidence to travel and develop new friendships. A forces childhood helped ground these women in discipline, comradeship, and the crucial understanding of when to obey orders and when to challenge them. It also instilled bravery and a sense of service.

Publisher **Judith Kendra's** father was a chaplain in the Army and, like so many forces children, she experienced life in other countries and was therefore more open to new challenges in later life.

Maja Daruwala and **Venu Dhupa** both came from Army backgrounds, with Maja's father Sam Manekshaw becoming the first Field Marshal of the Indian Army, in 1972, and Venu's a Colonel in the British Army. Both spoke about army life and how it taught them to be adaptable, proactive and at ease with all classes of people, all vital ingredients for a successful modern life.

Maggie Bellis, Managing Director of Corporate Services for Transport for London, was aware that her forces background gave her both confidence and self-reliance, although it had been difficult at times. *'I find it very easy to make new friends now because I had to when I was young. We changed schools so often and I had to make new friends and be adaptable. I always had that ability to be self-contained which is a quality one learns when one keeps going into new schools. Children can be quite cruel and so you have to be able to also stand up for yourself.'*

Convent girls

The grown-up 'convent girls' recognized that they had been taught to understand and appreciate a common humanity and an ethic of caring. Like the women who had experienced early life in the forces, convent girls acknowledged the value of discipline. So many of the women I encountered were either Catholic or benefited from a Catholic education.

Martina Milburn, Chief Executive of The Princes Trust, explained why she felt that her strict Catholic upbringing had been good for her. *They certainly taught us discipline and I am not talking about army style discipline'*. Although Martina confessed to being quite a rebellious teenager, she also added*: 'I do remember looking after my youngest sister as there is a fourteen-year gap between us and I even remember cooking Sunday lunch'*. The caring ethos and strong sense of duty with a purpose that the convent education offered to young people was evident in the way Martina approached life. Her strong personality has impacted on the lives of many young people who seek support and encouragement at a crucial time in their lives. Prince Charles' commendable choice of Martina to head his groundbreaking Trust has sent a clear message that women's particular qualities of leadership are to be recognized. The excellent work that The Prince's Trust does to expand young people's life opportunities is crowned by Martina's focused and inclusive direction.

Both design architect **Beverly Payeff-Masey** and President of the Indian Women's Press Association **Coomi Kapoor** found that convent schools stressed modesty and encouraged a very sheltered outlook on life. Beverly went to a convent in New York run by the sisters of St Francis, *'who were extraordinarily intelligent women, enormously disciplined in that they pressured us to learn a lot about world history and very little about the world'*. Coomi felt more ambivalent about the blessings of the convent ethos. *'There was a lot of stress on discipline, doing good to the world and putting yourself down, which is very nice but it took away your self-confidence. They gave you a lot of modesty and concern for your fellow men.'* Coomi's embedded sense of decency has enriched her work as a journalist and made her stand out as both a responsible and a respected figure in the world of contemporary media. There is no doubt that she is modest but that modesty adds to her character.

Scientist **Mae-Wan Ho** did not learn English until she was sent to a Catholic convent run by Italian nuns in Hong Kong, but she was also ambivalent about the values she was taught. *'The replacing of rationality with fundamentalist faith accounts for a lot of problems in the world. This is why I think I became a scientist.'* She defined her identity against the one she was encouraged to adopt in the convent but still valued spiritual depth. *'I am a misfit within the scientific community because scientists have no souls. To be a really good scientist you have to have the soul of a romantic poet.'*

Tricia Sibbons, social and charity entrepreneur, remembers that the nuns who taught her were *'radical feminists in the Catholic movement. They were interesting role models who made you think for yourself'*.

Maleeha Lodhi, Pakistan's High Commissioner to the United Kingdom, also received an excellent education when she went to a convent run by Irish nuns. She remembers the exposure that she had to all the great religions. *'Going to a convent taught me how to respect people of other faiths and our nuns never tried to convert us. They promoted common values of humanism; these are universal values.'* Like other successful women her courageous feistiness is based on a sound and liberal education that trusted her judgement and allowed her to flourish and show early signs of her destiny to be a key player in world politics.

So many women spoke with warmth and real affection about the nuns who taught them and how they gave them time and care. The Catholic Church was seen in a gentle and loving light because of them.

Maleeha Lodhi | Maggie Bellis

'Going to a convent taught me how to respect people of other faiths and our nuns never tried to convert us. They promoted common values of humanism; these are universal values.'

Maleeha Lodhi

Martina Milburn | Judith Kendra

Coomi Kapoor | Mae-Wan Ho

Education, education, education

For very many women education had offered the route to a different life. It was significant that one of Britain's most accomplished educators, the late High Mistress of St Paul's Girls School, **Elizabeth Diggory**, emphasized the importance of a rounded education: *'Education is about much more than exams. It is partly learning about what is within you, as well as branching out and looking at things that you otherwise would not have looked at, like new languages, other cultures and scientific concepts'.*

Helen Alexander, Chief Executive of the Economist Group, has herself benefited from an education at St Paul's Girls School. Helen was born in Geneva where her father was working for the United Nations High Commission for Refugees. She was a prototype European with a mixed European background, and was at ease with different nationalities, cultures and languages. After reading geography at Oxford, studying for an MBA and a short stint at Harvard, it seemed natural that she would join the Economist Intelligent Unit and finally be appointed the Chief Executive of the whole Economist Group. Helen is the enviable model of a classic education, a balanced home life, and a successful professional career.

While everybody thought education was important, ideas on what made a good education did differ. Author and Agony Aunt **Katherine Whitehorn's** seemingly simple comment, *'You can never educate the same child twice'* set me thinking about the tremendous responsibility that parents have in educating their children, not just academically but also emotionally and spiritually. It is often only when you look at your children as adults that you can see clearly what sort of education they needed and would have benefited most from. Although we are no closer to unlocking the perfect recipe for a stimulated, curious, balanced and happy child, there was a feeling that too much attention to purposeful activity may not be productive in the long term. Boredom may be the essential catalyst to creative and imaginative play and just staring at flowers or watching ants may offer a combined sense of concentration and wonder that reciting times tables can never deliver.

To be of value, an education must perform two major functions. One is to enlighten the individual by giving them an understanding of themselves and the world they live in and the other is to enrich the character. For many women in the world, education is not a right and mothers often have to demonstrate both determination and self-sacrifice to offer this privilege to their daughters. Judge **Leila Seth** shared her own story. *'My mother, who became a widow at the age of thirty-five with four children, said that whatever little money there was would go towards education. There would be no money for the wedding, but that doesn't matter.'* Her mother's investment was wise. Leila won a scholarship to university and went on to become the first woman Chief Justice to the High Court in India.

South African High Commissioner **Lindiwe Mabuza** also shared her own powerful story about gaining an education. *'My grandmother used to have girls from the countryside to stay with her so they could have their education. I really wanted to go to boarding school as I would have my own bed and there would be electricity. But my mother did not have the money to send me to boarding school. However, destiny worked for me. I travelled on a train and, as no one came to the station to collect me, I was put on the bus going to the boarding school. From the school I wrote to my mother and during the years I was there she worked very hard to ensure that the fees were paid for me to complete my education. After school I applied for nursing and during the waiting period I went with my friend looking for a part-time job. For some unforeseen reason, I entered a restaurant and asked to see the owner as we had only one shilling for food. The owner recognized me and asked me what I wanted to do. I said I wanted to study. He asked me to return with my mother as he wanted to repay the kindness my* *grandmother had shown his wife by helping to educate her. She was one of the five girls from the country that my grandmother had helped to get an education. He asked me to choose any university in South Africa and I chose Roma University, which is Catholic. This man and my education opened up the way for me.'*

Barbara Stocking recognized that her self-confidence only began to mature once she had achieved external recognition within the education system. *'Being picked to be Head Girl at school was a critical moment as I was picked out as having the qualities needed for leadership.'* Barbara did not come from a privileged background but, against the social odds of her time, she was encouraged to apply to Cambridge University. *'The fact that I got into Cambridge was a complete shock to me and my parents. Cambridge opened the door to a very new world.'* Being able to access opportunities through merit gave Barbara a sense of the possibilities for a more equal world. It was this sensibility of justice, along with her very positive outlook on life, that continues to inform her work as the British Director of Oxfam.

Several women still held strong memories of those special teachers whose lessons genuinely made all the difference to their lives. Thespian **Kusum Haider** recalls with gratitude her extraordinary drama teacher, Mr Kazi. *'He made me understand that, in the theatre, all the arts come together, so you learn you appreciate painting, architecture, music, and dance. That was one bit of crucial learning.'*

Peace campaigner **Eirwen Harbottle's** influential teacher was a rather daunting headmistress. *'She was a tall and handsome woman, a friend of the poet Walter de la Mare, George Bernard Shaw, the artist Robert Gibbons. She used to preside over the boarders' luncheon table. I remember her asking me "Will you have rice pudding or custard?" When I replied "I don't mind" she retorted "Don't mind? Haven't you got a mind? Now, which would you prefer, rice pudding or custard?"'*

Leila Seth Lindiwe Mabuza

'… in the theatre, all the arts come together, so you learn to appreciate, painting, architecture, music, and dance.'

Kusum Haider

Kusum Haider Eirwen Harbottle

Lila Poonawalla Isabel Morgan

No education is wasted

Lila Poonawalla was the first woman mechanical engineer in India and went on to become Indian Managing Director of the Swedish multinational Alfa Laval for over twenty years. She has received numerous awards, including the prestigious Royal Order of the Polar Star from the King of Sweden. She also runs her own foundation, which gives financial support for post-graduate studies to girls who are economically needy.
'I wanted to motivate women to step into the next millennium with confidence and encourage them to meet the challenges. I recognized the need to provide financial assistance to deserving girls in pursuit of higher education, and in shaping their own destinies.'

Lila is intelligent, charming, courageous, vivacious, steadfast, dynamic, takes no rubbish from others and to top it all is a great dancer. She and her husband Firoz have designed their own home, an Aladdin's cave which is stuffed with memories and memorabilia and unexpected collections of all sorts of things from match boxes to cows and a variety of clocks that all keep perfect time. Lila is a stickler for punctuality and discipline. Her sofa set was owned by the great Muslim Emperor Tipu Sultan, who was killed fighting the British in 1799 and known for his famous saying, 'Better two days as a tiger than two hundred years as a sheep'. Tipu Sultan also had the distinction of being the great-great-great-grandfather of my heroine Noor Inayat Khan, the British radio operator and spy, who was killed by the Nazis in Dachau and received the George Cross and the French Croix de Guerre for her heroism and self sacrifice in the Second World War. Lila, like my heroine Noor, has an energy that radiates action. She has a brilliant brain and a warm heart. Yet Lila's early childhood was not privileged. She spent her formative years in a refugee camp with her family near Pune in India. They arrived there after Partition in 1947, fleeing from their home in Pakistan. Her father had died in a train accident when Lila was only two and a half and so the family had to survive on his meagre pension. Attending the municipal school, she learnt Marathi, which at that time was looked down upon as a vernacular of the indigenous people, without the same status as Gujarati or English. Years later, as managing director of an engineering firm, it was a great asset for her to be able to speak Marathi, as that was the language of the workers. It helped in negotiations with the trade unionists and made the workers feel they were really valued, and she understood their issues and spoke their language. As Lila knows from first hand experience no education is ever wasted. When and where it will be useful is just a waiting game.

Jai-Hind Madam

The historical author of *India in Britain, India – British-Indian campaigns in Britain for Indian reforms, justice & freedom* and *An Indian Portia*, **Kusoom Vadgama** grew up in an atmosphere where there was great respect for British education and deep hatred for the British rule in India. *'I went to the Government Indian Girls' High School in Nairobi. Anti-Empire views could only be expressed outside the school boundaries. The English principal gave a guideline that "Jai-Hind" was not to be uttered in the school. It enraged me and I had to disobey. A plan was devised. At the next school assembly, instead of saying in unison "good morning Madam" we should all say "Jai-Hind Madam!" When the time came, others got frightened and decided to keep quiet when I alone shouted loudly, "Jai-Hind Mrs Lincoln!" I expected to be escorted to the school gates for immediate expulsion. Instead I was politely told that I was too young to get involved with politics and should stick to my studies. I did. At the age of twenty-one I began a new life, studying optometry in the country of my dreams, Britain. I developed a deep desire to know about the history of Indians in Britain during the Raj and have been obsessed with the subject ever since.'*

A child's gift

Sadhvi Bhagwati Saraswati grew up in a privileged area of Los Angeles. 'I don't remember seeing poverty in my early years. However, we used to go to New York every year for thanksgiving, to be with my grandparents. As we walked the streets of New York (I was probably about eight) I asked my father if I could have my own money. In that innocent state of the young child wanting to be independent, I wanted to personally be able to buy myself a pretzel, or hot chocolate, or chestnuts. So he gave me $20, in a mix of $1 bills, $5 bills and a $10. But by the time we got to the stand for hot chocolate and pretzels, I had to ask him to buy them for me. "What happened to your own money?" he asked me. I admitted that I had given it all out, in a few short blocks, to the beggars on the street. I couldn't bear to say "no" to any of them. Rather than scold me for going through $20 in less than ten minutes, and belittle my charity, Father said, "That must have made a big difference to the beggars," and promptly bought me my hot chocolate and also gave me another $20 to use as I saw fit. So, right from the beginning, my nature was encouraged and nurtured. Who I was and the decisions I made were respected, and I was never made to feel that I was making a wrong decision.'

Hard lessons in the classroom

A few of the women felt that their schools had failed them, often by not showing confidence in them or by overlooking their achievements. Very few, however, did not want to succeed at school and it is perhaps ironic that the woman who scorned her school education most openly is now one of the most powerful women in the world. **Indu Jain**, Chair of *The Times of India* group, was quite plain about her rejection of a conventional education: '*I never enjoyed school – I never wanted to study, so I got married. I was very happy to get married. I hated studies*'. It is a truism that you will always do better if you direct your energies at those activities that bring you joy, and in Indu's case it certainly proved to be true. She went on to excel in real life.

Who wants to be a millionaire?

Isabel Morgan is one of the kindest women I know. She has had a life that's included some spectacular highs as well as lows as one story serves to show. Isabel was going through a tough time financially when she saw a young woman use a cash machine but forget to pick up the money she had withdrawn. Although Isabel chased after her, the woman jumped on to a bus, leaving Isabel with a handful of crisp £20 notes. Her family could certainly have used such a windfall but Isabel instead handed it into the station manager's office. Within a week, the gods gave their judgement. Isabel and her eldest son, James, took part in a special Mothers Day edition of *Who wants to be a millionaire?* and won £250,000!

Isabel, now head of the broadcast unit at Christian Aid, was brought up by a strong, supportive and loving mother, who always made the best of any situation, however difficult or challenging. When her mother divorced and moved eight-year-old Isabel and her older sisters to London, she provided a home for the family by working as a live-in housekeeper for Sir Alun and Lady Pugh. In an example of how our lives are often strangely 'and wonderfully' interconnected, it was during this period that the Pughs' daughter, Bronwen, married Lord Astor. On her wedding day, Bronwen needed to pin on her corsage and the only small gold safety pin that could be found was the one holding up the hem of Isabel's Brownie uniform!

Sadly, the warm and creative atmosphere of Isabel's childhood home was not echoed in the classroom. Isabel was bright and won a scholarship to a top London girl's school but neither of these factors protected her from the class prejudice of 1960s Britain. When she decided to apply to Oxford University she faced outright opposition from her teacher. *'There was a huge stigma. My first application form for Oxford came through and the form mistress said "this is ridiculous, why are you applying for Oxford?" I said "because it is what I want to do". In front of the class she said "Your mother can't even afford the uniform for this school" and she tore the form up.'* Undaunted, Isabel sent off for another form and succeeded in winning a place at St Hugh's College, Oxford, where she was to learn more hard lessons about social barriers. She became friends with one of the young women who cleaned her room and encouraged this woman, who loved books, to approach the bursar about an opportunity to study. There was to be no Cinderella ending to this story though, as the girl was dismissed from her job, and Isabel was reproached for her friendship with the *'wrong sort of girl'*.

After graduation Isabel was determined to work in international television news and current affairs but this was the era just before the sex discrimination act and it was an industry beset with male prejudice. As one BBC executive told her during a job interview: *'we have no intention of ever using a woman as an overseas correspondent'.* The reputations of war correspondents Christina Lamb and Barkha Dutt prove the nonsense of this view and, thankfully, by the end of the 1970s, things were beginning to change. Isabel was one of the pioneers as a TV journalist, producer and commissioning editor, who opened up opportunities for other women and young film-makers. After eight years in the newsroom of Visnews, now Reuters TV, she moved to Worldwide Television News, now APTN, and became Editor of *Roving Report*, a weekly programme that brought issues of injustice and global inequality to an international audience in more than 40 countries. After two decades of working in broadcast television, combining a full-time job and foreign assignments with a happy and supportive marriage to Rob and the birth of their four sons, Isabel moved to her present role with Christian Aid. There she has developed innovative ways to use video to bring voices and stories of people in the developing world to viewers in the UK and Ireland. *'It's only by drawing upon the commonality of human experience – the hopes, fears and joys we all share whatever our circumstances and wherever we live – that there can be the growth of understanding needed to bring about change.'*

Kusoom Vadgama

Sadhvi Bhagwati Saraswati

Wendy Fortescue-Hubbard

Sister Cyril

'Rather than scold me for going through $20 in less than ten minutes, and belittle my charity, Father said, "That must have made a big difference to the beggars," and promptly bought me my hot chocolate and also gave me another $20 to use as I saw fit. So, right from the beginning, my nature was encouraged and nurtured. Who I was and the decisions I made were respected, and I was never made to feel that I was making a wrong decision.'

Sadhvi Bhagwati Saraswati

LIFE'S LESSONS

Maths Agony Aunt

Wendy Fortescue-Hubbard teaches and inspires the unsuspecting audience, making mathematics accessible to the masses through a variety of avenues. Her dyslexia, she believes, enhances her ability to inspire people in mathematics. This includes working with a cross-section of society, innovatively adapting more traditional methods through to utilizing the newest technologies to inspire the audience. Wendy has written a Mathagony Aunt column, responding to readers' problems about mathematics and mathematics education in *The Times Educational Supplement* and is the Mathagony Aunt on Teacher's TV. She often uses poetry as an illustration of the mathematical concepts. Her pioneering work has led her to give workshops in deprived areas of the UK, resorting to teaching maths in people's sitting rooms and kitchens, training them to deliver mathematics to others in their community.

Wendy has more recently been using the latest in collaborative video webcasting to teach. This experience has given rise to 'Learn and Earn', which combines peer mentoring and live delivery over the internet, in which young people are being trained to support other younger pupils in mathematics at various levels, receiving payment to do so. This offers them a way not only to extend their own mathematical understanding through having to teach, but also provides them with a revenue stream for accessing higher education for themselves.

Like **Sister Cyril** in India Wendy knows that young people can be excellent teachers, and indirectly teaching makes them excel in their subject. Wendy is very clear that her philosophy is: '*If a seed is sown it grows and scatters its fruit to the ground, some of which in turn grows to maturity, disseminating its seed to new grounds in a continuous cycle*'.

serious scholars

Scholarships have been a key to transforming many of the women's lives. They open up new horizons and take people into new environments which allow them to try out different ways of thinking and being in the world. They also affirm people's value and give them the confidence to see themselves and their achievements in a positive light. For many of the women I met, winning a scholarship enabled them to access an education and ultimately a life that would otherwise have remained out of reach.

Editor of *The Times of India*, **Dina Vakil** recalled her own experience. '*I was sixteen when I won an American Field Service Scholarship that offered students a year in America, living with a family and attending High School. I had this extraordinary opportunity to go and live in Iowa. We flew to Amsterdam and then to Rotterdam to get in a boat called the* Seven Seas. *It was like a junk ship that had been converted into a floating university and we floated from Rotterdam to New York. It took us ten days and it was wild and wonderful because there were kids from all over the world. It was my first experience out of Shivaji Park, an enclave of Bombay. It was magic.*'

Oscar-nominated screen writer and photographer **Sooni Taraporevela** related a very similar experience of leaving India for the first time on a scholarship in America. For her, a scholarship to go to Harvard was ' *"The New World" for me. It was while at Harvard that I met Mira Nair, the producer and director. The two of us became friends and that developed into our successful partnership and collaborations on films such as* Salaam Bombay, Mississippi Masala *and* My Own Country'. Harvard was also the launch pad for Sooni to enrol at New York University where she studied film theory and criticism. As she said, '*My introduction to films did not happen until I got there. I didn't know you could actually study films*'. It is through Sooni's films that many people in the West have come to a new understanding of India and so her work has completed the circuit of carrying knowledge across continents.

While studying at Oxford, lawyer **Ashminder Kaur Dhadialla** decided to start the Sikh scholarship foundation, Mata Sahib Kaur Scholars. This enables Sikhs to aim high and benefit the whole community. Despite the usual fundraising miseries, the project is succeeding and the first scholars have now graduated from Oxford. *'Sikhs are under-represented at leading institutions and tend to be poorly educated in relation to their own religion and history. As such, students who get our scholarships, have to take a course on Sikh history, religion and social issues. This provides the community with a group of informed educated young people who are clued into Sikh issues and willing to work on them.'* Ashminder is also aware that other minority groups would also benefit from similar schemes and she hopes to expand the scheme to provide scholarships to Australian aborigines and the Bushmen of South Africa. *'They are also 'stateless' people whose identity, way of life and image are degraded and they are often a soft target for the majority to push around. Sikhism is a religion that stresses helping the underdog and a Sikh Scholarship Foundation should do just that.'*

University challenge

Oxford and Cambridge may be known as the intellectual home of the élite, but the Oxbridge scholars that I was fortunate enough to meet had often broken social and attitudinal barriers to gain entry to these historic institutions. It struck me that their success was not attributable to an Oxbridge education as much as to the spirit that had taken them there. All the same, the benefits of a university education and real intellectual stimulation were clear.

For Managing Director of Sky TV, the charismatic **Dawn Airey**, school life was tedious and it was only after seeing a TV documentary on 'A Week in the life of Girton College, Cambridge', that she realized that she wanted

Dina Vakil   Sooni Taraporevela

'Oxford changed the way I looked at the world and myself. I was given the confidence to believe that I could do anything, go anywhere and be what I really wanted to be.'

Christina Lamb

Ashminder Kaur Dhadialla

Christina Lamb

Kate Parminter

Wendy Savage

to go to Cambridge and that the power of television was also to be her destiny. '*Cambridge was transforming. We were looked after and taught individually. You met interesting people and you were treated as if you were special.*' Her stellar career is certainly a glittering testimony to both her own ambition and the stimulating environment that she embraced.

Women's campaigner and gynaecologist Professor **Wendy Savage** also recalled the challenging and supportive environment that Cambridge offered. '*It opened up a whole new world to me. In many ways my adolescence had been sheltered and restricted, and meeting people from all sorts of backgrounds, talking late into the night, and having a chance to be taught by stimulating and unconventional people was a wonderful start to adult life.*'

While young girls in East Africa, both **Ashminder Kaur Dhadialla** and Professor Dame **Meher Master Moos** decided that they were going to go to Oxford to read law. Meher remembers the extraordinary Lord Denning asking her to sit on his right hand side at college high table, an unbelievable honour for a sixteen-year-old from the then Tanganyika.

Think global, act local

Oxford also gave **Kate Parminter** self-belief and confidence that she had previously lacked (as the product of the local comprehensive) to set out to achieve her goals. At Oxford Kate was given excellent private tuition by academics who believed in her. She also spent time with other bright young people who believed they could change the world and went on to do just that. '*I felt if they could, so could I.*'

'*I wanted to get involved in the running of my town. The policy area that particularly interests me is the environment. I came across the issue seriously at Oxford – with dynamic protest campaigns from Friends of the Earth and Greenpeace. I hadn't picked up on them until then. This interest burgeoned when I became a local district councillor on coming down from Oxford in the mid-1980s. The maxim 'think* global, act local' was almost made for conscientious councillors like me who were determined to do something to protect the local environment. You started out thinking about bin collections and realized there was a much bigger picture to address. My key achievements at the time were to persuade the council to adopt a CFC free policy and to protect a key large local area of land from development. I wanted to campaign for the environment and went on to run the CPRE (Council for the Protection of Rural England). I wanted to influence public policy. At CPRE I successfully led the organization to overturn the government's plans to weaken public engagement in deciding on the location of large-scale infrastructure projects (like airports) and to maintain a strong policy on the Green Belt. As an organization we championed the value of planning as a tool for securing environmental goals and the value of local people having a say in decisions which affected their local environment. I guess you could say that mirrors what I stand for. I'm now a Trustee of the IPPR (Institute for Public Policy Research). Without Oxford these would never have happened.'

Licensed to thrill

Award-winning foreign correspondent for *The Sunday Times*, the formidable **Christina Lamb's** whole being changed when she recalled the thrill of going to university. *'It was a complete eye-opener for me. Oxford changed the way I looked at the world and myself. I was given the confidence to believe that I could do anything, go anywhere and be what I really wanted to be. No one in my family had been to university so I knew nothing about Oxford, and chose a college because it was on the High Street between the bank and the pub, everything you could need! I had always wanted to write and became editor of the university paper* Cherwell. *I had a licence to go and interview anybody I fancied and of course I could ask them anything. It was wonderful training to be a foreign correspondent.'*

Life's lessons

While the benefits of a formal, academic education were a major factor in making many women's success possible, others were keen to point out that the 'life lessons' learnt beyond the classroom were often as valuable. Determination, imagination and confidence had inspired and steadied these high-achievers through a series of obstacles and made their triumphs and achievements all the more glittering. It was by stepping outside the comfort zone that these women actually learnt the most.

For **Anne Perchard**, it was not that she shunned a conventional education but rather that the circumstances of her life encouraged her to learn differently. Anne excelled at school and won a State scholarship to the Jersey College for Girls. However, her parents were very short of money because her father suffered from a debilitating illness throughout the German occupation of Jersey during the Second World War and there was no free National Health Service to pay for his care. Anne took the decision to stay at home and work for her parents, as most farmers' daughters did in those days. She harbours no regrets at having missed out: *'It was no pain for me – I loved the soil, the cattle, hard physical labour and working with nature, learning all its whims and fancies'*. The land itself was an excellent education. Belonging to a strong, settled community meant that Anne was able to gain the skills and knowledge to succeed without a university education.

Claire Bertschinger, the Red Cross nurse who featured in Michael Buerk's harrowing 1985 report from Ethiopia and inspired Bob Geldof's Live Aid, could not read until she was fourteen because of her dyslexia. *'I was not good academically but only excelled in caring.'* Claire's vocation for nursing grew from an encounter at the age of seventeen in Switzerland when she met missionaries who were spreading the word of God. It was then her *'mind became focused on medicines and health'*. Claire has life force, a golden aura that is undeniable. She has saved lives under fire in many of the world's most desperate trouble spots. Indeed, while award-winning war correspondent Christina Lamb was reporting to the world about the violence in Afghanistan, Claire was picking up the wounded. Although she

Anne Perchard

Dina Glouberman

Claire Bertschinger

Eirwen Harbottle

'Many people today have come to a moment in their life when it doesn't work any more, either because they have changed or because the situation has changed. They don't step back and rethink, but instead they drive themselves harder. It's like driving a car with the accelerator and the brake on at the same time. So they burn out and then they find out what they are really about. They have to move from wholeheartedness through burn-out to wholeness, which basically is about knowing who you are.'

Dina Glouberman

was not an able pupil at school, Claire learnt life's most profound lessons through her devotion to nursing. As well as educating through her own example, she now teaches at the London School of Hygiene and Tropical Medicine. In 1991, she was awarded the prestigious Florence Nightingale Medal. Ironically Florence Nightingale is remembered for nursing during the Crimean War, yet she never saw the battlefield. Claire has been at the heart of the madness of war. She has seen first hand the cruelties of war and famine and has demonstrated that a woman who never excelled at school, but who has passion and compassion in her heart, can change the world.

For **Dina Glouberman** the lessons of her early life were central to her adult career path. *'My childhood was in many ways an experience of isolation. In my family, although there was love there was not much overt loving, and very little communication about what was important. I also went to a school which was a conventional religious Jewish school, while my parents were unconventional and not religious, so I was always a bit of an outsider, a stranger. I was lucky enough to go to summer camps with the ethos of the socialist Zionism of the 50s, where the community atmosphere and the natural warmth brought out the best in me. I later also became involved in the personal development movement of the 60s, where communication, loving, and our inner truth were valued and where, once again, I blossomed.'* Reversing the old adage, Dina believes that 'we learn what we teach'. She learnt that she could create the changes or provide the tools to make a better life possible and this is what she also teaches through Skyros Holistic Holidays. As Dina says: *'We aim to create a community atmosphere and a sense of belonging and authenticity such that no one who came there need ever feel a stranger nor pretend to be what they aren't. Many people today have come to a moment in their life when it doesn't work any more, either because they have changed or because the situation has changed. They don't step back and rethink, but instead they drive themselves harder. It's like driving a car with the accelerator and the brake on at the same time. So they burn out and then they find out what they are really about. They have to move from wholeheartedness through burn-out to wholeness, which basically is about knowing who you are.'*

Global footprints

Often the opportunity to travel and take advantage of being in another place provoked a turning point in these women's lives. Adapting to a new context and living in a new place may have seemed daunting, but almost without exception every woman who had spent time living in different countries had benefited enormously from this experience. The energy that they had invested in the move seemed to be more than returned by new friendships, different outlooks and new worlds. Travel not only brought fresh insights but it created opportunities to break with the past. It taught self reliance, adaptability and a sense of daring.

Quite a few of the women had international childhoods. Both **Pim Baxter** of the National Portrait Gallery and **Eirwen Harbottle**, founder of the Centre for International Peace-building, travelled from the 'colonies' to school in England as young girls. Pim remembers being included in lots of different social events while her parents were working in the Caribbean and Africa and how it gave her a real advantage in later life. *'My parents took me to a lot of things with friends, so I became used to dinner parties at quite a young age. That ability has taught me confidence with my current job. That ability to talk with someone you've never met before and create a bond with them started very young.'*

Although Eirwen was lonelier, she also emphasized the benefits in terms of social skills. *'At twelve I left our home in Cyprus and had to travel to King's High School for Girls in Warwick, where my sister was head girl. I was a lowly "new bug". I only saw my parents in the summer holidays, travelling alone on a P&O liner, and transferring to a smaller boat bound for Cyprus. This taught me to become confident about travelling alone and being responsible for myself, which was a valuable lesson.'*

Both **Julie Mellor** and **Rosalyn Dexter** had travelling parents but both families took their daughters along on their travels. Now a Partner at PriceWaterhouseCoopers and former Chair of the Equal Opportunities Commission, Julie travelled with her father who was in the RAF and thrived on the variety that it brought. *'It was a fantastic experience being in Aden and East Africa. I think I was in ten schools before the age of eleven.'*

Hither and yon

For some women travel was an end in itself, whereas others crossed continents to study or work.

In many global industries travel is simply part of the job, as fashion designer **Nadya** explained. '*I spent six months of the year in Bali, four months travelling in the States doing showings in seven cities, and two months visiting other parts of Asia and Europe. It's not consecutive travel, and I'm back and forth a lot. Once I actually visited five continents in five days!!!*' The stunning international model **Ana Lucia** has also travelled the globe as 'a dedicated follower of fashion'. '*With my modelling career I have travelled the world from my little town Barretos in Brazil. I was always seeking adventure and love. I soon realized that the places and faces changed but the goal was always the same. We are all looking for the same thing and funnily it is right under our noses. It is in our hearts.*'

It was in her capacity as a teacher that the Director of the Institute of Science in Society, **Mae-Wan Ho**, fulfilled her distant dreams that brought together travel, environmentalism and inner harmony. '*I led a group of students on global ecology, integrating nature and culture. We travelled to Mexico, which had always been a dream of mine. Another dream of mine had been not to split my scientific persona and my private persona. I wanted to be a coherent being. What I believe in science is what I believe in private. It is my feeling of being at peace with myself, at peace with the whole universe. Which is the ideal of the Chinese.*'

Interdisciplinary artist **Radha Chandrashekaran** was born in India and now lives in America. But it was a trip to Australia in the year 2000 as a visiting artist that had a profound affect on her award-winning works. During her time in the Northern Territory of Australia, Radha made the connection between Kolam – a traditional Southern Indian ritual art form which involves decorating the entrance of homes with rice powder every day and for festivals – and the patterns on bark paintings created by Northern Territory Aboriginal women from Arnhem Land. This cultural

crossover became the subject of Radha's doctoral research. 'The similarities were striking. In our present world we have been bombarded by the media's relentless assault on our spirituality. The role of art expression in daily lives has the potential for human healing. It is fascinating that most cultures use art in its many forms to express something deep in their very being.'

Artist **Ruth Uglow** also drew attention to small, but significant, awakenings from her time in Namibia when she was there on a Royal Overseas League travelling scholarship. *'When you are away and you see things in new environments, you open your mind to all these different experiences. It might be something very small, just different vegetations that inspire you, different colours. Just seeing and being in different places, just broadens your horizons and part of my work is about putting yourself in other worlds and other places. When you draw, you spend time in an environment and you draw what is in front of you and you start to observe minute details, and then you become heightened in your awareness. You are then tuned into looking very intensely at what's around.'*

Those who have had experience of living and learning in different countries and cultures have clearly been at an advantage in the increasingly global world of work. **Marian Rivman's** working life has been extremely eclectic. As a student she read anthropology and then took a series of jobs as a consumer researcher, an advertising agency executive, and a school teacher, before settling to become an influential public relations consultant in New York. Moving across such a varied career landscape gave Marian a breadth of experience and sensitivity to her clients' varying needs. However, it was her time spent as a Peace Corps volunteer in the Philippines that she regards as most influential. *'Going to the Philippines was the first independent decision I made as an adult. It was pivotal in my life. I had lived at home when I was at college. It was the first time I had full reign over my life. I was living 10,000 miles from home in a culture vastly different from my own seminal experience that has shaped my world.'*

Global gourmet

Karen Anand is known as India's global gourmet and referred to as 'the Martha Stewart of India'. Recently she won France's prestigious 'Trophée 2006 Pour la Culture' for her work promoting French food and wine in India over the last twenty years. She is truly an international citizen. Of Goan origin, educated in England and France, with time spent in Russia and Spain, she is a perfect example of cross culture and fusion. Karen prefers to call what she creates *'borrowing from different cultures to create harmony, balance and excitement'*. And with her constant drive and eagerness to learn, she forced her way into every kitchen she could, whether it was in Bangkok, Bali or Sydney. She returned to her roots in India as an adult, armed with her travelling taste-buds and her ability to show-case and present with flair.

Karen is a one-woman business success story. A dynamo, she writes books, presents television programmes, created her own brand label, sets up top class restaurants, holds master classes in culinary magic and yet manages to be a loving and devoted mother, wife and daughter. Karen says that after all the cookery books she has authored she wants to write a humorous one called *How to cope from Monday to Friday*, as a tribute to how working women have to 'muddle through' life and be a success at the end of it! The book would be a best seller as Karen is seen as the food guru for India's middle classes who she has introduced to lean cuisine, crunchy salads and her individual flamboyant style of east-meets-west contemporary Indian food. She is a one-woman food and lifestyle experience and has that much sort after commodity personality which is stamped on all her work. It even shines through her pretty jars of preserves, salad dressings and speciality sauces, and signature style food. She shares the benefits of her own success within her wider community. She only employs women at her production unit and ensures that her business supports them.

For Karen, *'success does smell sweet and it's good to have money in the bank, and the freedom it gives to travel. Also the confidence that you've achieved something, brought up children who are decent human beings and that you have friends who love and admire you, makes all the hard work worth while'*.

Mother tongue

When **Taleya Rehman** was in her late teens the political situation in Bangladesh was focused on nationalist issues and in 1952 there was a big language movement, which culminated in the separate state movement. She was an active participant but she then moved with her husband, the journalist Shafique Rehman, to England. Although she was at a distance from the politics of her home, as a deputy head teacher in London she found that she was still very much involved in the debates over language politics. *'While in school, I was doing social work also. In selected communities they can't speak English and I used to go to my students' homes to assist and that's how I got into women's issues. I started campaigning for mother tongue teaching.'*

When Taleya went back to Bangladesh she continued her campaigning at this grassroots level, working with her husband whose paper was very popular with the young population. Taleya's work as a teacher and broadcaster, working for over thirty years with the BBC in London, enabled her to intervene in issues relating to human rights at a very practical level. She founded Democracy Watch in Bangladesh, an organization that campaigns for popular education and female empowerment. It advocates studies on democracy and good governance and is linked with a training institute to discover and train future leaders. As Taleya argues: *'Education is first and foremost. We need to educate people to be involved in world issues and to communicate with the world'.*

Queen of Fringe

Sometimes the significance of the journey is not measured by its distance. **Thelma Holt** had a successful career as an actress and went on to found the Open Space Theatre in London, but her most significant achievement was to give a new profile to community theatre and to bring regional theatre to London. She has been dubbed the 'Queen of Fringe'. Thelma later joined, as Executive Producer, the Theatre of Comedy, where she produced *Loot* by Joe Orton and was also responsible for major tours of National Theatre productions abroad. Thelma brought great theatre from other parts of the world and helped change the direction of British theatre. As **Kazue Hatano**, the founder of the Society of Japanese Theatre Designers, and herself a pioneer in production who has worked at the National Theatre in England said, *'Thelma deserved to receive the Olivier/ Observer Award for Outstanding Achievement in the Theatre. She was a force to engage Japanese theatre, which I am involved with, to come and perform in England and for English theatre to perform in Japan. She is the actor's ambassador'.*

Tales of the unexpected

For some women, the desire to explore the unknown, challenge themselves and learn from the unfamiliar, was a strong motivational drive.

Meher Heroyce Moos is not known as India's most intrepid traveller for nothing. Her extensive travels to over one hundred and fifty countries of the world has still not quenched her thirst for meeting people, seeing new places and eating exotic delicacies. In fact, eating with Meher is an unforgettable experience which will probably be written up in her weekly society column for Mumbai's glitterati and those who aspire to join them. No matter what restaurant she enters she engages everyone, from the waiters to the chefs to all the other diners. She is a one woman show on gastronomic delights that must be promptly conjured up by the unsuspecting chef while she recounts tales of the unexpected that will be lapped up by the other guests. Meher has experienced the diversity of the globe and has travelled right up to the Antarctic continent on board the famous liner *Lindblad Explorer*, sailing from Cape Town to Cape Horn, as well as deep into the jungles of the Amazon. She has literally crossed continents, covering the length and breadth of South America and journeying right across Central Asia, following the ancient silk route of Marco Polo. As a true traveller, Meher has always sought destinations off the beaten track and in 1981 she embarked on a five-month solitary exploration of over thirty-five countries in Africa. Bent on discovering forbidden and inaccessible interiors, she marched across the Sahara to fabled Timbuktu, home of the Tuaregs; and went on to live with the Pygmies in the dense equatorial forests. It was a veritable odyssey, demanding exceptional endurance which Meher showed with her usual bravado.

Around the world in eighty ways

Another adventurer, **Caroline Casey,** founder of the Aisling Foundation, made a life-changing decision to leave her job and follow a dream at the age of twenty-eight. That dream was to travel across India on an elephant and become a mahout, an elephant trainer. She trekked 1000km across Southern India. This challenging journey was a long-held personal dream of hers but it was also a way of shaking herself out of the negativity she had begun to feel about her visual impairment. *'It was a way in which I could regain confidence in myself but also a way in which I could raise awareness about the ability of people with disabilities.'* Although she had consciously pursued the unexpected, what she discovered was still a surprise: *'More than anything I would never have believed, until I lived it myself, just how much I had to learn. And I did learn it but, then again, I did have the best teacher. Just who would have thought that teacher would have been an elephant!'*

Taleya Rehman

Caroline Casey

Kazue Hatano

Meher Heroyce Moos

'More than anything I would never have believed, until I lived it myself, just how much I had to learn. And I did learn it but, then again, I did have the best teacher. Just who would have thought that teacher would have been an elephant!'

Caroline Casey

Caroline's adventures abroad and her ventures at home have made her a great success story in Ireland. However, like many other women who have genuinely embraced life in all its dimensions, she remains open to the possibility of failure and its own rewards: *'I think it is important not to be frightened of mistakes. It is how you get over them and move on that makes you a person. Failing, though hard, is about learning'.* The *Irish Times* cleverly titled their article on Caroline, 'Blind Ambition' but I could tell immediately that there was a real vision to her work.

In 2002 she became part of a team going *'around the world in eighty ways'*, a twenty-first century version of Jules Verne's novel. With two other disabled adventurers, Caroline left Britain for Ireland, France, Monaco, Italy, Egypt's Red Sea, South Africa, India, Thailand, the Malay Peninsula, Singapore, Hong Kong and the United States. Not only did this intrepid journey give Caroline another chance to travel by elephant, but also to adventure by ostrich, camels, a cardboard boat, canoes, Chipmunk planes and tug boats. Her resolve to use her personal strength and immense energy for the benefit of others places her alongside so many other women, who emphasized that personal empowerment must also be directed at the empowerment of others if it is to be experienced as real fulfilment.

Gli uomini: la sorprendente ricetta per vivere felici

رجل: السر المدهش للحياة السعيدة

Miesten suusta: Onnellisen elämän yllättävä salaisuu

男人是幸福生活的奥妙

Men: the surprising secret to a happy life

Yes my darling

Most successful women I met had men in their lives that they were deeply in love with. Young men and toy boys seemed never to have been in fashion. For nearly all of them it was the older man. He had a lifetime of experience, was confident, considerate to their needs, and guided them in their careers. Although new masculinity is the term used to indicate men who are caring, involved and active partners, many older men were described as nurturing and able to show their loving support. Indeed, the amount of praise that the women heaped on their men was one of the most surprising discoveries!

The trailblazer in maths teaching, Maths Agony Aunt **Wendy Fortescue-Hubbard** – who has broken new ground in the teaching of maths and making it accessible and fun – recounted how her first father-in-law used to say that if you want a successful relationship you should always say *'yes dear'* to your husband. Wendy went on to divorce her first husband. She is now happily married to a delightful man who likes to support her and say *'yes my darling!'*

As ever I turned to my mother and enquired *'is it really true that the secret to a happy relationship is to be a "yes" person?'* Mother said *'no'*. The secrets were much more complex. To have a perfect partnership you needed to be friends and lovers. There had to be a physical attraction, along with respect and understanding for the other person's independence. Shared interests and values were vital, as well as a sense of humour. Mother's last piece of advice was to give the other person space and avoid *'always being on top of them!'*

In praise of the older man

Sarah Miles followed her mother's example as well as her mother's advice. *'Both mother and I preferred older men. My father was twenty-four years older than mother; he was a Renaissance man. I also loved older men like Robert Bolt, my husband, and Larry (Laurence Olivier).'* Although a compelling pairing, the relationship between Sarah Miles and Robert Bolt, the Oscar-winning screenwriter was more unusual than many of the marriages I heard about. As Sarah explained *'Robert had been the most eloquent man in England. He had written the scripts for* Lawrence of Arabia, A Man for All Seasons, Dr Zhivago, Ryan's Daughter *– all the great movies of our time'*. They were married for seven years, divorced for seven years, and then Sarah decided to return to her love, Robert, because he was paralysed and couldn't speak and needed her. Sarah's devotion to Robert, and her experience of nursing him for fourteen years until his death in 1995, had clearly given her the ability to pass positive energy on to others. Despite being one of the silver screen icons, Sarah was very clear about her achievements in life: *'I am not really proud of anything I've done except looking after Robert for fourteen years, being faithful, loving and being jolly. Life is far more important to me than a mere career. Lately people who come into my presence go away happier. I'm good at that, whatever that is and I love to see somebody that has become unhappy leave feeling okay'*.

Sheer magnetism attracted prima ballerina **Wendy Somes** to Michael when she saw him on the stage at Covent Garden. *'I saw Michael and it was like an electric shock, a bolt of lightning.'* Michael may have been most famous as the partner of Dame Margot Fontaine but his marriage to Wendy was equally well choreographed and harmonious. *'He had tremendous inner strength and he told the truth which frightened a lot of people. He taught me everything in the ballet field and about life. He was my mentor, teacher, friend; he was my lover, my everything. He was quite an extraordinary person. Michael kept me a little bit wrapped in cotton wool as he didn't want anything to hurt me. He looked after me almost too much. We used to do everything together, we worked together, and we lived together. Everything he liked, I liked. It was just incredible.'*

Sarah Miles   Wendy Somes

'He is so confident about himself, he has no insecurities... and no ego I have to massage. I am quite in awe of his intelligence, and hugely dependent on him for his inputs. He's a friend, a good live-in mate, with no strings attached.'

Renuka Chowdhury

Renuka Chowdhury

Zandra Rhodes

Diane Burton

Kate Harcourt

This ability to move in tune with each other, to feel guided and enlightened was also mentioned by several other women who had married older men. Artist **Diane Burton** remembers how mature and knowledgeable her husband seemed when she was a young woman. He had first hand experience of the world of cinema and had mixed with artists; he had travelled and was a raconteur, but more importantly, he shared her love of art.

Older men cherished and valued women; they wanted them to achieve their potential. Younger men all too often needed to have their egos stroked or their careers prioritized. Fashion designer **Zandra Rhodes** cut the perfect cloth of words to describe the competitive partnership that she and many others consciously avoided. *'My present partner is older than myself. I never thought there was any point in going out with someone your own age and equal calibre, it becomes too competitive. Men are a bundle of inferiority complexes; if you go to a dinner and they have a place tag "partner of Ms Rhodes" they can't take it. How many women have had name tags as "partners of Mr Rhodes"?'*

Indian Minister of State **Renuka Chowdhury** made a similar observation about the strengths of her marriage to an established industrialist who was older. *'He is so confident about himself, he has no insecurities that I have to sit and pander to, and no ego I have to massage. I am quite in awe of his intelligence, and hugely dependent on him for his inputs. He's a friend, a good live-in mate, with no strings attached. He refuses to be in competition. He is that cool and when people say, "What's your name?" he says "Never mind, think of me as Mr Renuka Chowdhury". He has got a fantastic sense of humour, which is the greatest attraction between us.'*

Dame **Kate Harcourt**, who was honoured as Dame Companion of the New Zealand Order of Merit for her outstanding contribution to theatre, also confided that her marriage had been a great source of strength to her: *'My husband supported everything I did. We both needed to work to bring in an income, so that there were no tangible difficulties to overcome. Ours was a particularly loving and supportive relationship. Our lives were complementary in every sense of the word'.*

Barbara Stiocking

'I was lucky to have a husband who is completely committed to women's equality. He was prepared to take time off when we had our first child, to work part time and play a major part in bringing up our children.'

Barbara Stocking

Marjorie Scardino

'I'm married to an absolutely perfect husband so there you go. How much more lucky could you get?'

Marjorie Scardino

Barbara Follett

'Ken has backed me; he's supported me, financed me, and advised me. He's just been there for me.'

Barbara Follett

Helena Kennedy

'My husband makes me feel just the way my father did, very special.'

Helena Kennedy

What's it all about?

Oscar Wilde said *'Men want to be a woman's first love – women like to be a man's last romance'.* Actor and heart throb Michael Caine had been many a woman's first love from the moment he starred in the film *Alfie,* which transformed him into a twentieth-century Casanova. When he was famously asked in the film, *'What's it all about, Alfie?'* he hadn't met Shakira and therefore didn't know that when you meet your eternal love all desire for anyone else is extinguished. When **Shakira** fell in love with Michael Caine, for them the age difference didn't matter. He was able to show her a whole new world and she changed his world too. As she said, *'Michael showed me the way and I was there for him'.*

Best supporting role

The women I was fascinated with were not prepared to waste energy on difficult relationships. Those who married men of a similar age to themselves also chose reliable, supportive men who were proud of them. There wasn't any jealousy, just pride and devotion for the women they admired and adored.

Editor and broadcaster **Eve Pollard** spoke about her marriage to Sir Nick Lloyd in positive terms. She was also clear that women were more able to achieve if their husbands had a secure sense of themselves. *'Women whose husbands are right behind them do well and especially in Fleet Street. I think you have to have an exceptional man, who doesn't mind you being successful, who doesn't mind the fact that you are being written about. A successful man in his own right.'*

Holly Sargent was equally open about the fact that her husband played a starring role in her life. *'Robert has an integrity which is like a rock for me. He has always been incredibly supportive of anything I want to do, He would say to me, "Holly, if you want to do that, you set your mind to it, and you can do anything". Most importantly, I should say that*

Robert wanted to have children and I was so ambitious, so wrapped up in my career, that I really didn't see how I could have children. Today we have two beautiful daughters and Robert is brilliant as a father and husband.'

Julie Mellor, former Chair of the Equal Opportunities Commission, a strong advocate in promoting and supporting the changing role of fathers, acknowledged that her *'husband has been the nurturer of the whole family, who took time off from his work as a director to look after us'*. **Karen King Aribisala**, Associate Professor of English at the University of Lagos, Nigeria, similarly said, *'I am blessed with an understanding husband who "allows" me to be the me that I am and he helps me out with each and every conflict I encounter.'* Karen is also an accomplished writer and so it is not surprising then that she was able to express her mutually empowering and enriching marriage in such beautiful language.

'There for me'

Given the classic image of the successful woman as cold, hard-nosed and unemotional, one of the most fascinating findings has been how many of the women chose to emphasize their close personal relationships as being fundamental to their success.

The healing and transforming power of love, the selfless emotional commitment to another, is well-documented and so it is perhaps not surprising that women who share a loving relationship with a life partner were keen to draw attention to the huge advantage that they felt this gave them in all the dimensions of their life.

The distinguished Chief Minister of Delhi, **Sheila Dikshit**, praised her late husband: *'He was the one who encouraged me to come into public life. He made me understand so many things, my grasp of life, my grasp of human beings, my understanding all came from him really'.*

There for us

Frances Cairncross, Rector of Exeter College, Oxford, and **Helen Alexander**, editor of *The Economist*, spoke with obvious love when talking about their husbands who were true partners. Frances recognized that her husband *'was always keen that I should be an independent, intellectual force. He was always there for me and the girls'*. For Helen, the equal basis of her relationship was also translated into everyday living. *'My husband is a broadcaster and we live our life as equally as possible. We share various household jobs and take part equally in our children's lives.'*

Author and Agony Aunt **Katherine Whitehorn** emphasized the pleasure and reassurance of having a loving partner on whom she could always rely. *'Gavin, my husband, knew where he was going and I knew where I was going, in the same direction. He always wanted me to be everything I could be. He turned out to be brilliant with children, and as a writer who worked from home he was there from 10–3.00 every single day for seventeen years while they were growing up. Being bloody happily married for forty-five years does give you confidence.'*

There for my dreams

This same sense of sharing real closeness and yet allowing each other to develop was also highlighted by Baroness **Doreen Miller**: *'I so wanted to get into the House of Commons that I mortgaged our home. I thought "I'm mad, I have a successful young solicitor husband, three boys all down for private education and I was willing to risk financial security to make my dream of becoming a Member of Parliament come true". Henry, my husband, asked me how was I to pay for my campaign and I told him, "I had given our home as collateral". He said "of course, I knew you had the guts"'.*

Sheila Dikshit

Doreen Miller

'Not one day did I feel he doubted my credibility. That confidence and trust gave me so much courage. He is so proud of me. He is my inspiration.'

Lila Poonawalla

Lila Poonawalla

Karen King Aribisala

Helen Alexander

Jennifer Gretton

My inspiration

For industrialist **Lila Poonawalla**, her husband Firoz was more than special. *'When I became Managing Director of Tetra Pak, I was travelling nine months in a year and he was alone. Yet, not one day did I feel he doubted my credibility. That confidence and trust gave me so much courage. My mother used to ask him, "Are you mad, you are sending her alone, going and meeting men all over the world? You will lose your wife". Firoz's answer was "If she finds a man better than me, then she will tell me. What is the point of living with me and not considering me to be the best? I think she thinks I am the best and she will come back to me. Our relationship stands the test and I have no concern". He gave me total trust. He is so proud of me. He is my inspiration.'*

German born scientist **Uta Frith**, Professor in Cognitive Development, regarded her English husband as *'the greatest influence of all. He taught me the English language and cultural heritage, he shared and expanded my love of art, poetry, science; he was largely responsible for teaching me the basic methods of psychology, statistics and neuroscience; he not only encouraged me to be a successful researcher, but made it possible'.* Like others, Uta recognized that having a partner who supported her in both practical and emotional terms has been absolutely fundamental to her achievements and her enjoyment of those achievements. *'Both privately and professionally he made me a happier and more fulfilled person than I would have ever been. My husband is the main source of inspiration and all others pale by comparison. He has truly been instrumental to my success.'*

Steamy love

Lady **Jennifer Gretton** is the Queen's respected representative, Lord-Lieutenant of Leicestershire. She was born into a stable and loving middle class home and entered the world of the English aristocracy through a shared passion for steam engines. Her husband was a steam engine enthusiast and they fell in love through his hobby, giving an unusual meaning to steamy love.

Power couples

Many of the women I met may have had marriages made in heaven but their power was also felt firmly on earth. Among the many 'power couples' were **Eve Pollard** and Sir Nick Lloyd; **Coomi** and Virendra Kapoor; **Lila** and Firoz Poonawalla; **Barbara** and Ken Follett; **Uta** and Chris Frith; **Eirwen** and Lieutenant-General Michael Harbottle; Maharaja and **Maharani of Tripura**.

Fleet Street

Eve Pollard and her husband were the only British couple who edited national newspapers at the same time. '*I edited the* Sunday Mirror *and he was editing the* Sunday People *and then he edited the* News of the World *and then the* Daily Express *and I ended up editing the* Sunday Express. *Five papers in total.*'

Press corps

Former President of the All India Women's Press Corps, **Coomi Kapoor**, met her husband, Virendra Kapoor, while they were working on a newspaper together. Both are contributing editors now. Coomi's Sunday column 'Inside Track' in *The Indian Express* gives the background on what's happening in Indian national politics and is the touchstone for anybody interested in political personalities and party political manoeuvrings.

Ambassadors – two for one

Ambassador's wives actively worked to support their husband's lives and careers. They were very exceptional women, sophisticated, highly intelligent and effortlessly special.

Wendy Luers married Bill when he was the American Ambassador to Venezuela. Part of the strength of their marriage undoubtedly comes from Wendy's excellent understanding of her value as a partnership wife. *'The job of an ambassador is getting to know people in the country where they are. So, as a wife and partner in every sense of the word, the more papers I read, the more languages I speak, the more I understand about the country, the more likely it is that my husband is going to do his job that much better. We have mutual respect for each other's intelligence and networks, it's two for one. You're getting me free of charge.'*

Kusum Haider, wife of Salman Haider, who was also formerly Foreign Secretary of India and High Commissioner to Britain, was aware of her supportive role and yet she also continued to star in her own career. *'As a High Commissioner's wife, you have to have a public persona and do the correct things, which can cause stress. You meet interesting people; see the most amazing countries, so this is a small price to pay. I also was able to continue my acting and directing.'*

For **Arnaz Marker**, being married to Ambassador Jamsheed Marker meant she was a part of living history. They both served in postings to Geneva, to Bonn, to Paris, to Washington, and to the United Nations, where he chaired the Security Council. Jamsheed was later asked by the UN Secretary General to be his personal envoy in East Timor leading up to the independence of the territory. Arnaz was President of the UN Ambassador's Wives Association. They were seen as one of the most successful diplomatic partnerships.

Lady **Lynn Jones Parry**, married to Sir Emyr Jones Parry, UK Ambassador and Permanent Representative to the United Nations in New York, commented on how the role of an ambassador's wife has changed. *'I have travelled the world with my diplomatic husband. I had to adapt when we moved around the world and I left my teaching post which I adored. When we first started I was a mission wife. In those days during the first week diplomat's wives had a formal tea; that doesn't happen any more. There is certainly far less pressure on spouses these days and wives often have their own careers.'*

Zeba Kohli Naina Lal Kidwai

'I couldn't have done anything if I hadn't had the implicit and explicit support of my husband. That support meant not just that I went and did my own thing, but that he adapted his life to mine.'

Aban Marker Kabraji

Angela Morris Aban Marker Kabraji

Shusha Guppy Angela Lennox

The King and Queen

Maharani Bibhu Kumari Devi of Tripura is married to the last ruler of Tripura, who became King at the age of thirteen. His throne is as old as the Sanskrit epic, the *Mahabharata*. The Maharaja traces his ancestry back to those ancient times. The Maharani is not only a mother and champion of tribal people, but an extraordinary politician. A remarkable power couple, the King and Queen understand the words of their family friend Tagore, the first Indian writer to receive a Nobel Prize for Literature, in 1913, '*We are nearest to the great when we are great in humility*'.

Modern day Ruth

The Very Reverend Canon **Vivienne Faull** said that the book of Ruth was her favourite book in the Bible. It reminded me that so many of the women had spoken about being 'outsiders'. They had taken extraordinary risks, committed themselves to other peoples and causes and had gone on to make an impact beyond their own ambitions. The biblical Ruth had left her own people and returned with her mother-in-law to the country of her husband, undertaking a huge venture that carried her across barriers of religion, culture and tradition to become one of the ancestors of Jesus. While these women had not quite endured the trials of Ruth, they had often gone against tradition and family expectation in order to marry the men they loved.

Editor **Sathya Saran** really did run away from home to marry her love. '*I left my home and married in secret and then returned. My parents tried to match me with another man, and I had to reveal my secret eventually. As I had not consummated the marriage, they spoke about annulment. It was only when I said that annulment would bring even more publicity because I had married outside the community, to a man who was neither a Brahmin nor a South Indian, that my family accepted the situation.*'

Both **Zeba Kohli**, the chocolate queen, and **Naina Lal Kidwai**, Head of HSBC in India, married out of their communities. As Zeba recounted, '*I married the most exquisite looking Punjabi Hindu. His family were Hindu refugees from Pakistan and my father-in-law was to have been beheaded during partition. They managed to escape and come to India. He now has a Khoja Muslim daughter-in-law whom he loves*'. For Naina too, her happy marriage has been a great reward for the risk of breaking traditional barriers. '*I married out of my Hindu community, my husband is a Muslim, and he is completely supportive of what I do. He is my severest critic, my sounding board, and shoulders the responsibility of bringing up our daughter.*'

Author and singer **Shusha Guppy** wanted to be her own casting director and saw her opportunity by marrying out of her Iranian community to an Englishman, a Byronic figure who never had a second-hand opinion. He was an explorer, lived in a jungle and was a great writer. '*A friend gave him my telephone number and he rang me up and when we met each other that was it.*'

Yes Minister!

For years, Indian Minister of State **Renuka Chowdhury** '*tried to be stereotyped. I wanted to be the girl every guy wants to take home to his mother. That all changed when I had a look at the mothers and said, "Oh God, perish the thought, I can't bear it". It took a while to get used to breaking that mould, because there is so much peer pressure, so much family pressure around you that tells you to belong to their ideals. Praise, remuneration, recognition, is all there only when you are the sausage in the factory. You have to be marriageable, affordable, and accessible, with modest skills and modest means and I wasn't having any of that. I rebelled against it. Why should I demean myself? What was I looking at, some guy waiting to pay my bills? Forget it, I can make my own money and pay my own bills and pay his bills too*'.

Weekend husbands

For quite a few successful women a weekend husband was the answer to a life without strife, as you had no time to fight. In fact leading lives apart in the week led to an unexpected satisfaction. As Dr **Angela Lennox** explained, it can be a good recipe for maintaining the romance and excitement that daily living erodes. *'Our interests complement each other; we usually try and have a week or two together on holiday but most of the time we are apart and that is very exciting.'* She added *'For our first six years of marriage we used to meet up once a month for weekends; it was like a Hollywood movie. In fact my neighbour once asked me the name of the gardener who came once a month. I know why she said it; because I would shout down the garden "Do you have sugar in your coffee?" I was married to him but I had no idea'*.

Minister of State **Renuka Chowdhury** was keen to point out the positive aspects of a weekend marriage. *'We are weekend husband and wife, who over a period of time, have a rather comfortable relationship, because there is really no time to fight.'*

Obviously couples who live apart for long periods need to have a strong and trusting bond. **Rachel Oliver**, Director of Communications at the National Farmers' Union, really valued this in her own marriage. *'My husband and I have a real partnership where we can disappear for four or five days and there is no resentment. A total give and take.'*

For **Aban Marker Kabraji**, Director of the World Conservation Union, the give and take of a travelling marriage was central to its success. *'I couldn't have done anything if I hadn't had the implicit and explicit support of my husband. That support meant not just that I went and did my own thing, but that he adapted his life to mine. When the children were young we had a basic agreement; if he was travelling, I was at home. If I was travelling, he was at home. Now that I work in Thailand and he runs his law practice in Pakistan, we meet at weekends and holidays to suit our own timetable.'*

What's in a name?

People ask 'what's in a name?' Many women felt that their education and career mattered less than they would have done if they had been men. They chose to keep their own names and identities when they married and resented being seen as 'other halves'. Academic Dr **Angela Morris** expressed this perfectly. *'I hate that the only thing that distinguishes me from my husband is the 's' in "Mrs". I've been reduced to an 's!'*

Peace activist and founder of the Kesher Project **Sallie Gratch** had a similar message to her story. *'My mother came from a generation that protected its women. She chose to be at home and to "run the household". Naturally, she wanted my life to be like hers. Perhaps the best example of the initial congruence of our lives and the eventual shift that occurred were the note cards my mother had made for me when I got married. The cards had engraved on the face, "Mr and Mrs Alan Gratch". I recall that, at first, I felt wonderful with my person being consumed by my husband's name. It seemed secure, comfortable. It was part of what I had observed, learned about married life growing up in my family. And it felt OK. But years into my married life I began to feel uncomfortable with this imposition of his name into mine. I could assume his last name, but not his first. While many of those cards still sit unused in my drawer, their presence reminds me that change is always possible; and that the most important thing is to embrace what works for you while keeping a comfortable balance with those whose dreams you have replaced with your own.'*

With or without you

Rosalyn Dexter was married for seventeen years to a successful doctor and, although she had made millions by then, she remarked that in those days she thought she *'couldn't have done it without him'*. In fact, her great entrepreneurial and creative skills had made her successful. Her husband was never involved in the business. Yet she used to tell herself that she would give up everything to support him and desperately wanted him to be the breadwinner and look after her. It was only later that she dropped the idea that power was something to do with being masculine. '*Power in the right people is what the world needs.*'

Fashion designer **Nadya's** troubled marriage empowered her in an unconventional way. '*As difficult as my marriage was, I learned invaluable lessons primarily relating to differences in thought processes and natures. It was a PhD in human behaviour, and I've applied those lessons to many other areas of my life.*'

Sex and the single girl

German disability champion **Dinah Radtke** was told to forget men as no man would be interested in her on account of her disability. Although separated now and enjoying her own company, Dinah lived with a partner for twenty years. Editor **Dina Vakil** also enjoys her independence and in her classy way frankly told me '*I don't miss not being married. I wanted very much to get married when I was in my thirties; at that particular time you may have set your heart on somebody then other people came into your life. Anyway, I am married to the* Times *of India and when I'm asked, "What is your husband's name?" I say "Mr Bennet and Mr Coleman" (the founders of the newspaper). They are my two husbands!*'

Broadcaster **Carole Stone**, now happily married to author and veteran television journalist Richard Lindley, looked back on her unmarried life with sound advice and spoke for so many other women when she recalled '*When I was single I used to sit by the phone at night waiting for some man who wasn't going to ring me. I should have said, "That one didn't work" or "If he wants to ring, he knows where I am", and gone out and enjoyed myself'.*

Secretary-General of World Federation of UN Associations **Pera Wells**, made an important point about the new 'single women' of our time. '*Single women do live a different kind of life and I don't think we have acknowledged the benefits of what that kind of life brings into the twenty-first century.*'

Sue Stapely   Pera Wells

'Single women do live a different kind of life and I don't think we have acknowledged the benefits of what that kind of life brings into the twenty-first century.'

Pera Wells

Amisha Patel

Kiran Bedi

Jackie Ballard

Bani Dugal

For Falkland Island representative **Sukey Cameron**, and Chair of the United Kingdom Overseas Territories Association, being a single woman was also empowering, but she was incredibly open about the sense of aloneness that not having a loving partner often evokes for men and women. 'It does sadden me at times to think I don't have that someone at the moment to share and enjoy the wonderful life I have.'

As somebody who almost single-handedly made being a single girl a fashionable status, by writing her book *Sex and the Single Girl*, **Helen Gurley Brown's** view on marriage was instructive. 'I think marriage is insurance for the worst years of your life. During your best years you don't need a husband. You do need a man, of course, every step of the way, and they are often cheaper emotionally and a lot more fun by the dozen.'

Soul mates

Eirwen Harbottle's second husband, Lieutenant-General Michael Harbottle, was an inspiration to her and vice versa. '*Michael needed a woman to believe in him. He needed to be taught to think holistically which he wouldn't have done without me. He kept me on the straight and narrow and aligned my thinking. I do dash about all over the place in my mind and, being a very well trained military administrator, he knew that things had to be in a regular pattern in order to be effective. We were soul mates actually, which was very, very lucky because we had both been starved before in previous marriages. We gave each other mutual recognition and support and loved working as peacemakers together.*'

Ideal man – Bollywood style

Bollywood superstar **Amisha Patel's** *'ideal man will respect my profession and respect my independence. He would have to respect my mind. He would have to be family orientated. I would have the freedom to work and not be restricted to doing housework only. That is not to say that I would not shoulder the responsibility of running a home beautifully and play the hostess. I would love to keep a beautiful home, that's every girl's dream and I have it in me. But my life can't centre on that. I would want to bring up children but they would have to be independent at a very young age. A sense of self is very important and I would want that to be instilled in them. He would definitely have to respect my mind. I do not want to be just there for procreation, to have a family heir and to run someone's kitchen. I have had zillions of proposals and have declined them all. I have proposals from men who are rich, poor, ugly and handsome, from sensible men to smart ones, from dumb ones to party animals. I have declined them all. It's easy for an Indian girl to be known as someone's granddaughter, then someone's daughter, then someone's wife. I wanted my own identity. I don't want to be dependant on any man. I want to secure myself financially in such a way that if tomorrow Prince Charles' son proposes to me, I remain independent'.*

Room for improvement

Police supremo **Kiran Bedi** was amusing when she said that if she was reincarnated and had to do it all over again she would want the same mother and father, but when I pressed her about her husband she laughed and said *'There's room for improvement there!'*

Unhappy endings

Just as the women were keen to acknowledge the great strength that they drew from their happy marriages, those whose partnerships did not offer a context of loving support were also honest.

Former MP **Jackie Ballard** had no support from her husband and was utterly frank about her disappointment in their marriage. '*I have always seen the biggest failure in my life as not having a happy marriage.*' **Marian Rivman's** equally candid but humorous remark, '*I went to bed with a virgin and did the right thing by him, I married him*', is how she described her brief and mistaken marriage.

Many of the social restraints that kept women in unhappy and unfulfilling marriages are now openly challenged. Fewer stigmas are attached to being divorced and women do not generally fear being shunned or losing their children. While there still seems to be a feeling amongst some divorcing men that '*my wife wants everything that belongs to me, except me*', such bitterness among women was rare.

Bani Dugal seemed to have escaped the negativity trap that divorce can cause. '*When my husband and I divorced it was because he was sick and things fell apart but I still have a great affection for him, and he for me. I'm sorry my children didn't have a healthy father who could be with them but I tell my sons, "You have a mother and not everyone has a perfect life. Everybody is dealt a hand of cards and how you play is the challenge".*'

Communications consultant **Sue Stapely** acknowledged that for her '*divorce, after a long marriage, was unexpectedly liberating and I relish my new independent life*'. However, she also recognized that her former husband had been '*supportive both emotionally and financially while I burnt the midnight oil for five years as a late qualifying lawyer*'.

The widow smiles

Many of the women I passed happy hours with were widows. One evening I had the pleasure to experience **Sarah Miles'** one-woman show *The Widow Smiles*. After a lifetime at centre stage Sarah was now able to view her life and widowhood with a gentle understanding. Writer **Katherine Whitehorn** said. *'Being widowed may be regarded as an intensely individual and intimate loss and yet it is also a powerful tie that binds women to each other. It is an issue that affects very many women's lives and yet the women's movement has been slow to take up the prejudices and obstacles that face widows'.*

The loss of a husband or life-partner is devastating, as **Sheila Dikshit**, the Chief Minister of Delhi, articulated powerfully, *'Somewhere, something inside you dies, never to come up again, and that becomes a dead portion of you'.* **Esther Rantzen** still has a strong sense of her husband's presence, and told me, *'My husband was a wonderful man'*, but she is also actively embracing life and taking on new challenges. *'I still celebrate his birthday by going to the place we loved and having a bottle of champagne.'*

When Dame **Mary Marsh's** husband died suddenly of a heart attack at the age of fifty-three, Mary had the dramatic realization that she *'had to build a whole new life. We had been together for thirty years and suddenly he wasn't there. I can't say I will never remarry but it seems unlikely that I'll find somebody that I'll want to be with all the time. I took on the job of heading the National Society for the Prevention of Cruelty to Children (NSPCC), after he died and it has kept me very busy'.*

Given the high value placed on having a happy and sustaining marriage, it was fascinating that the vast majority of the widows whom I met had not remarried. Instead, they had found a new and more intense focus in their working lives, challenging the entrenched and stereotypical view, that pervades most cultures, of a woman surplus to all requirements.

How am I supposed to live without you?

After her husband Rohinton died, **Anu Aga** took over as Chief Executive Chairperson of the Thermax Group, a major industrial company in India. Not only was her husband's death sudden but a year later her son died in a car accident. It is hard to imagine how someone can recover from such grief and still stay serene and focused but Anu did. She took time to learn one of India's most ancient Buddhist techniques of meditation, Vipassana, which means to see things as they really are. It focuses on an observation-based, self-exploratory journey to the common root of mind and body that dissolves mental impurity, resulting in a balanced mind full of love and compassion. Anu said *'In spite of losing two very dear people, I learnt to embrace life and to live fully'*.

When Anu stepped in as the Chief Executive the company shares were going down. Some people reassured her that it was due to the decline in the Indian economy, but she also received an anonymous letter from a shareholder. He was very worried because his livelihood was dependent on her and, although the company's success might not matter to Anu, as she was a rich woman, it mattered to him. Although she could have thought that her suffering was so much more than his, she didn't. Instead Anu was moved by the one shareholder's needs and brought in successful consultants from America to transform the company's profits. What they asked Anu to do as the Chief Executive was harsh. With calmness and compassion she had to find the courage to make some of the top people in the company redundant, in order to turn the company's fortune around. Today Anu Aga is one of India's most respected industrialists and known not just for her business acumen but for her courage and vision in speaking out against the communal violence of Hindu-Muslim riots in Gujarat. Anu, in a brave act, called for real action from other industrialists and opinion formers in the Confederation of Indian Industries. She also publicly denounced politicians who played the race card.

A life changed forever

Bronwen Astor was probably one of the most famous media-darlings of the 1950s, as Balmain's muse and one of the first women newsreaders on the BBC. Her achievements were often very public.

What was not so public was her inner spiritual life of a mystic and experience of union with God. The sudden death of her best friend from college changed everything. It led Bronwen on an inward journey to find answers to *'Who am I?'* and *'Why am I here?'* and after seven years she awakened to a new reality that is beyond reason and rationality, where everything is one and there is a unity of all things. With this inspiration she married an unhappy man, Viscount Astor, the eldest son of one of England's most renowned aristocratic families. After they married Bronwen moved into Cliveden, the Italianate mansion on the Thames which her mother-in-law, Lady Nancy Astor – who was the first woman to take her seat in the British Parliament – had made famous with her political salons. But within three years of Bronwen's marriage she and Bill were engulfed by the famous Profumo affair which deeply affected her husband and led to a series of heartaches, and ultimately, to his death. Bronwen was left to bring up their two children alone. She lived a life of paradox, outwardly normal but inwardly solitary, and with only God as her inspiration to survive. Converting to Roman Catholicism she joined the Charismatic Movement and eventually trained as a psychotherapist. Bronwen mentioned her friend, the spiritual teacher Andrew Cohen's perceptive understanding that there must be 'transparency, integrity and authenticity' in the soul. She has now been a widow for over forty years. She did not pretend that it was possible to recover totally from that loss or that being a widow is a comfortable status for a woman. *'I'm not scared but you never really get used to going through everything by yourself; it's quite difficult to motivate yourself to go to occasions on your own. And you do not have status in a lot of things because you don't have your husband's support, but I have learnt to live with that.'*

Bronwen has now been working for over twenty years as an analytical psychotherapist and is training as a spiritual director, which means someone who walks alongside people on their spiritual journey.

She is not only an acknowledged beauty but has a beautiful soul. Only special people are so blessed. She explained that *'when you experience a union with God and understand that all of life has a unity then you are completely changed. Maybe in years to come scientists will be able to prove that our actual DNA has changed when we have experienced this and contacted your divine self'*. I felt I had changed in Bronwen's company and maybe even my DNA might have been transformed by her special presence.

Cruel taboos

In many cultures and communities becoming a widow also means experiencing a loss of social meaning and value, as widows are regarded as unlucky and a burden on resources. When **Lily Thapa** was widowed in Nepal she experienced the pressure of these negative attitudes, but her remarkable response was to confront what is perhaps the last major taboo, 'widowhood'.

Lily was widowed in 1992 when her husband, Major Dr Amir Thapa, was killed serving as a Medical Officer in the Peacekeeping Force, during the Gulf War. Only thirty-two years old and with three small children to bring up, she was utterly bereft and yet found that no support was forthcoming on either an emotional or financial level. Her father, a General, Second Chief of the Army had also died young and left her mother widowed, but whereas she had never dared to revolt against the negative cultural practices she faced, Lily did. She fought for compensation through the United Nations and finally received it after three years of total persistence. But the lack of support within Nepal and her own community was also striking: *'There was not a single organization that can help the widows in my country and share my grief. There was nowhere where I could cry and get myself some support.'* Lily had already experienced the conservative prejudices of her husband's family when they had advised him to make a

Bronwen Astor

'I'm not scared but you never really get used to going through everything by yourself; it's quite difficult to motivate yourself to go to occasions on your own. And you do not have status in a lot of things because you don't have your husband's support, but I have learnt to live with that.'

Bronwen Astor

Lily Thapa

'Almost always widows are ignorant of their legal status and their rights to compensation or inheritance.'

Lily Thapa

Margaret Owen

'one of my Malawi students said, "You mean your husband's brother lets you stay in this house and keep all these things, even though you're a widow?"'

Margaret Owen

second marriage after Lily had a series of miscarriages. Although her husband had supported her, and eventually they did have three children, after his death she experienced the family's same harshness again. Her own hardship inspired her to address the problem directly: *'I endured discrimination from society and my family for being a widow but took charge of my life, by helping others in the same plight'.*

'When a woman becomes a widow in Nepal, the loss of her husband is not the only ending she faces. Immediately, special rules apply to her. She is different from other women. The particulars differ among different castes, religious groups, but always economic dependence dictates her options as do many other rules that effectively put her on the sidelines. Typically, among Hindus, the women are told they must stay in their husband's family home, where the family perpetuates the system of rules and separation. Widows are not allowed to wear red clothes, which is a lucky colour used on religious occasions. They are considered inauspicious, a harbinger of evil, and are not allowed participation in any religious functions, even the marriages of their own children. Almost always widows are ignorant of their legal status and their rights to compensation or inheritance. I would like to change all these discriminatory things against widows to make an equitable society.'

Widows' rights

Lawyer **Margaret Owen** was also provoked to campaign for widows' rights, although it was not on the grounds of her own experience of widowhood. She was moved to action when: *'The wife of one of my Malawi students came to our home with her sick baby and blurted out, "You mean your husband's brother lets you stay in this house and keep all these things, even though you're a widow?" These words were a catalyst which rang in my ears as I flew to LA to take up a post as a visiting professor, teaching women law, health and development. I decided to explore the issues of widowhood and have never stopped since'.*

Bettgeflüster
Κρεβατομουρμούρα
Racconti del cuscino
صحبت‌های خاله زنکی

Pillow talk

Secrets of life

They say it takes a lifetime to get to know someone but, often with only a couple of hours, I needed to fast-forward the conversation and get to the heart of the matter. I had to understand what turned women on, what turned them off and what really got them going. Delilah had pillow-talked her way to the secret of Samson's power and I too wanted to know the secrets of these extraordinary women.

Some secrets were surprising, some less so, but several phrases kept being whispered again and again: 'be kind', 'act without concern for results', 'surrender all attachments' and 'accomplish life's highest good'. It did not matter from which culture or religion the women came, they all articulated the same understanding – *give of yourself and do not expect anything in return*'.

The women mused on life, the world and the universe. Did God exist? Was it better to make a difference to one person's life or should one strive for larger visions which sometimes were not achievable? Was an unexamined life that did not question itself worth living? Should we stop questioning and just marvel at the mysteries we call life? These seemed to be the ultimate questions that needed to be considered.

As ever, my mother gave sound advice on how to approach life. '*Never harm or mock anyone because it will come back to you. Always be generous, because it too will come back to you a hundred-fold. If you cannot make sense of history and the world today, then take steps to make your life have meaning.*' She ended with the most simple and profound thought. '*If you can do one good deed a day before going to bed it makes for a restful night and a happy life.*'

The meaning of life?

The beautiful iconic actress **Sarah Miles**, who has seen more of the world than many, still felt it necessary to wonder, *'What is life? Is it a gift? A lesson? A curse? A blessing? A punishment? Is it a miracle? Karma? Or nothing more than random chance? Are we all part of some overall master plan, having our strings pulled by that great puppeteer in the sky? Or having our legs pulled, as the humanists would say?'*

These 'big' questions about life, the universe and our place within it, may never be answered definitively, but they provoked careful thought about who we were and how we should act. The Reverend **Rosemary Perry**, whose own life, like so many of the other women's lives, had been like a blockbuster, felt every life could have meaning because *'we are cosmic film directors in charge of our own destiny. Although some events and meetings can't be avoided, our thoughts are probably the most powerful and creative things we have. I've learnt that deep inner self-esteem is very important. As soon as the victim scenario appears then my ego is hijacking me to a hell of my own making'.*

Perhaps being grateful and just being happy to be alive was the simple answer to it all. The women I asked had an understanding of something greater than themselves but still acknowledged that destiny was a complex business which they had a hand in. Internationally acclaimed astrologer **Paula Garton** believed in an individual fate which *'pushed you into the right place at the right time, to allow us to complete our destiny'.*

Nearly everyone felt there would be some sort of judgement in life by either friends, parents or lovers and that finally the laws of karma and God would come into play. Many were confident that on death their souls would experience all the unkindness they had inflicted on others, as well as all the kindness they had shown. At this point they would truly understand how their actions, thoughts and words had impacted on other lives. There was no escape from the consequences of the life they lived.

Sathya Saran

Sarah Miles

'Karma is the only explanation for so much in life. I believe in a great Divine Plan which is unfolding at every moment ... We are put on this Earth for a reason, a purpose, and every day which is not spent fulfilling that purpose is a wasted day, both for our own spiritual growth and also for the world.'

Sadhvi Bhagwati Saraswati

Sadhvi Bhagwati Saraswati

Rosemary Perry

Diana Cooper

Paula Garton

No escape from karma

Editor **Sathya Saran**, one of India's acclaimed journalists, is also admired as a writer of short stories. She shows a deep understanding of the laws of Karma in her mesmerising book The Midnight Train. One of the short stories in her book is a modern-day version of Jason and the Golden Fleece. As she explains, eternity claims your thoughts and actions and every life is the unfolding of one's past.

For some, one's karma from past actions gave the definite answer. Californian-born **Sadhvi Bhagwati Saraswati** explained, 'I believe in karma and destiny. Otherwise there is no way that I personally could have ended up living in India, blessed by the teachings and wisdom of Indian culture, under the guidance and shelter of my Guru. Karma is the only explanation for so much in life. I believe in a great Divine Plan which is unfolding at every moment. It is almost absurd to assume that all of this divine creation and the divine plan is just random coincidence. It cannot be. We are put on this Earth for a reason, a purpose, and every day which is not spent fulfilling that purpose is a wasted day, both for our own spiritual growth and also for the world. This motivates me'.

Author Dr **Diana Cooper**, a power house of energy, explained how she understood the complex concept of karma to work. 'Our soul takes higher decisions, while our personality takes day-to-day ones. These become karma. Based on our energy, our angels and guides in spirit create the opportunities and challenges we need for growth.'

Shernaaz Engineer felt 'we created our own "karma" every minute of our lives with our own choices, thoughts, actions and perceptions and none of these are predetermined, so we have to take responsibility for what we do to ourselves. Good things did happen at the right time and the right place but we determined that time and place to a great degree by our own wisdom or lack of it'.

Wisdom of the ancients

Written on your hand

As a devout Muslim, **Parvin Ali**, who was born in Malaysia, and founded the 'FATIMA' Women's Network, follows her faith's teachings on the balance between determined and independent action. *'As a Muslim I strongly believe in pre-destination but this does not preclude self-will, as we are ultimately responsible for our choices. The trick is to know when to stop pushing against one's fate and just accept it. Many Muslims say everything is ordained, pre-ordained by Allah. But that can't be the whole answer because if it was why are we being told by the teachings of Islam that we are responsible for our own actions and we have to accept the consequences of those actions?'*

Only the angels don't have freewill as they serve God. One of the stories my mother used to tell me is about a noble emperor who went to see a wise man to ask him if it was a good thing to plan on invading a particular country. The sage looked at his hand and said *'Well no, it is not written on your hand because you haven't got a line just here'*. So the Emperor pulled out his sword and cut the line into his hand and said *'It is there now'*. He went ahead and conquered the country.

Written in the stars

Ninety per cent of people admit to reading their horoscopes, but most of these probably wonder if our fate can really be written in the stars. I decided to test the reliability of the stars and cross reference the findings with the renowned astrologer, **Paula Garton**. I was curious to know whether the women who fascinated me and were life's success stories shared any astrological qualities, as I had never seen this blind-tested. I gave Paula the women's birth dates but no names and no other information about them. Not only did she find that the women had intriguing planetary aspects to their birth charts but, much more interestingly, an astonishing number had fixed stars in their charts. In this way Paula was able to ascertain the women's fields of success in a way that was unnerving in its accuracy.

It was explained that the extraordinary women I had spent time with had fixed stars which related to their success. *'Fixed stars are stars not planets and do not orbit around the sun. They are in the heavens, positioned in various constellations and signs. They are called fixed as they do not move quickly like the planets. They give an influence throughout life as to whether you will be famous or successful in a particular field or have a problem that you have to deal with. It is part of your character make-up and is often the reason why people are successful for no apparent reason in the rest of their birth chart analysis.'*

Mullah Nasruddin

'Mullah Nasruddin was scrambling around on all fours on the street, searching for something. A passer-by asked him what he was looking for and the sage replied he was searching for the key to his house. Several villagers helped to search for the key but to no avail. Finally one of them asked the mullah where he had lost the key. The mullah replied that he had lost it inside the house. Then why are we searching for it out here on the street? "Because there is a street lamp out here and there is no light in my house", said the mullah! Similarly we rush around keeping ourselves busy with various tasks and projects. We think that by distracting ourselves with frantic activity we are changing the world and doing something worth while. All the while we are avoiding going within and finding the nature of our true self which is the actual key to happiness.' **Usha Devi Rathore**

Chinese pots

'An elderly Chinese woman had two large pots, each hung on the ends of a pole which she carried across her neck. One of the pots had a crack in it while the other pot was perfect and always delivered a full portion of water. At the end of the long walk from the stream to the house, the cracked pot arrived only half full. Of course the perfect pot was proud of its accomplishments, but the poor cracked pot was ashamed of its own imperfection, and so miserable that it could only do half of what it had been made to do. After two years of what it perceived to be bitter failure, it spoke to the woman one day by the stream. "I am ashamed of myself, because this crack in my side causes water to leak out all the way back to your house." The old woman smiled, "Did you not notice that there are flowers on your side of the path, but not on the other pot's side? That's because I have always known about your flaw, so I planted flower seeds on your side of the path, and every day while we walk back, you water them. For two years I have been able to pick these beautiful flowers to decorate the table. Without you being just the way you are, there would not be this beauty to grace the house." The lesson of the story is that each of us has our own unique flaw and you simply have to take each person for what they are and look for the good in them.' **Shyama Perera**

Sight and insight

'In Japan, an entire village pitied a blind woman who lived in the house by the sea. Her only daughter, a pearl diver, had died in an accident and she had no one to care for her. One day the old blind woman went to a merchant and held out a silken pouch. "Pearls," she said. "The special ones my daughter did not sell. The price I will get will let me pay for my meals as long as I live." The merchant asked, "How do you know what they are worth as you cannot see?" The old woman answered, "I have fingers and I have counted them and know their size. I know what they are worth." The merchant opened the pouch and held his breath. He asked, "Why did your daughter keep these pearls?" "I don't know" said the old woman. The merchant said gently, "Your fingers have counted the pearls and know their size, but your fingers have not seen their colour. They are the rarest black pearls and are worth a fortune. And I shall pay you exactly what they are worth." When the story got around, some people laughed at the merchant. They asked, "Why did you tell her the pearls were black as you knew she was blind?" The merchant smiled. "Yes, she was blind. That is why I told her". **Kazue Hatano**

Chop wood, carry water

'No therapist can actually heal us, we have to heal ourselves. God as a creator is brilliant. Do you think he makes a bad design? Do you think he can make snowflakes, trees and oceans and then make a mistake with us? He gave us self-will because he wanted to make life a choice. But we only want self-will at certain times. You either have self-will or you don't. The final chain of truth has to come from you. I have made three fortunes and sabotaged myself three times, from millionaire to dead broke, before I woke up. In life what matters is that you learn from the errors and from the successes. There's a great expression: before enlightenment, chop wood, carry water, after enlightenment, chop wood, carry water, and that's it. One day the light goes on and you know you don't have to ask any more questions. You've arrived at the place where you're ready for the next lesson.' **Rosalyn Dexter**

Leila Seth | Shyama Perera

'You are given periods in your life where you have to make decisions and you are given periods in your life where you live with the consequences of those decisions. Sometimes we have to think "Did I do the right thing?" Those are the periods when we grow into better, stronger, more human people.'

Tricia Sibbons

Tricia Sibbons

Parvin Ali

Rennie Fritchie

Lynn Jones Parry

Up to you

In contrast to those who subscribed to Hamlet's idea that there is *'a divinity that shapes our ends, rough-hew them how we will'*, many others expressed a strong belief that self-determination was the most important thing to focus on in life.

Campaigner for the displaced Chagossian people, and nominee for the Nobel Peace Prize, **Lisette Talate** affirmed a conviction in her own actions that had also inspired other victims of British colonialism. *'I do believe in destiny but at the same time I believe you make your own destiny. I cannot let life decide for me. I am the master of my life and I dictate its course.'*

Leila Seth, the first woman Chief Justice to the High Court in India, felt that whatever you want to achieve, you must do it now in this life. *'There is no afterlife for me, but I respect those who believe in it. There is no Judgement Day. I used to think so, but now I don't — dust thou art and to dust thou return.'*

For **Tricia Sibbons**, social and charitable entrepreneur, a woman who has helped to transform the lives of so many in modern Africa, the Day of Judgement must be understood as self-judgement. *'You are given periods in your life where you have to make decisions and you are given periods in your life where you live with the consequences of those decisions. Sometimes we have to think "Did I do the right thing?". Those are the periods when we grow into better, stronger, more human people.'*

For others still, having feet firmly on the ground and eyes set ahead was the right way forward. Historian **Kusoom Vadgama** asserted *'I am a realist. For me pigs never fly, they stay in the sty'.*

Claire Bertschinger

'I live life knowing that the goddess of opportunity only has one golden hair. You must pluck it when you find it.'

Claire Bertschinger

Elena Ragozhina

'Success doesn't come from the Communist State, it doesn't come from God, it comes from believing in yourself. I used to be a size 20 and now I'm a size 12 because I was determined to look good. God can't always help you, you've got to help yourself.'

Elena Ragozhina

'When you point a finger look very carefully, four fingers are pointing back at you.'

Anando Heffley

Anando Heffley

Maureen Mannion

'Life is not a lottery. You have to want to succeed. It is easy to "opt out". Say "yes" and carry the plan through. I agree it helps to be in the right place at the right time, but don't miss a chance.'

Maureen Mannion

Lady Luck

Rather than feeling the reassurance of a shaping force in their lives, such as God or fate or destiny, some women simply regarded life as a game of chance. German-born pioneering scientist **Uta Frith** saw life this way. '*Given the force of arguments for evolution of the species, it is hard to believe in a personal destiny and fulfilling a contract. Chance must be a major factor in our life. Some of us have been very lucky, others unlucky. We can influence and change our fate to some extent. Luck often attracts even more luck. Some people seem to attract good happenings and good people, others bad things. Everyone will experience some adversity in their lives and everyone will die. There are many ways to cope with the things that are apparently sent to try us.*'

Baroness **Rennie Fritchie**, whose own life led her from early struggles to being a distinguished Commissioner for Public Appointments and finally a rightful place in the House of Lords, believed that '*Life presents challenges and if you don't address them they keep on coming back in bigger forms until you do. I think we have a duty to give something back. I also recognize that some are more fortunate than others and I have been fortunate*'.

Iranian singer and author **Shusha Guppy**, known for her vitality and lightness of being, added her observation that, '*When you're young and struggling you think everything in life depends on you, but the older you become the more you realize it doesn't all depend on you. So much is lady luck*'.

Body-talk

Although it is rarely difficult to decide whether we feel comfortable with someone or not, working out how we arrive at that decision is much harder. Lady **Lynn Jones Parry** explained how instinct mixed with experience guides us, '*You learn how to recognize qualities. There is a sort of natural attraction*'. **Shakira Caine** believed that the natural attraction *'is a chemical reaction, an electric spark, an instant connection'.* **Dana Gillespie** says that she *'can hear a lie in a voice',* whereas **Maharani Bibhu Kumari Devi of Tripura** reacts instinctively on sight. *'I do judge by appearances. Your physical features reveal your personality. The eyes must be soft and steady and the smile should reach the eyes. That makes for a trustworthy person.'* **Julia Middleton** relied on her father's way to assess people *'to look at the amount of energy a person exudes'.*

Fascinatingly, fitness guru **Ramma Bans** believes that the body-talk philosophy can be applied to oneself, as well as others: *'If you want to see what your thoughts were like yesterday, look at your body today. If you want to see what your body will be like tomorrow, see what your thoughts are like today'.*

'Table talk'

Chatting with so many fascinating women over meals made me think of something my mother had said. *'I reserve judgement on an individual until I've seen them eat. It is the small things that give people away. Some people grab their food and get on with it; some people leave the best for the last. Some people only eat delicacies and leave the rest for others. For some, each mouthful is a balanced mini-meal, with the ingredients carefully chosen. Some push their food around the plate and really have no interest whatsoever in it. Some fill their plate up and always leave most of it behind. Yet more are totally distracted while eating and don't even know what goes into their mouth. How a person eats is a reflection on their character, how they approach life. You can observe whether, underneath it all, they are insecure, calculating, selfish, disengaged or horribly greedy.'*

Almost always it was a real pleasure to share good food, good company and good manners! Interestingly though some women found the dinner table a natural place to argue. I learnt about this behaviour pattern from two eminent women who explained that family meals had a defining impact on their approach to life. Both the brilliant Baroness Rabbi **Julia Neuberger** and the brilliant **Nafis Sadik**, one of the defining pioneers of the United Nations, enjoyed family meals where their parents encouraged them to talk, argue and debate. This, in turn, seemed to enable both women to express their passions and opinions at the decision-making tables of the world.

Modern-day goddess

Indu Jain, the Chair of the *Times of India* group, is an ardent believer in women's innate 'shakti' – if only they really believed in their own greatness. We first met over dinner, during the Millennium Conference of World Spiritual Leaders at the United Nations in New York. I was told that women had to reclaim their power and awaken the goddess within. Later, when I re-encountered Indu in her office in the *Times of India*, I was invited to join her for lunch served on the chairman's huge desk. Indu is a devout Jain and her food is strictly vegetarian. She selected my food from silver containers and each mouthful was carefully chosen as if it was my last meal. If it is true that you are what you eat then Indu Jain is the best advertisement for vegetarian food. She is stunningly beautiful. Upon asking her permission to record her views on life she wickedly proclaimed that *'Goddesses were not in the habit of giving interviews'*. I winked at her and said I had never spoken to a goddess and she would be my first. She agreed there must always be a first time. I was fed, charmed and now ready to bask in her heavenly pronouncements, with most of my critical faculties put to rest. Like the goddess she was, Indu cherished her inner wisdom and knew how to celebrate it. She was in control not just of a media empire that her two beloved sons ran but she knew the real meaning of power and was not embarrassed to express it. Power was taking difficult decisions, demanding action and being devoted to your ideals and religious passions; it was being decisive and daring in challenging people and their staid ideas about life. Most importantly Indu showed me that women had power in their homes and work, but they now needed the confidence to unleash it for the betterment of all as well as for their own wellbeing.

Julia Neuberger

Angela Lennox

'Many people who show great confidence in public are often torn with self-doubt and loss of confidence. Sometimes I fear I cannot do something and then suddenly I am overtaken by determination and I can.'

Angela Lennox

Indu Jain

Shernaaz Engineer

'My biggest challenge continues to be coming into my own as a person and not fighting shy of taking destiny between the teeth and racing on.'

Shernaaz Engineer

Barriers in your own mind

It was genuinely surprising how many of the women did not regard themselves as confident. I had assumed that, having made such great headway in their careers and set out as pioneers in their chosen fields, they would have a secure sense of self-belief.

Sue Stapely frankly admitted that *'my greatest obstacle is my lack of self-belief'*. Similarly editor **Shernaaz Engineer** felt that her greatest obstacle had been her own sense of vulnerability. *'My own fears held me back over and over again, when I should have been pushing ahead instead. My biggest challenge continues to be coming into my own as a person and not fighting shy of taking destiny between the teeth and racing on.'* **Sallie Gratch** recognized that she also lacked self-belief. *'My own inner resistance, my yet-to-be-developed self-confidence, my still uncultivated self ... in looking back over the years, I cannot point to anything in my life, beyond myself, that has kept me from moving ahead with my life.'* Even the admired industrialist **Anu Aga** experienced self-doubt, often agonizing over being selected as the Chairperson of Thermax, India. *'I kept asking myself whether the Board would have selected me if my family did not own a 62% stake in the business.'*

Although self-esteem is fundamental to a sense of fulfilment, it cannot be taught. Social changes have encouraged women to be more confident in the public sphere, but self-esteem cannot be guaranteed by legislating for equality or personal rights. This was made evident by **Anna-Liisa Fazer** who said that despite having been born and raised in Finland, one of the most gender equal countries in the world, she knew that the only obstruction to her success was her lack of self-esteem. Dr **Angela Lennox** summed up the confidence dilemma: *'Many people who show great confidence in public are, like me, often torn with self-doubt and loss of confidence. Sometimes I fear I cannot do something and then suddenly I am overtaken by determination and I can. When I talk to others who seem so high achieving, I find that we all suffer from both burning ambition and a total exhaustion and feeling that we just cannot do what the rest of the world expects of us!'*

Emily Payne

'The only way to be optimistic about the future is to invent it.'

Emily Payne

Zena Sorabjee

'Striving for one's own happiness, you find that happiness eludes you. But when you are bringing about happiness in the lives of many others then you are able to achieve satisfaction and joy in life.'

Zena Sorabjee

Leonora van Gils

'We have come to the Earth with a contract that we have a desire to fulfil. Therefore it is of the utmost importance to understand what the contract entails and the lessons we need to learn and fulfil.'

Leonora van Gils

Oonagh Shanley-Toffolo

'Let go and then the magic happens.'

Oonagh Shanley Toffolo

You can do anything

Among the many who constantly questioned themselves, there were a few who exuded the gift of total confidence. Neuro-design pioneer **Beverly Payeff-Masey** shared a particularly inspiring story. *'Don't let anybody tell you you can't do something. I was teaching a whole range of students from the American first grade to the eighth grade and I decided that traditional art and plaster was too boring. I was going to give them a taste of what real life was about, art and design in the real world. We had this industrial design project and I asked them to do something simple: design a steering wheel. It had to look beautiful, feel good and work effectively. I had a class of seven-year-olds take on the project and another class of thirteen-year-olds. I told the young ones about our project and said "Just do what you think would work!" and they did a beautiful job. I gave the same project to the thirteen-year-olds, but I told them just once that this was an industrial design project, usually done at universities. They gave me a very hard time and said it was a very difficult project. I was asking too much from them; it was too advanced for them. At the end of the week I said to them, "I'm so sorry you had such a difficult time with this project. I know this is a university level project, but I want you to see what the seven-year-olds have done with the same project that you were given". They were so excited about what the youngsters had done. I said to them, "The only difference is that I told you it was a university project and you believed that. Boundaries may be put on you but you don't have to believe in them. You can do anything you put your mind to and don't let anybody say otherwise".'*

'The first duty is if you have life live it. There is a prayer that says may you have all the tears and laughter in life. One of the greatest curses of Western civilization is you have to be happy all the time.'

Glenda Jackson

'You can be born with a lot of ability, a lot of talent, but it is what you do with it in life that is important.'

Sharon Choa

'I consider it a most valuable thing to be able to own and face one's own fears, because from passing through the fear we gain the ability to act freely.'

Marigold Verity

'Everyone has potential, a gift of some sort. The stars are those who translate this into discipline and dogged persistence.'

Shireen Irani

Persistence

Chief Justice **Leila Seth's** wonderful story of her experience as an aspiring advocate is equally inspirational. The head of chambers first instructed Leila, *'Instead of joining the legal profession, young woman go and get married'.* She replied, *'But Sir, I am already married'. 'Then go and have a child',* he advised. She responded *'I have a child.' 'It is not fair to the child to be alone; you should have a second child'.* Again she replied, *'Mr Chaudhuri, I already have two children'.* Taken aback for a third time, he finally said, *'Then come and join my chambers, you are a persistent young woman and will do well at the bar'.*

Fight another day

Life is to be lived and one has to experience joy and sorrow to really be a whole being. When you go to the pearly gates with no scars, no wounds and no disappointments, surely St Peter will send you back to live your life again. Arguably no one understands the special link between suffering and pleasure more than artists, and especially those who sing the blues. Blues singer and songwriter **Dana Gillespie** recognized that she had to go through a terrible period of suffering in order to understand life but this enriched her art. *'I could only sing the blues after I'd suffered – I'd been to hell and back. You have to experience life to be able to sing about it.'*

Britain's greatest leader, Winston Churchill, was no stranger to failure. He understood that *'success is the ability to go from one failure to another with no loss of enthusiasm'.* Many of the women showed this same humour and resilience. **Rifat Wahhab** said, *'Some of the best battles you will have fought will be the ones you lost'.*

Beverly Payeff-Masey

Madhuri Dixit

'Thomas Edison, when trying to find the right filament to make the light bulb work, did not succeed thousands of times. When asked about this supposed failure, he said he had not failed, he had just discovered thousands of materials that didn't work.'

Dorothy Dalton

Patsy Robertson

Dorothy Dalton

Maja Daruwala

Shahnaz Husain

Winner takes it all

Often in life failure stares you in the face, but it is your response that counts. Many of the women found a positive spin on a negative experience and saw failure as an important part of their development. As **Dorothy Dalton** so aptly commented: *'The great inventor, Thomas Edison, when trying to find the right filament to make the light bulb work, did not succeed thousands of times. When asked about this supposed failure, he said he had not failed, he had just discovered thousands of materials that didn't work'.* Dorothy Dalton remarked that in England if you had tried ten ways to do something new and worthwhile and nine had failed and one had been very successful you were still seen as a failure. Yet in some other countries like America you could fail nine times but if you succeeded once you were a winner. It was all to do with the mind set. It had to be a 'win-win' situation rather than 'the winner takes it all'.

Heroines

Whom we admire often reveals what we wish to become. It was no coincidence then that the heroines of the women I met were usually other women who dared to think differently, act differently and to put their heads above the parapet. They were big-hearted and valiant souls who had passion and persistence and even a bit of pragmatism.

Lucie Aubrac's heroines were three Simones whom Lucie, a Resistance heroine herself, had known personally: Simone Signoret, the great French actress whom Lucie taught; Simone de Beauvoir, the great French academic and author of *The Second Sex*, whom she worked with, and Simone Veil, the great French politician, former President of the European Union and survivor of Auschwitz-Birkenau, whom she campaigned with.

Mother India

Despite criticism, especially during India's period of emergency in the mid-1970s, many of the women cited Prime Minister Indira Gandhi as their heroine. Chair of the Commonwealth Association **Patsy Robertson** came in contact with Mrs Gandhi during her time at the Commonwealth Secretariat. She described Indira Gandhi as dignified and calm. *'She was always elegantly dressed with that distinctive white streak in her hair. Given that she was the leader of the biggest country in the Commonwealth and the biggest democracy in the world she showed no arrogance whatsoever. She was beautifully mannered. I remember the last conversation I had with her when she hosted the 1983 Commonwealth Conference in Delhi. We were walking together from the meeting and the wind was blowing and she was telling me about her hair and how when you grow older your hair thins. She was completely natural. Throughout the struggle against apartheid in South Africa she was absolutely supportive of what the Commonwealth was doing, which didn't receive publicity. She was a remarkable woman.'*

Ramma Bans's memories also struck a similar chord. *'For many years I used to be Mrs Gandhi's health adviser. She was a most refined and delicate person and I have great praise for her. She was totally down to earth. She was a weight conscious person and always wanted to look good because she was patriotic and wanted everyone to think the best of India.'* **Shahnaz Husain**, founder of the Husain Ayurvedic cosmetics empire and a household name in India, also admired her friend Mrs Gandhi. *'She was a woman of steel, with the power of an emperor and a heart of gold. Her dignity and courage made her an icon.'*

For Bollywood icon **Madhuri Dixit**, Indira Gandhi, her heroine, was powerful, witty and dignified.

Film producer and journalist **Elaine Attias** told a very fascinating story about Indira Gandhi, whom she interviewed. *'I had built up anger against Indira Gandhi as I'd spent a whole month interviewing people around her and I had this naive American belief of "Let's get rid of this person if they're the corrupt head". I saw corruption in India. It's not a good* idea to go and interview somebody when you have bad vibes because you can't draw them out. At one point I said to Mrs Gandhi that there was an editorial in the New York Times *talking about why the Egyptian Prime Minister, Anwar Sadat, had been killed. Even though he had tried to make peace with Israel, he didn't really bring his people along with him. I then put it to her that a true leader was someone who can bring their people along with them. I then looked at her and asked "Are you a true leader?" which was a kind of insolent question. She sensed the hostility in my question because she was very good at reading people. "Oh yes" she said "I do the best I can." Just like that!'*

Real life heroines

Strikingly, few contemporary figures were cited as heroines. Perhaps this turn away from an upward admiring glance is a symptom of our age. Everyone from football players to pop-stars are named as heroes by the media-machine, although they are often not very elevated in their standards of behaviour and self-sacrifice. Given that heroism involves putting the needs of others ahead of your own, it is not that surprising that many looked to those with ability to endure life without money, fame or power, for examples of genuine heroism.

Maja Daruwala, Director of the Commonwealth Human Rights Initiative, argued that the real heroines were the unsung young women who left their families and travelled vast distances to work as domestic helps in somebody else's home. These women had the courage to venture into somebody else's home and make their life easier, often with no companionship and no support system. '*They were elegant, polite, never subservient and always proud of their skills and service. It was a joy to see how their faces lit up when a little bit of help was given to them. They had so little from life and yet they were the real successes.*' I considered what Maja had said and tried to put myself in their shoes. I knew that I could not travel to a different country and work for someone I didn't know in a place where I couldn't speak the language. I agreed with Maja that their lives were heroic stuff. Feisty Indian Minister **Renuka Chowdhury** also articulated the heroism of the poor in even plainer terms. *'My heroines are the women who live in villages with no drinking water, no education for their children, no decision-making and who still dare to smile after that.'*

It was also interesting that many chose to emphasize the heroism of their own mothers. I have to admit my mother also comes top of my heroine list. Given the unconditional and selfless love that a mother represents it is understandable that nearly every heroine was a mother of some sort, whether the Virgin Mary, the Mother of God; Indira Gandhi, seen as the Mother of India or Mother Teresa, 'Mother to us all'.

Organizational consultant **Rifat Wahhab** is still inspired by her mother, the first Muslim headmistress of a Church of England school, whose place in history was hard earned. Dr **Jane Grant**, a former Director of the National Alliance of Women's Organizations, acknowledged her mother's courage in single-handedly bringing up three children and eventually pursuing her own dream. *'In her day, you had to fight for education but at the age of seventy she received her Open University degree. Mother was exceptional because she has enormous courage and is able to live alone.'* Historian **Kusoom Vadgama** also cited her mother who had been equally undefeated by age. *'My mother is one in a million. At nearly 100 years old, her energy and enthusiasm to cook, travel, exercise and do gardening, is undiminished. Her virtues of patience and tolerance are as remarkable as her ability to please.'*

When **Barbara Rogers**, the founding editor of *Everywoman*, sat her Foreign Office exams she was asked to write down the person she admired most and, even as a young woman, she wrote *'My mother'*. For others, it was only later in life that they fully realized the extraordinary virtues of their mothers. British Member of Parliament **Diane Abbott** recalls: *'As a teenager I looked down on my mother. Recently she came to stay with me. It's only since she was with me and was dying of stomach cancer that I realized how heroic she was. As a nurse she knew all* about illness. She never complained about her pain, she never took pain killers and she only took a little bit of morphine just before she died. Only now do I know how important it was for her when I got elected to Parliament'. Indian classical vocalist **Lakshmi Shankar** spoke for so many other women when she praised her mother's achievements, despite a hard life with little advantage but her natural gifts. *'She was an absolutely wonderful woman and the more I think of her, the more I see what a great woman she was. She came from a village where all the ancestors were hardly educated. She never learnt anything but she could sing.'*

Economist **Noreena Hertz**, who has been described as one of the world's leading young thinkers, spoke for the majority of women who said that their inspiration and heroine was their mother. When I was with Noreena it dawned on me that I had known her late mother in the early eighties as one of the leaders of the feminist movement. She was a woman who, at the age of forty, decided that she had made enough money from her trendy fashion company and studied for a PhD in law. Here was her daughter, a beautiful thirty something, who had taken the world by storm with her cogent arguments in favour of global responsibility and the potential of ordinary citizens to participate in ethical change. Noreena's whole being changed as she spoke about the loss of her mother, who was central to her identity, but I could see that she had many of the same heroic qualities as her mother and will undoubtedly make many women proud to name her as their inspiration in the future.

For film director **Sai Paranjpye**, having a truly heroic mother was a mixed blessing. Sai's mother was. *'at least one hundred years ahead of her time. She was the woman who launched the family planning movement in India when the word or topic was not discussed in polite society. She was also a writer, a dramatist, a social worker and, when girls of her age didn't even finish school, she went to Cambridge.'* She was offered the prized Indian award of Padma Shree before it was offered to her mother. Loyal to her mother, despite her exacting expectations that had often made Sai feel inadequate, she actually refused the award on the grounds that *'you have not honoured my mother who has achieved so much more'.* Her mother was awarded the higher Padma Bhushan award two years later.

Thelma Holt

Jane Grant

'Elizabeth I wouldn't have time to be Queen today. She would be receiving counselling, talking about her ghastly father to a psychiatrist. She was devious, cunning and did it all. She managed to survive and had a great sense of the dramatic, but initially she had to make enormous personal sacrifices in order to fulfil what she thought was her destiny.' Thelma Holt

Diane Abbott

Noreena Hertz

Sai Paranjpye

Rosa Maria Juárez

History's heroines

Theatre producer **Thelma Holt** also cited Elizabeth I as her heroine. 'She wouldn't have time to be Queen today. She would be receiving counselling, talking about her ghastly father to a psychiatrist. She was devious, cunning and did it all. She managed to survive and had a great sense of the dramatic, but initially she had to make enormous personal sacrifices in order to fulfil what she thought was her destiny.'

President of the Mexican Franchise & Networking Institute, **Rosa Maria Juárez** spoke about Mexican heroines she was brought up with, who were freedom fighters for their community. Iraqi judge and Member of Parliament **Zakia Hakki** was inspired by the Kurdish heroines, Princess Khan Zad and Kadam Khair. Lawyer **Ashminder Kaur Dhadialla** spoke of Mai Bhago, a leader in the Sikh Army. When Sikh men betrayed Guru Gobind Singh, and refused to fight the invading Moguls, the women stood up and told the men to stay at home as they were going to fight with the Guru's army, which they did. Mai Bhago became a symbol of the Sikh spirit.

Iranian singer and author **Shusha Guppy** identifies Persian women as remarkable, resourceful, forbearing and strong. 'There are so many heroines but my favourite is Manijeh, the daughter of the King of Turan, who fell in love and seduced her father's enemy Bijan, keeping him in her castle as her lover. Upon discovering Bijan, her father threw him into a well. Manijeh would beg for food, lowering it into the well and sacrificing everything for love. She contacted Rostam, the great Persian warrior, to come and rescue Bijan and herself, which he dutifully did.'

While some of the women admired drive and guts, others found heroism in a sense of selflessness borne from love and kindness. Red Cross nurse **Claire Bertschinger** spoke of how, when she saw the film *The Inn of the Sixth Happiness*, it had a profound effect on her. It was a true story about Gladys Alywood, an English missionary, who in 1930 travelled to China and was caught up in the Japanese invasion. She led a group of orphaned children across the mountains to safety. 'I remember thinking "That's what I want to do".'

Lynne Franks

Audrey Kitagawa

'We must stay attentive and true to ourselves and not give our power to gurus, businesses, institutions or politicians, but understand that we are our own and each others' teachers.'

Lynne Franks

Leonora van Gils

Miranda Macpherson

Anando Heffley

Sadhvi Bhagwati Saraswati

Gurus

The Hindi word guru has now passed into the global language as a shorthand for an expert or leader. However, embedded in the word guru is more than the idea of instruction or expertise. True gurus offer their followers a sense of protection and grace alongside guidance, a very powerful cocktail for those seeking personal transformation. For some spiritual traditions, the idea of a guru figure can be seen to stand in the way of an individual's relationship to God. Former attorney, Hawaiian **Audrey Kitagawa**, now loved as the Divine Mother, believes that each person should be true to themselves, and realizes that the true guru is within. *'The Kingdom of God is within, the scriptures are within and so we have to come within our own hearts and look within our own selves.'*

Similar to Audrey's belief, the PR consultant **Lynne Franks** also believes that we must focus on our own potential, although in a more secular frame. *'We must stay attentive and true to ourselves and not give our power to gurus, businesses, institutions or politicians, but understand that we are our own and each others' teachers.'*

However, as the Reverend **Miranda Macpherson**, founder of the Interfaith Seminary, explained, *'If you want to find your way through the jungle, you take a guide who knows the way. If you want to know about spirituality, you go to someone who knows about it'.*

The avatar Sri Sathya Sai Baba

For many women, the guidance and emotional energy offered by their guru has had a very profound effect on their sense of being. The Reverend **Leonora van Gils**, founder of a Dolphin Therapy Centre, affirmed what so many women told me, *'The turning point in my life was meeting the avatar Sri Sathya Sai Baba. For the first time in my life I came face to face with a divine being who would change the lives of millions of people for the better and was about to change mine as well.'*

Osho

Anando Heffley's account of her spiritual awakening under the guidance of her guru, Osho, was equally powerful. *'He touched something in me and millions of other people. He was like a wind that fired me up. He triggered something in me that was dormant and then showed me how to develop it. For him, life was not a problem to be solved, but a mystery to be lived and enjoyed. People came to Osho's ashram for different reasons, some because they realized there was something missing in their lives, some because they had a kind of crisis in their lives and were ready to look for change. Some just came to look for a band-aid. They were into exploring themselves.'*

His Holiness Pujya Swami Chidanand Saraswatiji

Sadhvi Bhagwati Saraswati, American by birth, was raised in Hollywood and prior to meeting her guru was completing her PhD at Stanford University. Travelling to India, she met His Holiness Pujya Swami Chidanand Saraswatiji, and pledged her life to service, taking the official *Sanyas diksha* (vows of renunciation). *'The blessings of my guru have been* *essential to the success of both my own spiritual growth and also all of the work I do. My guru lives only for others and for God. Regardless of the situation, regardless of the presence of an audience or no audience, regardless of His own state of comfort, regardless of the "dignity" of the situation, He is always the same, always calm, always peaceful, always loving, always thinking about others rather than Himself, never fatigued, always one with God. To me, this has been the most inspiring lesson. Particularly since I come from the West where service is frequently relegated to a few hours one Saturday a month. Where work is what you do because you have to support a family, where we spend a great deal of energy learning to assert ourselves and our needs better.'*

Someday my prince will come

For generations, fairy tales have been used to teach and terrorize children at bedtime. It was curious to learn of the impact that these stories had made on successful women throughout the world. Unlike other childhood literature, fairy tales are intimate and magical. They portray a dramatic world, divided into good and evil, princesses and witches, fairies and ogres. They occupy a special place in memory, eliciting nostalgia of both the security of childhood and the pleasure of fear without real danger.

Many fairy stories have often been cautionary tales that warn girls about the price to be paid for freedom or escape from family and marriage. For this reason many women did not identify with traditional Western fairy stories. **Frances Cairncross** thought they were destructive, and depicted women as passive creatures. Baroness **Rennie Fritchie** agreed with this, and was, instead, fascinated by the Greek tale of Ariadne, who found her way out of the labyrinth with a hidden ball of thread. Here was a woman who had foresight and was pro-active. Although fairy stories often have an obvious moral message, they are also open to many different types of readings.

Frances Cairncross

Rennie Fritchie

Parvin Ali

Shauna Crockett-Burrows

Diana Cooper

Rosemary Perry

Dorothy Boux

Alison Donnell

Far from being immersed in a romantic idyll, waiting for the Prince to come, **Parvin Ali** simply liked Snow White because she was the only Princess with black hair! However, Parvin continued, *'It was only when I was much older that I recognized the strong symbolism and parallel purpose of fairy tales. I did object to the fact that the heroines were always passive, beautiful women whilst the witches and hags were always ugly. Any knowledge possessed by women was always seen as being used for malice and mischief, like Snow White's vain stepmother. The heroines were the ignorant ones, from whom knowledge and information was withheld. They were always waiting for the Prince to come'.*

Fairy stories

For those who were charmed by fairy tales, 'Cinderella', followed by 'Snow White' and 'Sleeping Beauty' were the most popular stories. But how these stories were read, was as important as the stories themselves. 'The Princess and the Pea' was cited by a few women as it could be seen as an uppity young lady complaining about her sleeping conditions or, as the founding editor of the pioneering paper *Positive News* **Shauna Crockett-Burrows** thought, the princess was such a sensitive soul that even the slightest imperfections impacted on her.

Dr **Diana Cooper**, the author and founder of Angel Day, chose 'Jack and the Beanstalk' because she identified with Jack being a seeker of truth. In contrast, lawyer **Maja Daruwala**, who has dedicated her life to justice and human rights, sees Jack as a thief because he runs off with someone else's gold. Morality has many faces.

The Reverend **Rosemary Perry**, hypnotherapist and homeopath, found 'The Ugly Duckling' the most appropriate story for her. *'We are all swans. It is only the ego, circumstances and ignorance that make us feel like ugly ducklings. Swans have the ability to siphon milk molecules from water, symbolizing an ability to recognize and discriminate truth within the illusory 3-D world. The Sanskrit for swan is Hamsa which is also 'Ham*

'I love Cinderella because deep down every woman dreams of being discovered.'

Helena Kennedy

'Bless Cinderella's heart. The abused child who became a princess.'

Esther Rantzen

'I was the youngest of three sisters and used to imagine I was Cinderella. I always wanted to go to their parties but I was five years younger so was often left behind.'

Marigold Verity

'As a hopeless romantic, and having been a Latin ballroom dancer, I love the idea of "going to the ball like Cinderella".'

Zenobia Nadirshaw

– Sa', the sacred breath in, then out. The Hindu goddess Saraswati, who fosters the Arts and education, rides upon a swan, symbolizing the mastery of that sacred breath that inspires all such activities.'

Some look to fairy tales for picaresque adventures, and escape. Such stories launch the reader into an unknown realm, away from the familiar monotony of everyday life. Author and calligrapher **Dorothy Boux** enjoyed stories, *'where people set out on a quest and are subjected to extraordinary happenings, but given a talisman to hold on to. The talisman is their wisdom. You secretly know that they are going to go through difficult situations and desperate times. Yet you know, because they have that magical presence and inner strength, they will survive and live great and memorable lives'.*

Scheherazade

The escapism of fairy stories attracted Iraqi-born Judge **Zakia Hakki**, for very different reasons. *'I was born in Baghdad, the place of flying carpets and the magic lamp, the home of Scheherazade. All my childhood I dreamt of finding the magic lamp and having all my wishes come true.'*

Neuroscientist Professor **Uta Frith**, read the story of *1001 Arabian Nights* and loved the character Scheherazade. *'She was so resourceful that she invented story after story to profoundly change and improve a cruel ruler and to stave off death. I think of myself as a person who makes stories of strange and often cruel facts of nature to fight against ignorance and to buy time to improve our condition.'*

As academic **Alison Donnell** explained, *'The importance of Scheherazade is not simply that she keeps herself and the other virgins alive by telling her stories to the king, but that she uses these stories to teach the Sultan Shahryar a better understanding of life, so that he no longer wishes to murder her. It is this capacity of stories to help us understand something more about our lives and make changes for the good that underlines the appeal of these tales.'*

دعاها بر آورده میشه

Respuestas a sus oraciones

苍天有眼

svar på deras böner

Answers to their prayers

Good God

Throughout my womanising it became clear that I had serious competition on a number of fronts, loving mothers, wonderful husbands, and my greatest rival of all, God!

I have always been a believer in God but, like everyone, I have moments of doubt. I believe that you reap what you sow and that there will be a day of judgement. Naturally, I was very conscious that my womanising might catch up with me. But who would ever have thought that womanising would bring me to God? As they say, *'God works in mysterious ways, his wonders to perform'*.

Many of the women I spent time with had a strong faith, even an absolute belief. As jazz singer **Dana Gillespie** pointed out, *'Why have faith when you know for sure?'* Perhaps their secret to success in life boiled down to the wisdom I first recognized on an embroidered cushion in my mother's sitting room: *'In everything you do, put God first, and He will direct you and crown your efforts with success'*. Proverbs 3:6.

Enlightenment

My womanising initially started in the pursuit of happiness but this path was soon linked to a spiritual quest. I learnt that happiness was about overcoming your own limitations; learning how to accept yourself; being proud of what you achieved, even if it was something small; giving happiness to other people and being in a deeply loving and compassionate relationship with them. Those who were happy were disciplined; they had a sense of morality and did not abuse their own bodies with drugs, alcohol or cigarettes. They saw a purpose to their lives and were wise enough to see the unity of the universe. They appreciated that every little action, every thought, had a consequence for good or evil. It was the ripple effect.

Spiritual quests have always been seen as the necessity of the poor for whom earthly pleasures were denied, as if the reward of the spirit made 'drudgery divine'. Now, however, there is no denying that spirituality has become the quest of the rich. The pop star Madonna, the original material girl, is just one well-known personality to have embraced a new belief system, in her case the ancient Kabbalah. It is nothing new to suggest that this yearning for spiritual fulfilment is a symptom of an age in which the worship of money and media fame has devalued life. But perhaps the link between materialism and spirituality goes beyond this. For the wealthy (and those who live off credit!), there is no saving up and looking forward to treats and moments of special pleasure. Champagne is no longer the savoured drink of significant celebrations. Children no longer wait for months until birthdays and festivals bring new clothes or presents. Apart from the poor, life is swollen and bloated with material goods and we seldom deny ourselves anything we 'feel' we need. Nothing is deferred except enlightenment and therefore its value shines out at us more and more as the prize really worth waiting for.

As the Reverend **Miranda Macpherson**, Founder of the Interfaith Seminary, explained, *'There is a feeling of loss and a yearning for something that you can't put your finger on. I think that is part of what is driving this really extreme materialistic debt culture that we are in at the moment. People are hungry for something and what they are being told by the media is buy this new skirt, it will make you feel sexy, go on this holiday, buy a new car: that is the God – but en masse people are searching for meaning and not finding it in traditional establishments'.*

The spiritual women I met had no doubt found a path through which to combine centredness with the great cause. Although they did not seek earthly rewards or recognition, they had a deep personal stake in what they did and their passion seemed unequalled.

Sister Nirmala

Sister Cecily

'My daily prayer and quiet time with God recharges me and fires me with energy and passion to go out each day and make a difference to the life of at least one person.'

Sister Cecily

Phyllis Krystal

'We have to live in the world. We are in bodies and our duty is to share what knowledge we have been given and also to help other people. It is about giving people the opportunity to work on themselves and to learn to serve joyfully.'

Phyllis Krystal

Sister Cyril

Meeting **Sister Nirmala**, Superior General of the Missionaries of Charity in Kolkata, and the successor to Mother Teresa, at five in the morning was memorable. We respectfully said prayers over Mother Teresa's tomb and asked for her blessing. For Sister Nirmala, Mother Teresa was her mother and she follows in her footsteps with immense humility. Indeed, her life was so centred on the idea of selflessness that she found it almost impossible to talk about herself.

Sister Cecily also has an innate humility coupled with a timeless serenity. A renowned educationalist in Singapore, she has dedicated her life to teaching and empowering girls. Indeed, it is her firm belief that has guided her life as an educator. *'It is truly my life of consecration to God that prompts me to want to make a difference to the world. My daily prayer and quiet time with God recharges me and fires me with energy and passion to go out each day and make a difference to the life of at least one person. I believe that every person is an image of God and is deeply loved by Him. As such I cannot but respect and revere everyone and strive to love as God does. My philosophy is to love and give and serve unconditionally, and not to seek reward because the joy and thrill is in the giving and serving'.*

Sister Cyril in Kolkata is another nun and educator who has transformed the lives of so many young people by offering them a valuable education, and her own example of spiritual wholeness. She is a radiant and feisty headmistress, a supercharged saint in the waiting. Although Sister Cyril was the only woman I met who had taken on a man's name she was all woman. She has a maternal and passionate nature that is electric. She is also a pioneer in delivering education. Sister Cyril insists that all pupils at the famous Loreto School, where she is the head, whether rich or poor, teach their peers who are less fortunate. A simple but effective formula in encouraging educational excellence, because not only do deprived children in the villages benefit from a basic education but all Loreto students learn to work in their community, helping to empower their peers. In turn it encourages the student teachers to excel in their studies so as to be able to teach other young people less fortunate than themselves; a win, win, educational system for the rich and the poor.

Economic giantess

Sister Cyril's joy for life and unstoppable goodness were confirmed when I met **Naina Lal Kidwai**, Chief Executive of HSBC India, in her office in Mumbai. Naina's personality is a fine balance between being very shrewd and yet responsive. She mentioned how she needed to excel at school and how she became the first Indian graduate from Harvard Business School. Described by *Fortune* magazine as one of the world's 50 most powerful women in business, and in the first three in Asia, Naina is an economic giantess who is able to anticipate new trends and has that rare intuitive understanding of how the markets will react. She is astute at reading the markets, people and situations. Naina has the golden touch. She also has a singular way of interacting by responding in a measured but enthusiastic way to what you are saying. We were saying our *au revoir* by the lift when I happened to mention that I had met Sister Cyril of Kolkata and what an impact she had on me. Naina's whole demeanour changed. She was a different person; not the financial whiz that the world knew but a star pupil of her old headmistress the same Sister Cyril. I, who had seen the world and knew that fame and fortune were as transitory as life, was moved by Naina's genuine gratitude to her old teacher. I left thinking that life was magical.

Spiritual giantesses

This same magic informs the work of **Dadi Janki** and **Phyllis Krystal**, two spiritual giantesses. Like the three nuns, Sisters Nirmala, Cecily and Cyril, it would be almost impossible to measure the breadth or depth of the influence that these two women have had on others' lives. For both women, their links to the social world are strengthened rather than diminished by their links to God. Both Dadi and Phyllis are in their nineties and both women continue to travel extensively and work tirelessly to inspire and be of service to others. The Brahma Kumaris World Spiritual University is known both for its grass roots work in spiritual education and for its role as a convener of international projects and dialogues dealing with issues of world transformation. As a founding member, joining in 1937 at the age of twenty-one, Dadi has been centrally involved in developing both the social projects and the spiritual conversations of the university, becoming one of the world's first female spiritual leaders. Indeed, Dadi's understanding of the crucial links between spirituality, the enrichment of human consciousness and the improvement of human lives, continues to inform much of her work today. She was designated a Wisdom Keeper at two United Nations conferences, becoming part of an eminent group of religious leaders advising on the spiritual dilemmas underpinning global issues of the environment and human settlement today. Together with Archbishop Desmond Tutu and the Dalai Lama, Dadi is an international patron of Rights and Humanity, an organization promoting respect for human rights. She is also the founder of the Janki Foundation for Global Health Care, *'dedicated to positive human development and whole-person healthcare, an approach that considers the needs of patients at the levels of body, mind and spirit'*.

Phyllis Krystal's contribution to spiritual development has centred on her teachings of Higher Consciousness. In the late 1950s she studied the work of Edgar Cayce and was regressed into past lives. Inspired by her experiences, she worked with a friend on developing a method for contacting the inner source of wisdom which they called the Hi C. The techniques received from the Hi C have been used to help those who wish to release themselves from attachment to, or reliance on, outer security or control. Phyllis has written extensively about her visualization method, including her seminal *Cutting the Ties That Bind* and *Cutting the Ties of Karma – understanding the patchwork of past lives*. Her own spiritual pathway has also been enriched by her encounter with the Indian avatar Sri Sathya Sai Baba, whose life and teachings are an inspiration to her and millions of devotees around the world. Like Dadi, Phyllis sees her spiritual work as connecting to the human world and its needs. 'We *have to live in the world. We are in bodies and our duty is to share what knowledge we have been given and also to help other people. It is about giving people the opportunity to work on themselves and to learn to serve joyfully.*'

Mata Amritanandamayi

'love is the cure.'

Amma

Audrey Kitagawa

'I was told that everything in life is recorded – every thought, every word, every deed. I felt God's loving presence as he shared this secret, this act of love with me.'

Audrey Kitagawa

Dadi Janki

'I have committed myself to working for God and wanting others to experience the same happiness as I do in my spiritual life.'

Dadi Janki

Jackie Ballard

'While I was queuing in a bank in Tehran, a prayer of mine was answered and I realized then that I believed in God.'

Jackie Ballard

spiritual mothers

It is no coincidence that female spiritual leaders are usually known as Mother. The selfless devotion and love of others that directs their lives embodies a maternal ideal of unconditional care.

Simply known as **Amma** (mother), Mata Amritanandamayi is dubbed the 'hugging saint' because she offers the simple and fundamental reassurance of mother's embrace. When I met Amma I was bewildered as to why people might come from such distances to be hugged by her; yet when she hugged me I felt completely at peace and did not want her to stop. Amma was born in a poor fishing village in Kerala on the west coast of India. It is said she arrived in the world smiling, and she spent her childhood meditating. Dark skinned and unconventional as a child, the local villagers considered her crazy, but even then she was slipping into what she and her followers recognize as profound and God-intoxicated states. Now she channels this energy towards the happiness of others through her loving gestures. As Amma says, *'love is the cure'*.

For **Audrey Kitagawa** the call to spiritual work came after she ran a successful law practice in Honolulu. A devotee of the Japanese Divine Mother, Audrey was asked to carry her light into the world, upon her death in 1992. As Divine Mother, Audrey has devoted her life to sharing her gift of love. Like nearly all mothers, Audrey is aware that one loving heart increases the possibility for more loving hearts. *'The love that we already have within us becomes magnified many times over when we reverse the flow from one of grasping to one of giving, sharing, and allowing freedom.'*

Finding God

We tend to think of faith as a given, rather than a process, but I was fascinated by the stories of finding God.

Jackie Ballard's promising political career with the Liberal Party was cut short after she lost her seat in the 2001 British elections, brought down by the hunting lobby. With courage, she left her political career behind and went to live in Iran for almost a year, challenging herself by studying the Persian language. While there, she also had an unexpected life-changing experience in one of the most unlikely places, a bank. *'While I was queuing in a bank in Tehran, a prayer of mine was answered and I realized then that I believed in God'*. When she returned to Britain Jackie's inclination and ability to campaign for others' rights was directed in her work as Director General of the Royal Society for the Prevention of Cruelty to Animals.

Several women had experienced profound shifts in consciousness or intense moments of spiritual being that changed their lives. Calligrapher **Dorothy Boux's** awakening to God came even earlier, at the age of three. *'To me it was the most extraordinary moment of beauty. I knelt down in the grass and I just looked at it and I just knew God existed. There is no other word. I just knew at that moment. I hadn't got a name for Him, I didn't know he was called God but I knew there was love and beauty and there was a creator. After that nothing could shake me from that belief.'*

Spiritual Leader **Dadi Janki** remembers her experience of a deep love for God from the age of two, although her search for truth began at the age of eleven. *'I was challenged from within my family and from my community, asking me why I was following this spiritual path from such an early age which was very unusual for a female. But whenever anyone opposed me, I just maintained my resolve not to be shaken and also not to feel any bitterness towards them. Physically I would get sick quite often from a young age, so I often wondered how I could serve the world and I decided that the best way was serving through my mind.*

I remember having a vision, where I saw myself carrying a ball of light and I was showing this ball of light to the whole world. I have never forgotten that vision from all those years ago. When I was twenty-one, I met Brahma Baba (founder of the Brahma Kumaris World Spiritual University) and, through his inspiration and example, I felt that my aim was given a determined focus. It was probably the single most important turning point in my life. Ever since, I have committed myself to working for God and wanting others to experience the same happiness as I do in my spiritual life'.

Divine Mother **Audrey Kitagawa** also shared a strong consciousness of God from an early age. *'I had this remarkable experience when I was in first grade. I was very ill with a high fever, and I was lying all by myself when I actually felt my body leave, and I was in the presence of God. I was told that everything in life is recorded – every thought, every word, every deed. I felt God's loving presence as he shared this secret, this act of love with me. I was very comforted by his presence.'*

Finding Jesus

Sister Nirmala heard the name of Jesus and his stories in school at the age of seven. *'A few years later I went with my entire family to a temple of Shiva at the outskirts of a village in Bihar. When I came out I saw a huge statue of Jesus. There was a church near the temple. I was fascinated by the statue. Two or three years later, I brought a Bible home and when I opened it the first line I read was, "Love me because I am meek and humble of heart". And I remember saying to myself, "how proud is Jesus. He is boasting of himself". I closed the book and never looked at it again. Later on, after I finished school, I went to Sri Lanka for a family holiday and one night we were discussing which was the best religion. My cousins said Christianity is beautiful and I said what* rubbish, it is Hinduism, and I said all the negative things that I had heard and read about Christianity. Soon after that my father brought me back to Bihar and I was admitted to a convent college for further education. On the third day I saw my friend, who was Hindu, kneeling down and praying and something happened to me. Jesus became alive for me. I started reading books and worshipping him. I received baptism and joined Mother Teresa.

Finding Mary Magdalene

Liz Jackson, Managing Director of Great Guns Marketing, movingly recalled her conversion to Christianity as a young woman. 'When I went to work in America, the director of the company I worked for was the pastor for the Evangelical church. I went to church with him and his family a couple of times and found it an interesting environment, people jumping up and down and rock bands, very, very lively. My boss and family were going to Memphis for the weekend and asked me if I wanted to go and I agreed. It was an experience that I shall never forget. I was filled with the Holy Spirit in the church. I remember I cried and suddenly found a longing for something beyond myself. I heard a voice in my head saying "Don't worry my child, my feet are being washed". I had never really read the Bible before and after that experience someone in the church read the scripture where Mary Magdalene washed Jesus' feet with her tears.'

Growing through grief

For some of the women the death of a loved one triggered deeper questions about the existence of God and how to live a good life. Neuro-design pioneer **Beverly Payeff-Masey** lost her second child in a dangerous childbirth and almost died herself. Her story is compelling. *'I managed to survive but the marriage didn't. It was at that period of my life that I used my art to start a career in design. I had a partner who was a photographer and one day I found him dead on the road, involved in a car crash. It was too painful so I shifted again to interior design. When I met my husband Bill Payeff in Paris he was in charge of North Africa and the Middle East for the US Information Agency. We travelled to many places together. In Indonesia, in 1984, Bill was the public face of the American Embassy. It was at that time the Islamic Jihad blood curdling message that embassy staff and their wives and children would be killed, was delivered. The letter changed our lives. At the time we were working on security aspects of design for the Embassy itself. We were living under a dreadful death threat so the two older children were sent back to the United States for safety. It was there that my eighteen-year-old daughter was killed. She was run over by a habitual offender who had already lost his licence four times. I remember coming home and shaking my fists at God and saying "You son of a bitch, how dare you do this?" And then I thought, "Well, who are you yelling at? You must believe in a God, you can't yell at nothing, you clearly are a fraud; you do believe in God!" I had to return to the United States for the trial of the man who had killed my precious child. I became extremely ill. This was a dreadful time in my life and yet another gentle turning point when I decided to work with other parents whose children had been killed and had problems with flashbacks.'* Beverly's life experiences provoked her to research the neuroscience of trauma to understand how it connected to design and architecture. She became a pioneer in the field of neuro-design and developed ArchiMap®, the first successful neuro-science-based application for architects and designers to map the specific needs of individuals and especially for victims of violence and natural disasters.

Anu Aga

'We do not think about death at all. We take it that life will go on and we give hurtful meanings to death. We don't accept that everyone who is born is going to die. When and where and how, we don't know.'
Anu Aga

Beverly Payeff-Masey

'… my eighteen-year-old daughter was killed … This was a dreadful time in my life and yet another gentle turning point.'

Beverly Payeff-Masey

'I began to realize the enormous importance of silence if one wishes to commune with God.'

Oonagh Shanley-Toffolo

Oonagh Shanley-Toffolo

Having experienced the sudden and tragic death of her son, as well as her husband, **Anu Aga** came to a realization that we need to embrace the reality of death as a part of human life. Her words were heartfelt: 'We do not think about death at all. We take it that life will go on and we give hurtful meanings to death. We don't accept that everyone who is born is going to die. When and where and how, we don't know, but death is inevitable. Every day the sun rises and sets. When it sets we do not start mourning and crying, because we have accepted this process but we haven't accepted death as a natural process and we make up belief systems that say that the young don't die. If you go to any hospital you see the young dying. I used to touch wood like crazy if ever the thought of death was there, but today I know, even if I carry a log of wood, I cannot alter my destiny'.

Given that it is commonplace to regard people in a state of grief as being less themselves, absorbed or even lost on account of the intensity of their emotional state, it is important to acknowledge that experiencing a very heightened sense of loss may actually peel back layers of habit and custom to reveal a sharper sense of what is important and even healing.

Healer and spiritual guide to the late Princess Diana, **Oonagh Shanley-Toffolo's** own crisis moment came when she was almost five. 'My dearest brother and playmate, Kevin Patrick, was accidentally killed while harvesting hay. Many people were there when a sudden downpour sent the men running for cover. My eleven-year-old brother took shelter in the hay and when the rain ceased the men resumed work. One man accidentally dug the pitchfork through Kevin's right temple. I remember running out when I met a neighbour carrying my brother in his outstretched arms. I started to cry and scream and somebody whipped me up in their arms and carried me to my bed. Through the window I could see men's heads; they must have been trying to resuscitate him.

Dorothy Boux

Ashminder Kaur Dhadialla

Mae-Wan Ho

Tricia Sibbons

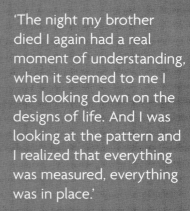

'The night my brother died I again had a real moment of understanding, when it seemed to me I was looking down on the designs of life. And I was looking at the pattern and I realized that everything was measured, everything was in place.'

Dorothy Boux

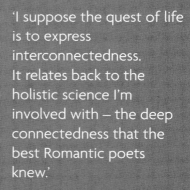

'I suppose the quest of life is to express interconnectedness. It relates back to the holistic science I'm involved with – the deep connectedness that the best Romantic poets knew.'

Mae-Wan Ho

I was taken to a neighbour's house that I might calm down, but nothing would console me. Later that day my father came to take me home. Still in his arms, I was taken to say goodbye to my beloved brother, who was laid out on my parents' bed. My mother had made a beautiful pale blue habit and a neighbour wove a crown of white roses for his head which symbolized love and purity. I was desolate. I wanted to lie down beside him and to go to heaven with him.' Although the trauma had a very deep effect on Oonagh and has left a scar for life, the grief was also instrumental in her spiritual growth. *'After my brother's death I grew very reclusive. I had a favourite hiding place between two double ditches where I played at being a hermit. It was here I began to realize the enormous importance of silence if one wishes to commune with God.'*

Dorothy Boux's brother also died young when he was shot down during the Battle of Britain in the Second World War. The trauma provoked a crisis in her faith but also a strengthening of her spiritual connection. *'He was a wonderful young man, caring and very peaceful by nature. He was nine years older than me and therefore an intermediary between my parents and myself. I was left heartbroken. I loved him deeply. That was the only moment when I went through a real crisis of belief. I had been praying that he wouldn't be killed and my question was why was he taken away? The night my brother died I again had a real moment of understanding, when it seemed to me I was looking down on the designs of life. And I was looking at the pattern and I realized that everything was measured, everything was in place.'*

Human rights lawyer **Ashminder Kaur Dhadialla** similarly recalled that the most critical event in her life was when a close family member was murdered at the age of twenty-three. *'It is one of those events that turn your world on its head and it takes a long time to re-balance. Ambition and the things you thought were important somehow fade away and you both harden and soften in certain ways. It changed who I was and how I saw the world forever'.*

'Mother said "Think of death, once a day". It makes a good human being out of you. When you realize that you could be gone just like that, and anything can happen to you at any time, you tend to lead a better life.'

Farzana Contractor

'We should determine our way of living and plan our life by imagining how we will feel when we look back from our grave.'

Sue Stapely

'Actually we don't know if there is life after death and a world to come. Worrying about it is pointless since there's absolutely nothing we can do about it. What we should do is just get on with doing good things in this world.'

Julia Neuberger

'Death has inspired me to live and enjoy living. Since I was very young I am conscious of life and death. I define myself as a true survivor in all fields.'

Rosa Maria Juárez

I will survive

Mae-Wan Ho felt she should have died many times. 'When I was born, it was during the war. My mother was escaping the Japanese invaders and she was with me in a boat with one hundred other people. I started to cry. Of course everybody said, "Smother her!, Throw her overboard". I could have died then. My mother saved me the first time. The second time, we were living in Hong Kong and a bomb was dropped outside my home and was intercepted by a big banyan tree. The tree is still there but the house was eventually bombed, and you can still see the damage done to it. Luckily the first bomb didn't explode; otherwise we would have been killed. The third time was much later. I was visiting one of my graduate students in Wales, near Snowdonia. My husband and I thought "let's go for a stroll". We didn't know that Snowdonia is really serious mountain climbing and when we were out there I took a step, just stumbled, and fell down this very steep slope. I had this inspiration and just hugged the mountain which actually broke the fall. My husband eventually managed to get me out again. It was almost as if there was some love between myself and the mountain. It was a very eerie experience because I didn't panic. I just thought, now, what can I do? I suppose the quest of life is to express interconnectedness. It relates back to the holistic science I'm involved with – the deep connectedness that the best Romantic poets knew.' I knew why Mae-Wan had to live. She is blessed with a dazzling mind and passionate personality. She is the heady cocktail of a Romantic scientist blended with an artistic realist, and what more could anyone ask for?

Faith in action

Faith comes in many forms, either faith in God, faith in yourself, or faith in other people. There's also an interesting division with those who have total faith in God and those who had an equal faith in humanity.

Teresa Hale, the pioneering founder of the Hale Clinic for Complementary Medicine, arrived at her faith through spiritual practice. '*Greatness has to have a spiritual connection; deep down there has to be a heart to serve. The most important thing for me is to go back to God. That is the most important divine contract. But I definitely think I made a contract to serve in the area of health. It is the spiritual work that gets you through the difficult part. I just wish that I had a stronger spiritual understanding when I was a bit younger.*'

Tricia Sibbons, social and charitable entrepreneur, recalled a meaningful encounter that confirmed her humanity and recognition of spiritual duty. '*It was Christmas and I was coming out of St Martin-in-the-Fields church in Trafalgar Square when I was confronted by a tramp who asked for money. I have this principle of not giving money. I told him about going to the charity for the homeless, Crisis at Christmas, if he was homeless; basically I was trying to tell him how to survive Christmas. I then had my Christmas lunch and I felt uneasy. I could have taken him to Crisis, the homeless shelter, in my car, but I didn't. It was more about me than him. I didn't connect with him. I had been given an opportunity to respond and I failed. The encounter was important because I'm much more careful now. When I was in Johannesburg I went for a meal with a friend and when I came back to the car there was a little street child who had not eaten properly and wanted some food. I went to the supermarket and bought food and then sat with him because I wanted him to eat the food and nobody else to come and take it away from him. It took half an hour of my time but there was preciousness to that engagement. The more you respond to each other, the better the world will be – that is my deepest spiritual belief and that is where my spiritual journey has brought me. To understand the Gospels in a deep, meaningful way, we have to respond kindly to each other.*'

Faith in miracles

Spiritual faith was not confirmed for disability champion **Dinah Radtke**, who remembers with sorrow her family's failed quest to cure her of disability. *'My mother believed very much in healing powers. When I was ten all the family travelled to Lourdes because she thought the Virgin Mary would heal me. All the way to Lourdes she prayed the Rosary. I was so excited that I would be healed that I got a high fever. The procedure with the bath and the holy source, the nuns and the holy mass outside on the lawn with hundreds of disabled people was a nightmare. My smaller sisters cried so hard in the next bathroom when they had to dive in the ice cold water that I thought they would be killed. Anyway there was no miracle in Lourdes.'* I had to disagree with Dinah. I thought that there had been a miracle. Even though Dinah was still wheel-chair bound, she had the most extraordinary strength of spirit and a determination to challenge the crippling prejudice that others have towards the disabled. If Dinah had walked away from Lourdes, she would never have developed her distinctive way of seeing the world and of helping to cure the emotional disability that such prejudice causes. Nor would she have had the empathy to empower others with disabilities throughout the world.

Faith in life

For Professor Dame **Gillian Beer**, faith was firm but not divine. *'I have faith in life. That is why I found writing about Darwin fascinating.'*

Rosa Maria Juárez although brought up as a Catholic in Mexico, admitted, *'I am not a religious person, but I consider myself a woman with great faith in human capacity to survive and make a better world to live in. We need to balance right and wrong, good and evil, feminine and masculine, light and darkness'.*

Was hat Liebe damit zu tun
Причём здесь любовь?
¿Qué tiene que ver el amor con est
ما علاقة الحب به!
Was hat Liebe damit zu tun
Причём здесь любовь?
¿Qué tiene que ver el amor con est
ما علاقة الحب به!
Was hat Liebe damit zu tun
Причём здесь любовь?
¿Qué tiene que ver el amor con est
ما علاقة الحب به!
Was hat Liebe damit zu tun
Причём здесь любовь?
¿Qué tiene que ver el amor con est
ما علاقة الحب به!
Was hat Liebe damit zu tun
Причём здесь любовь?

What's love got to do with it?

Love me do

Any self-respecting womaniser will tell you that love's got everything to do with it. Deep in our hearts we all know that it's the only thing that really matters. All we really do need is Love.

The call today is to learn how to love ourselves. This latest love-fad is aimed at giving self-confidence, teaching you how to develop and search for your true self in the hope that if you love yourself then everyone else will love you too. I tried to follow the self-help love manuals. I stood in front of the mirror for lengthy periods, telling myself *'I was worth it'*, but it was dreadfully tedious.

When I asked my mother to explain love to me, she replied *'I've spent my whole life trying to work it out'*. She warned me not to expect that every love would be perfect. Often one person gave more than the other and that I should always take W H Auden's beautiful words as my advice: *'if equal affection cannot be, let the more loving one be me'*.

Love is a many splendid thing

It was an inspiring experience to hear so many women talking openly about the significance of love. Not the highly-charged and often temporary love of romance, but the steady, sustaining and connecting emotion that enables people to extend their own understanding and compassion for others; love as an emotional gift that never detracts from the giver.

Sister Cyril was the personification of great love. As she explained, *'There are two kinds of people, one who lives by love, the other by law. In our school each teacher has fifteen days of casual leave. The teacher that lives by the law will definitely take those fifteen days off. The one that lives by love will need to be bundled into a taxi with a 105° temperature as she feels that even taking an hour off, her students will suffer. Every teacher in my school lives by love'.*

It is not only the spiritual giantesses such as **Phyllis Krystal**, **Dadi Janki** or **Amma** who are able to translate their love through their living. Prima ballerina **Wendy Somes** understands her art as an expression of her love. *'I love what I do. I think love is the strongest thing in the whole world. Love will never die, love will always shine through and that's what I wanted to show when I produced the ballet* Cinderella *at Royal Covent Garden.'* At the end Cinderella is with the Prince and, although her ugly sisters have made her life a misery, she has the capacity for love and so can kiss them and include them in her happiness.

Expressing love through art is also part of life for classical singer **Lakshmi Shankar**. *'My guru said to me "when you sing one note, put your heart into that note. It doesn't matter how many skills you have, unless you really love people, those communication skills don't mean anything. It's sort of cold. It has to come from the heart."* However, it is not only artistic stars who can express this love and Lakshmi remembered how tears would come to her eyes when she saw her mother, an untrained singer, singing to her son in his cradle.

The gifted communicator and author of the best-selling spiritual guide *Boundless Love*, **Miranda Macpherson** explained: *'There is no difficulty that enough love cannot conquer, no pain that enough love cannot heal, no problem that enough love cannot tear down, it matters not how muddled the tangle, difficult the circumstance, a sufficient realization of love will dissolve it all.'* Miranda's message had echoes of TV personality **Esther Rantzen's** stories. When Esther was hosting her weekly talk show *That's Esther*, she met an unusual couple whom her producer and researchers thought would be laughed at by the audience. *'One was a little person, a dwarf, and the other was a 6ft transsexual bus driver.'* They had underestimated the communicative ability of real love that the audience was quick to feel. *'They had a real emotional relationship. They had come together because of their moving experiences of being bullied and ridiculed all their lives. The audience absolutely understood their bond. It was very moving.'*

'My guru said to me "when you sing one note, put your heart into that note. It doesn't matter how many skills you have, unless you really love people, those communication skills don't mean anything. It's sort of cold. It has to come from the heart".'

Lakshmi Shankar

'it matters not how muddled the tangle, difficult the circumstance, a sufficient realization of love will dissolve it all.'

Miranda Macpherson

Working with children in a burns unit in Quito, Ecuador, brought **Sadhvi Bhagwati Saraswati** to a full realization of the healing power of love. 'Love is not about language. Love is about touch and about the eyes and heart. And people do not necessarily need sophisticated therapy to heal from their wounds. Rather the power of pure love, of tender touch. This is enough to ease the pain of third degree burns, to quiet a tantrum, to put a hyperactive child into a meditative state, and to heal most of what ails us all.'

Embracing life

Conversations with most of the women seemed to follow the way of the Buddha; they did not look for refuge to anyone besides themselves and they embraced life because they genuinely loved that sense of being alive and making an impact. Even though many had gained material wealth, few were motivated by money nor did they see financial gain as any criteria of being successful. They focused on the end product of any venture and placed more emphasis on the process and the act of involvement. They embraced every experience, whether positive or negative, and lived through these experiences with grace. It became evident that what a woman thought and felt was largely coloured by her experiences and how she reacted to them.

Sadly many people who have talent do not always have courage, confirming the adage *'a great deal of talent is lost to the world for want of a little courage'*. Inspirational women seem to have immense courage that goes beyond themselves. Often, this courage is fired by a sense of responsibility and love. As scientist **Mae-Wan Ho** explained, *'I am conscious of following a path of love. I want a science, a way of knowing, that enables me to love what I am doing and love the world. I don't want to be separated; I don't want to be fragmented. I want to be a part of the whole'.* In the simplest but profound way they demonstrated their love of life by seizing all the opportunities that came their way. They genuinely relished life.

High C

Author **Phyllis Krystal** pointed out that the value and capabilities of love have always been played down in favour of the merits of material resources. 'Caring, compassion, empathy and love are qualities that have always been denigrated, particularly by men, and considered to be weak; but they are actually very strong and the most important of all is love. In the face of a global world that is increasingly saturated in material goods and crying out for emotional and spiritual wholeness, the significance of loving can no longer be dismissed. I try and explain my work with the "High C", through the words of Jesus, "Ask and it shall be given unto you. But it should always be thy will and not mine". The "thy" represents your own real self, what we call the High C, which does know what is best for you, whereas your ego or your mind or your desire can be very deceptive.'

We get in touch with the High C, which is the real self of everyone, and then ask love, the unconditional love, to flow to each one of us. Then we send this unconditional love, this perfect love that we can get from within ourselves, first of all to the people we know; particularly people with whom we are having problems. We send this love and if the people are open to receiving it they will and if not, they won't. We also send love to people in prisons, refugee camps and orphanages. Anywhere where there are people gathered together who are unhappy, lonely, depressed. We send them love and anyone in that group who is open to receive it will. They will never know where it came from. Then we send it to different parts of the world where there is terrorism, or war, or torture, or oppression.'

As well as working at a cosmic level, Phyllis also stresses the importance of loving interactions between individuals and the need to really communicate with others. *'Look at any two people, usually one is speaking and the other is really not listening; they are usually waiting for an opportunity to talk. You see listening is hard. In fact one woman pinpointed it, and said, "What you are really saying to us is that we must all develop a loving ear" and I thought that was so perfect. We really do need to develop a loving ear. We are so involved with what we want to say that we are not listening to other people. We are so busy doing what we are doing that we are not really seeing what other people are also doing. We need to pool our knowledge for the good of all.'*

Fortune smiles

Lyutha Al-Mughairy has a personality and personal style that is both charming and has a sense of purpose. She took all her opportunities to work in new fields and establish new organizations, which led to a remarkable and varied career. After Lyutha graduated she started a radio and television programme in Abu Dhabi, which was very popular all over the Gulf region. She simultaneously helped launch the first women's society in that country. When she returned to Oman, her home country, in 1975, Lyutha established and ran the English Radio and Television Services. Her next career change came at the end of 1979 when she accepted the invitation of the United Nations to serve as Information Officer for the International Year of Disabled Persons. Since then she has taken on several different major projects within the United Nations and, in 2002, she accepted the position of Chief of the Information Centre's Service. While these achievements may lead others to regard her as a rare high-flier, she does not see herself as being innately special. *'I believe there are a lot of women who are like me and I don't think I am better than so many women. I was lucky and I worked hard. I have achieved whatever I sought out to do. I believe that in life you reap what you sow.'*

This maxim was a repeated conviction for many. If you have a positive attitude, application, and a good heart, things will work out in the end. Most women advocated having magnanimous ideals, but with feet firmly on the ground. **Hilary Blume**, founder and Director of the Charities Advisory Trust, has worked in the voluntary sector for thirty-five years and yet she confessed that whatever she did, she thought she could be

Lyutha Al-Mughairy

'I believe that in life you reap what you sow.'
Lyutha Al-Mughairy

Rennie Fritchie

'Life presents challenges and if you don't address them they keep on coming back in bigger forms until you do. I think we have a duty to give something back.'

Rennie Fritchie

Teresa Hale

'… and when something goes wrong I wonder what I was being taught from the situation. What did I have to learn? What was I missing from this situation?'

Teresa Hale

Hilary Blume

'Principles are only principles when you stick to them.'
Hilary Blume

doing more. Hilary is the grandchild of Jewish immigrants whose parents worked hard to achieve a level of middle-class comfort. She inherited the pragmatism, strong moral sensibility and work ethic from her family. Her guiding values are simply expressed, *'Do right. Seek justice and be fair. Principles are only principles when you stick to them'.* Her equally achievable idea that we should seek to help just three people to really make a difference to their lives, was a realistic vision of a better future.

Opportunity for equality

Clearly, there is nothing like equality of opportunity. For many women the daily struggle for survival is all consuming, but there is a value in understanding how certain opportunities can suddenly open up at particular historical moments. When I met Baroness **Rennie Fritchie** she explained that *'some are more fortunate than others and I have been fortunate'.* Certainly Rennie has had a wonderful career and is an astonishing woman who has received rightful recognition for her work in the public arena. However, it was not good fortune alone that had shaped Rennie's life. She had lived by her core philosophy, *'Life presents challenges and if you don't address them they keep on coming back in bigger forms until you do. I think we have a duty to give something back'.* Rennie was tenacious and held on to a sense of her own value, despite not having taken the usual route into a high-profile career. She was appointed to her job as Commissioner for Public Appointments by Sir John Major, who had never benefited from a university education, yet had ended life as Britain's Prime Minister. He wished to demonstrate that it was the quality of the person that mattered and their past record of service and not just an Oxbridge degree and the old boy's network. Rennie was a perfect example of his point. She had never had the opportunity to read for a degree while a young woman and as a single parent she had no choice but to earn a living. Yet she had used every opportunity that life had afforded her to contribute to others' lives. Rennie is admired for her emotional maturity and equanimity. She was a perfect choice to hold such an important public appointment.

'I've learnt that nothing matters more than love and nothing is harder to offer unstintingly.'

Frances Cairncross

'There's no love anymore just sex.'

Sarah Miles

'The most important thing that is missed out in the modern medical world is love.'

Wendy Savage

'We are divine beings with the unconquerable power of love available to us. How often do we live fully in that knowledge?'

Rosemary Perry

Carpe diem

Many of the women followed every opportunity given them. They understood the true meaning of *carpe diem* and seized each day with a passion.

Teresa Hale, founder of the Hale Clinic in London, is one of the world's leading 'health visionaries'. She has played a major role in the growth of complementary medicine over the last twenty-five years. Despite unquestionable success, Teresa remains alert to the need to reflect on, and learn from, life as it unfolds. She described how, through daily meditation, she writes down what each day's lesson is, *'and when something goes wrong I wonder what I was being taught from the situation. What did I have to learn? What was I missing from this situation?'* As Teresa reminded me, the Dalai Lama said that your enemies are your greatest teachers; they teach you compassion. It is this ability to welcome life as an uneven terrain of good and bad experiences, friendly and hostile influences, that seems to enable certain women to evolve and enjoy the fullness of life.

All Greek

A truly open-minded set allowed **Aliki Roussin**, the Greek award-winning photographer, painter, poet and journalist to maximize her love of life. She continually reflected on her understanding of living and how best to link her own grasp of life both to her work and her relation to a world of habit and tradition. *'My philosophy is close to what Socrates said: "A life that does not question itself is not worth living". Yet, there might be another way too. To appreciate and accept what there is. Simply to marvel at the mystery of what we call life. Being Greek I choose to believe in many gods, but what I believe mostly is that life is a wonderful gift. Of course there are negative and destructive situations in life as there are positive and constructive. One has to cherish and learn from both.'* In order to capture this sense of animated and ever-expanding appreciation of life, Aliki combined elements of photography and stucco paint-

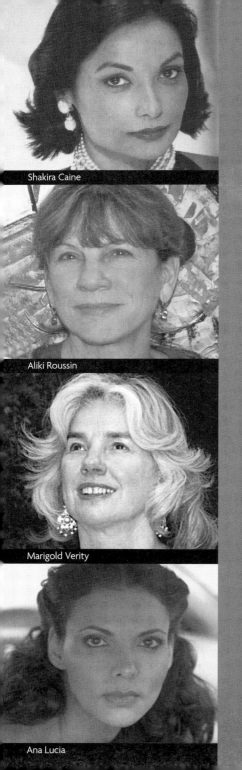

Shakira Caine

Aliki Roussin

Marigold Verity

Ana Lucia

'My philosophy is close to what Socrates said: "A life that does not question itself is not worth living". Yet, there might be another way too. To appreciate and accept what there is. Simply to marvel at the mystery of what we call life. Being Greek I choose to believe in many gods, but what I believe mostly is that life is a wonderful gift.'

Aliki Roussin

ing, bringing her own personal history to the canvas: *'Stucco contains elements of my country's geology and history, dehydrated limestone and marble dust glued together'*. Her art is designed to encourage contact as well as visual stimulation. *'The paintings can be touched and felt, establishing a tactile communication; they can be re-waxed and polished, exactly as an old piece of furniture, sealing the memory of the hand that fingered it.'* In this way her works literally embrace life. The canvas becomes a contact zone between the artist and her public, translating Aliki's love for others. *'I would describe myself as a person of action who has both loved and has been loved by people. Whatever I have done is just a demonstration of that. Nothing more and you call it art. Art after all is a way of life if not life itself and life is about love. If it sounds too abstract, then call it the instinct of life.'*

Although her sense of peace with herself and easy relation to life may seem enviable, it has not been effortless. Aliki, whose beguiling vitality was evident, told me that, apart from being born a girl, when she saw the light of day she was a cross between an ugly duckling and a monkey. Her grandfather who loved her dearly, when he looked at her for the first time gasped, *'A girl, ugly and cross eyed ... there is no hope'*. She felt that *'the Greeks were to blame for this obsession with youth and beauty'*. It was not until she suffered from an eye condition that almost led to partial blindness that she came to her own rejection of this superficial creed, which is all too easy for women to internalize. *'When I had my eye operation I remember coming home, looking through the new eye and being shocked by the brightness of it all. Finally I found the courage and after a whole day went to meet myself in the mirror. I did not know what I looked like since, before, I could not distinguish any details. It was a weird reaction because it was the first time I could see wrinkles. I remember I smiled and said out loud: "I do like this person". From that time onwards I was at peace with myself.'* When Aliki told me this story I was able to say without any hesitation that I liked her too.

Beyond the beauty myth

Regardless of their physical features, women who have verve and vitality are beautiful to me. It is difficult to describe how vitality looks but, at the same time, everyone recognizes vitality when they see it. It's a spring in the step, a sparkle in the smile, an extra burst of enthusiasm. To people who possess it, scents are more powerful, sights more vivid, and the senses more finely tuned. All these features correlate with a life that is full of love and overflowing. It truly takes your breath away.

Women have made real gains over the last thirty years in terms of control over their reproductive rights, access to education and to careers, but women's relationships to their bodies still present a major obstacle to self-acceptance. Judging by the increased turnover of the beauty and slimming industries, the sharp upturn in so-called 'ordinary' women opting for plastic surgery, it seems that the female body remains a subject still fraught with anxieties and loaded with unrealizable ideals. In a world where media attention is given to celebrities and pop stars more often than to those who serve, it is easy to see why an emphasis on physical beauty may have been mistaken as a pathway to success. If there is one area where more self-love is needed, it is real women's bodies.

Nearly all the women I met placed little significance on physical beauty. When asked to send a photograph so that their portraits could be painted, I was heartened by their lack of vanity. They had a confident sense of being which was more than their appearance – it was a deep-rooted understanding of inner beauty.

French author Stendhal stated that beauty is the promise of happiness. Surely that was true, yet even those women whose physical presence was central to their careers, did not relate happiness to beauty. When asked what beauty was, the **Rajmata of Jaipur**, celebrated as one of the worlds' most beautiful women, answered *'I have never thought about it'*.

Shakira Caine thought beauty did not always bring happiness but could be a trap to attract negative aspects and people. She defined great women who had a beautiful presence as those who danced lightly through life and were able to move gracefully with the music, yet capable of leaping into action at the right moment and for the right reasons. Beauty was bound up with living intuitively. Unwittingly, Shakira had described her own loveliness.

Harpist **Marigold Verity**, herself a naturally good looking woman, felt *'beauty came from inspiration and was linked to the spirit. It was magical'*. Model **Ana Lucia** recalled the simplicity of her life in a small town in Brazil and how her great grandmother, a native Brazilian, had a charismatic beauty that was bewitching. She was small, didn't speak much, but her power and loveliness was palpable. Ana Lucia felt *'that so much modern hype about beauty is surrounded with ornaments that are supposed to make you feel better and prettier. It is a marketing ploy. Real beauty is not sophistication, it is simplicity'*.

Venu Dhupa and **Dana Gillespie** both commented that to be a compelling and attractive person, *'one has to be comfortable in one's own skin'*. Professor **Zenobia Nadirshaw** added, *'An early concept of being at home with my body allowed me to develop the understanding and respect for myself and others'*.

For actress and sixties icon **Sarah Miles** beauty was a mystery. *'Things that are hidden are beautiful. Glamour, beauty, charisma, these things have nothing to do with labels. If you're looking at labels on shoes and neatly cut hair, you're just looking at the outward show, but I don't look there. I look into the face. Recently I saw a nun and she was quite stunning to me. She was as glamorous as you can get. She had stillness, purity, a shimmer coming from within and that's beauty.'* Mauritian Member of Parliament **Nita Deerpalsing** agreed. *'When you are at peace with yourself, you are beautiful.'*

Pheroza Godrej believed that *'a woman should sparkle with her intellect and not her jewels'*. Fellow Mumbaikar and Director of Fantasie chocolate **Zeba Kohli** added that *'It is easy to find a woman who walks into a room and is exquisite looking. That is not difficult once you have been*

Nita Deerpalsing

Rajmata of Jaipur

'When you are at peace with yourself, you are beautiful.'

Nita Deerpalsing

'A beautiful woman lights up the room when she walks in. Beauty can encompass charm and sexual attraction. Charm is for everyone. Sexiness is for a potential partner.'

Lindsay Rosenhead

Madhuri Dixit

Lindsay Rosenhead

Pheroza Godrej

Barkha Dutt

under the cosmetic surgeon's knife. I mean it is the most common thing today. A beautiful woman to me is charismatic in her actions and her presence'. **Shahnaz Husain**, who founded the Shahnaz Husain Ayurvedic Herbal Cosmetics empire, is today a household name in India. She traces her ancestry back to the Moguls who came from Samarkand and from an early age she was conscious of her rich heritage which understood the value of Ayurveda and herbal treatments. For Shahnaz, 'Beauty is a complex mix of beauty power, brain power and spiritual power'.

Fashion executive and educator **Lindsay Rosenhead**, who had worked for twelve years for *Vogue* and whose life had been involved with fashion, its creating and selling, said 'a beautiful woman lights up the room when she walks in. Beauty can encompass charm and sexual attraction. Charm is for everyone. Sexiness is for a potential partner'. Lindsay then went on to explain that captivating women made you want to be with them. They were wonderful and they, in turn, made you feel wonderful too. That was the secret. To make others feel good about themselves.

Beauty to be marvelled at

Someone who makes the world feel good is the Bollywood heroine **Madhuri Dixit**, recently voted as the best Bollywood actress ever. There is no questioning her off-screen presence. Madhuri lights up the room when she walks in. She is a true Eastern beauty, soft, sensual, with a regal elegance. She is not a made-up product of Western commercialism – tall, painfully thin and a carbon copy with no distinctive attributes. Like every beautiful woman I met Madhuri does not think she is stunning but she did admit that it was an advantage to be attractive as it pleased others to be with you. Her exquisiteness is so fabled that the Picasso of India, MF Hussain, whom I consulted on women's beauty, explained how he had painted a series of portraits of Madhuri and that her loveliness was unsurpassed. Beauty was not to be explained, it was to be marvelled at. Hussain had also painted a series on Mother Teresa but it was Madhuri who had bewitched the heart of the artist. He spoke with reverence when he told me about the beauty of Bollywood's most adored idol and the spiritual strength of Mother Teresa. Interestingly, both modern icons shared other things in common. Their hero was God and they both had a beguiling wish to help others in their own unique and beautiful way.

All the women saw compassion for causes bigger than themselves as being far more significant than their looks and they had found that happiness came from pursuing their passions with love. War correspondent **Barkha Dutt** commented that *'often classically beautiful people are very busy being beautiful. They are not able to let go. What compels me and holds my attention is the kind of beauty that embraces life'*.

Beauty talk

As a professional make-up artist, **Patricia Daver** may be seen to confirm the current obsession with limited ideals of physical beauty. In fact it was a frustration with this attitude that prompted Patricia to change direction and train in camouflage make-up for people with disfigurements. *'What has happened with facial beauty is that people now aspire to what they see in magazines. I kept saying to myself, there is more to this than just trying to make someone look like some movie star.'* Patricia works with people suffering from burns, scars, skin discolouration and birth marks, not because it makes them more beautiful in conventional terms but because it empowers them by *'taking them from a world that won't accept them into a world that will'*. She herself was also keen to stress that to her physical beauty has never been a fixation and not being as beautiful as her girlfriends was never a problem for her. *'I always knew that if we met some guy, even though my friends might attract him first, I could keep him. And you know why? I could talk to him. I had a brain and knew how to use it and without that men get bored.'*

Body talk

Ramma Bans, India's keep-fit guru, was the diet and fitness consultant to India's former Prime Minister Indira Gandhi, and worked with Rekha, the legendary Bollywood actress, as well as training Miss World contestants. She is renowned for establishing fitness clinics in India's luxury hotel chains, and has an uncompromising view on healthcare for the body. *'Only fat, stupid, rich, lazy women use pills and machines to reduce weight. They make a fool of themselves and the media should stop encouraging them. Women should exercise, shut their mouths and not eat junk food. You have no business to be fat. It looks ugly. Nobody who is overweight can make an entrance. To be fat is sinful and brings disease. God has given us an infrastructure that serves us 24 hours a day and we had better serve the infrastructure one hour a day.'*

At first Ramma's attitude may seem shocking in its forthrightness, but her conviction that women can take back control of their bodies in a way that will bring them happiness, as well as health, is inspiring, if rather bracing. She is not interested in creating clones of an ideal body shape, but rather bases her approach on identifying each person's 'body print' by listening to their body's needs and adjusting their lifestyle accordingly. *'We cannot set universal norms; as such conformity is not nature's plan.'* Her advice to women is to set aside their ideal image and work with reality: *'Let go of yourself; too much control and self-criticism aggravates 'imbalance'.*

The secret of dieting

Like so many woman I know, **Carole Stone** had dieted all her life. As she said, *'I have put on and lost stones. If a girlfriend says "I've just lost 6lb" you can't help but think "damn". But if she said "I ate two bars of chocolate and I put on 3lb this week", you feel better. It's ridiculous because my hips are the same whether my friends have eaten or not, but you feel better if somebody else is as weak as you. Anyway I think that when I'm big my girlfriends like me more'.*

Patricia Daver

Sathya Saran

'Only fat, stupid, rich, lazy women use pills and machines to reduce weight … Women should exercise, shut their mouths and not eat junk food. You have no business to be fat. It looks ugly. To be fat is sinful and brings disease. God has given us an infrastructure that serves us 24 hours a day and we had better serve the infrastructure one hour a day.'

Ramma Bans

Ramma Bans

Nafis Sadik

Yue-Sai Kan

Margaret Sheehy

Me

The first thing that strikes you about **Sathya Saran** is her youthful, understated elegance. Her long pigtail that touches the floor, her wide smile and quirky sense of humour touch you immediately. It doesn't matter who you are, even a womaniser can talk to Sathya without reserve, share her innermost concerns and be sure of empathy and pragmatic advice. Sathya is the editor of India's first weekly magazine for women, *ME*, and formerly editor of *Femina*, India's leading women's magazine that pioneered Indian women's access to discussions and information on the issue of beauty. '*The magazine evolved to meet this need, and we grew the two pages on beauty into ten, and then twelve. It was our duty to inform and educate, so the woman could marry style to beauty and emerge the complete woman. Of course the value system, the relationship see-saws were all part of the sub text, but the main message emphasized the fact that we knew the Indian woman wanted to love herself too, and we were there to help her do so! I encouraged young women to look their best, to walk with pride and emphasized that pretty women need not be bimbettes and that intelligent women need not look like housemaids.*'

Sathya is also well-known for her involvement with the *Femina* Miss India Pageant and Contest. Although beauty contests are now commonly regarded as a rather uncomfortable way of assessing women's value in the West, the enormous popularity of the event showed how some women in India regarded it as liberating. Rather than seeing the pageant as a parade that objectifies women, Sathya was aware that the contest offered Indian women a platform to demonstrate their talents and strong sense of self-esteem.

Her understanding of beauty has always been holistic. During her time as editor of *Femina*, Sathya responded to the increasingly complex fabric of the Indian women's lives by including reports on environment, business, enterprise, money management and relationship management. She felt a responsibility both to reflect the changing social expectations of Indian women and perhaps to help shape these expectations as well. '*Women have to know that they are not secondary citizens; that things are not forbidden; that they should reach out and work together. They don't need the approval of men in what they do. I have changed lives and I have reached out and used the magazine as an agent of change. And where I have not succeeded, I have not changed enough.'*

China doll

Living legend **Yue-Sai Kan** is one of the most famous women in China and her face has even graced postage stamps. Her books are bestsellers, her television programme *Yue-Sai's World* reaches over 800 million people every week. *Time* magazine has called her the 'Queen of the Middle Kingdom'. Her passion has been to help the Chinese regain their self-confidence as a people and she believes that one of the biggest contributions she can make is to change how they think about their appearance. She brilliantly marketed the Yue-Sai Chinese doll, and set a beauty standard that *Forbes* magazine claimed had literally 'changed the face of China!' Stunning and poised, Yue-Sai felt that the drabness had to go; Chinese women should look good, feel good about themselves. Yue-Sai has brought make-up to China, where it is now a multi-billion-pound industry, and her beauty brand has been bought out by the French cosmetic giant L'Oreal for millions. They, like me agreed that she was worth it!

The real thing

Even though the women were not concerned to dazzle others with their beauty, they were well aware that most people made assessments of others quickly, often in a blink of the eye. They were concerned to present themselves well and those in the public eye knew that they were under constant scrutiny. They knew that their abilities would be read from the way that they looked, that the whole package counted. Their good taste, individual style, and refinement, were appreciated. They were not Barbie doll imitators, but the real thing. Philippine educationalist and President of Miriam College, **Patricia Licuanan**, summed it up, *'great women have a certain class and style about them'.*

UN Director **Nafis Sadik** mused *'Many people complimented me on my beautiful saris. Some women used to wonder why I was interested in clothes and jewellery. You don't have to look like the back of a bus if you are professional. Appearance is part of how you judge people. If you are untidy and unkempt maybe that is how your mind is. Pride in your appearance makes you have pride in what you are and what you do'.*

In disguise

Connie Jackson remembered, *'When I first started working, wearing heavily starched suits and these bow ties that looked like men's ties, and stiff suits, was the norm. Everything was to disguise the fact you were a woman. I remember one day my mother gave me this beautiful dress and I wore the dress to work instead of a suit. I didn't have any client meetings and the reaction was "Wow, where are you going?" My boss said that it looked very attractive but asked "Do you think it is appropriate for work?" Twenty years later women do not need to be in disguise. I see women going to work in all kinds of clothes'.*

Cultural animateur **Margaret Sheehy**, who grew up in Australia, turned the tables on the idea of women's power-dressing with a perceptive comment on male dress codes. *'Interestingly, it is men who use dress for status, they're the ones who use fancy uniforms, bits of braid in their caps, give themselves medals; they are much vainer, they get their portraits painted and put up in public places. Women dress to feel good, men dress to make others think they are good.'*

Τά Εργαζόμενα Κορίτσια Τα
Flickor i arbete
دختر های شاغل
Tytöt töissä

Τά Εργαζόμενα Κορίτσια Τά
Flickor i arbete
دختر های شاغل
Tytöt töissä

Τά Εργαζόμενα Κορίτσια Τά
Flickor i arbete
دختر های شاغل
Tytöt töissä

Τά Εργαζόμενα Κορίτσια Τά
Flickor i arbete
دختر های شاغل
Tytöt töissä

Τά Εργαζόμενα Κορίτσια Τά
Flickor i arbete

Working girls

Working late

They had the most unoriginal alibi in the world. *'I'm working late tonight darling'*. It was an airtight excuse because everyone knew that work was their magnificent obsession. Individually they were highly-motivated, super-charged and determined to succeed. Collectively, they have been a powerful force within the male-dominated world of work.

The opening up of the workplace provoked one of the most profound changes in women's lives and identities in the twentieth century. Although women had worked for centuries and many unacknowledged lives had been given to service and servitude in different contexts across the globe, this kind of work had rarely been empowering. It did not give women more life choices, a sense of having achieved their potential, or the chance to make their mark in history. Often, it did not even give them economic security or the resources to support their families. For very many women work remains unrewarding and exploitative today. However, as more women have benefited from educational opportunities and other measures of social equality, albeit unequally across the world, women's career aspirations and achievements have shifted significantly.

The women I spent time with helped to record the history of a changing workplace. Many of them are trail blazers, the significant firsts in their fields who have exploded the myth that certain jobs are naturally destined for men. Many also acknowledged that they were daughters of history. They realized that the opportunities they seized and the difference they made to their professions and disciplines was only possible because they arrived at a particular flashpoint in history when the seals were peeling off the locks, what several refer to as a 'golden moment'. Despite having won prestige and recognition, they also spoke about how the workplace can still feel like a man's world and how women usually carry the particular strain of trying to achieve a balance between work and family life.

There was also a sense that women's attitudes to work may be changing. The generation of over-achievers who carried the hopes of so many women before them into the bastions of male power had not found career success to be all it promised. Some of these women have shifted from the power professions of politics and law to the empowering sectors of charity and community work. It was not so much the cost of personal success that provoked this shift as much as their desire to make a difference to others' lives in a way that would also fulfil their own.

Blood, sweat and tears

Women still face serious barriers in seeking equal opportunity, participation and pay in the workplace, and not one of the women questioned said that career success had been easy, although almost all felt that it had been worth while.

It cannot be overstated how phenomenally hard most of the women worked. They were 'action women' but not in the macho sense of action men. Their action was purposeful and often directed from the heart, as well as the head. There is no question that their success in the workplace was the product of hard work, endurance and the ability to catch their moments of opportunity, but the hard work could not be avoided. For some, this ethic of complete dedication was almost a way of life.

Dr **Angela Lennox**, pioneer of multi-agency health and community centres, admitted *'I have given up my life to do this, I am driven to do it, and I don't have a life'*. Internationally acclaimed designer **Zandra Rhodes** also confessed *'I am a workaholic and would self-destruct if I was not working'*. Managing Director of BSkyB TV, **Dawn Airey**, was similarly passionate about her work, *'I seldom take a no. I don't take defeat. I have worked very hard but I've had some fantastic lucky breaks'*.

One of the world's most successful working girls, **Lila Poonawalla**, the first woman in Asia to act as Chair of a multi-national, admitted, *'Hard work, hard work and more hard work, even when you are sad work,*

Dawn Airey

'I seldom take a no. I don't take defeat. I have worked very hard but I've had some fantastic lucky breaks.'

Dawn Airey

Lila Poonawalla

'Hard work, hard work and more hard work, even when you are sad work, when you are happy work, there are no shortcuts in life.'

Lila Poonawalla

Connie Jackson

'After you live a little of life you know how little of life you have any control over.'

Connie Jackson

Sallie Gratch

'… learning any new task, with the support of a group, helps bring about change.'

Sallie Gratch

when you are happy work, there are no shortcuts in life'. Although one or two women had a slightly different take: 'hard work, hard work and then more hard work in bed!'

For **Connie Jackson** work had become a treadmill that she had tied herself to, through her own expectations. *'I had been on a course from the age of fifteen of going to business school; going to Harvard; going to Wall Street. I was going to be the first black woman to be Secretary of the Treasury; I mean I had this whole thing planned. Then I would have four children who would go on to do great things. I would die at ninety. It was just so ridiculous. After you live a little of life you know how little of life you have any control over. I got there and I met all these interesting people who had done all these really interesting things and they had wound up in the same place as me and I was really depressed because it was like "God, I could have looked at a lot of other things and I could have still wound up here". I was very much "no, no I can't get off track".'*

Sallie Gratch managed to combine her own love of running with her therapeutic work. Her personal experience of the benefit of building up a literal sweat enabled her to bring life and work together in a positive way. *'I created a program called "Run for Your Self", a running-therapy program that combined a group run, followed by an hour of group psychotherapy. The objective was to create a short term intervention (8 week session) for people with mild depression and anxiety. Being a runner myself, I fully understood the psychological and physical benefits of running. I also believed in the effectiveness of the group model in bringing about personal change. I understood that learning any new task, with the support of a group, helps bring about change. Running became a metaphor for change.'*

Lindsay Rosenhead

Ramma Bans

Eve Pollard

Kirsten Rausing

'I had to deal with a room full of noisy men, who were all determined that if you produced a good idea, they would ignore it. Later some man would come out with it and it would be his brainwave.'

Lindsay Rosenhead

'Take a typical meeting, men come in and they fluff themselves up and they say "When I was a director of this", and they care where they sit at the table. Women arrive and they just want to get on with it. Women want to change things.'

Eve Pollard

Job satisfaction

The emphasis on sheer hard work certainly does not mean that these women did not enjoy their jobs or thrive in the workplace. In fact, it was this real devotion to a profession or a job that made hard work both possible and pleasurable.

As fitness guru **Ramma Bans** confessed, '*Work has become a big worship for me*'. Feeling that you have given of your best is deeply satisfying as **Maggie Bellis** stated, '*I am proud that every job I have done, I've done to the best of my ability*'. Taking on a job and knowing that you have done it well is a big factor in women's self-esteem, as well as having clear benefits for employers. Baroness **Usha Prashar** took well-deserved pride in the fact that '*Whatever job I have undertaken, and often they have been difficult, I have done them well, made a difference and achieved objectives that I have set for myself*'. It has long been a saying of the workplace that if you want a job done quickly give it to the busiest person, but one could also add that if you want a job done well, give it to a woman!

Many women spoke eloquently and at length about how women's attitude to work was significantly different, and how they were usually more conscientious than their male colleagues. At the same time they did not brag about their own achievements or moan about being exploited.

Kirsten Rausing, Worldwide Director of Tetrapak, gave a note of encouragement to all women when she told me '*If you are efficient at meetings they'll make you the chairman!*' **Eve Pollard** not only bore witness to this difference, she also understood it. '*Take a typical meeting, men come in and they fluff themselves up and they say "When I was a director of this", and they care where they sit at the table. Women arrive and they just want to get on with it. Women want to change things.*'

The most effective strategies that fashion executive **Lindsay Rosenhead** found in her years in the workplace was that of persistence plus real conviction. That was the double whammy. *'You can't promote change if you don't believe in it.'* Lindsay admitted that she was often asked *'Did you ever feel it was a disadvantage being a women, and a pioneer? and I always said "Never". Of course I had to deal with a room full of noisy men, who were all determined that if you produced a good idea, they would ignore it. Later some man would come out with it and it would be his brainwave. The way to deal with them is to lower your voice, speak slowly and rather quietly and adopt a physical posture of intensity and domination. No yelling, for God's sake; it never got anyone anywhere, except with a bull. After that you've got to have the muscle behind it and see it through if you are to be taken seriously. Throughout my fifty years of working life I have been the expert, the specialist in my field and I have known no other way than to work and to be responsible for my family, myself and my community'.*

This sense of a responsibility to make a difference unites all the women in this book. Collectively, twentieth-century women carry the burden of history inasmuch as they are often the first in their families to enter university, the professions, or to gain well-paid work fitting to their abilities and ambitions. Their expectations, like their energy cells, are often switched to power-surge and they have a strong sense of wanting to make an impact, of settling a score with history. Living up to the hopes of their mothers and grandmothers and creating a new environment for a new generation, their achievements are never purely personal.

Jobs for the girls

In the Western world, the majority of women entering the workplace during the 1950s and 1960s were encouraged to become secretaries or to join the caring professions, mainly nursing and teaching. If they were pretty, they may have been directed towards being an air hostess and modelling. A high proportion of exceptional women had begun their working lives in these conventional and somewhat low-profile 'female jobs'. While attitudes to 'women's work' were often rather staid and limited, there was fluidity and flexibility built into workplace structures that enabled those with ideas and ambitions to develop their confidence and trade their skills to get right to the top.

Aesthetician **Patricia Daver** expressed it perfectly. *'It was good years ago, because you could go into a job as Girl Friday and find out what you really wanted to do. Nowadays young people have a harder time. They have to have fifty million degrees for this and that.'* The defining separation of high and low ambition that now operates means that many young women shun the idea of learning to type or taking on caring work for fear of being ranked as 'low-fliers'.

Women welcome women

Frances Alexander, who was born in 1935, may be regarded a model for women of her time as she trained as a nurse, a midwife and a teacher – two of the big three job opportunities for girls of her day. The resilience, inner confidence and empathy that these jobs demanded were undoubtedly useful when she stood for Parliament three times unsuccessfully for the Liberals, but it prepared her for eventually becoming the Chair of the council. Her term as Mayor resulted in trees being planted, gardens being laid and many small projects completed as part of the year for 'Loving High Wycombe,' her home town. These days she spends time in the Environment Centre on Holywell Mead, one of the projects she visualized and helped build to encourage good environmental understanding and involvement – a local way to save the planet and reduce mindless pollution. The optimism essential to nursing, teaching and politics, perhaps showed most inventively when she started the organization 'Women Welcome Women' from her spare bedroom. Today it has almost 3000 members in around seventy-five countries. Women from all over the world become friends and stay in each others' homes and experience life in another country. One member, a Russian doctor, who could never

Karen Cox

Patricia Daver

Claire Bertschinger

Frances Alexander

'It was good years ago, because you could go into a job as Girl Friday and find out what you really wanted to do. Nowadays young people have a harder time. They have to have fifty million degrees for this and that.'

Patricia Daver

'My mother brought me into the world but you Frances, have opened up the whole wide world for me.'

A Romanian woman

afford to leave her country, was able to visit Germany and stay with another WWW member whose father was also a doctor. On her return home to Russia she was greeted with a huge box of medical supplies for her hospital; a bond that had been forged through real friendship. Frances' whole being lit up when she remembered another member, a Romanian who blurted out: *'My mother brought me into the world but you Frances, have opened up the whole wide world for me'*. Frances is one of the world's quiet leaders and doers. A woman of vision who has not only helped create a 'future village' in reality with the Eco-environmental Centre in High Wycombe but, in a larger sense, has created another 'village' of like-minded women from around the world. She is like the person who throws little stones into the sea causing ripples. Her actions have spread far and wide, touching every corner of the world.

Healing lives

For both **Karen Cox** and **Claire Bertschinger** nursing has itself proved a profession to grow within. Karen was drawn to nursing but took a traditional route with a modern twist by studying for a nursing degree and staying at university to write her doctorate. She is now Professor in Cancer and Palliative Care and Head of the School of Nursing at the University of Nottingham, which has 350 staff and 4000 students.

Come fly with me

In a different way, **Maggie Bellis**, Director for Transport for London developed the same interpersonal skills as an air hostess for BOAC, which became British Airways in 1974. *'We had to deal with many famous people in first class. You knew instinctively who wanted attention and who didn't want to be recognized. You learnt to understand your colleagues and the different people you worked with. You recognized what actually worked for them and what didn't.'*

Taking notes

The high-heeled, smart and sassy secretary who really aspires to be the boss has become something of a stereotype, but there were certainly many high-powered career women who began their working lives behind the secretary's desk.

For **Sukey Cameron** secretarial work was a positive choice. Sukey was home educated in the Falkland Islands with the support of the Parent National Education System and was then advised by her mother to train at secretarial college in London. Although she did not greatly enjoy being a secretary, she proved herself as highly competent and became Executive Secretary of the Falkland Islands Association from 1979 to 1982, moving to the Falkland Islands Government Office when it was established in 1983. She was appointed as the Falkland Islands Government's London Representative in June 1990. Today Sukey also holds the Chair of the United Kingdom Overseas Territories Association.

Pim Baxter of the National Portrait Gallery also trained in secretarial work, as did **Carole Stone**, who went on to produce BBC's political debating programme *Any Questions*. And PR guru **Lynne Franks** told me how *'secretarial skills always held you in good stead and could lead on to great things'*. This certainly proved true for Lynne who became the model for the brilliant but totally zany Edina in the hit TV series *Absolutely Fabulous*.

Publisher **Judith Kendra** explained her decision to take a secretarial course after graduating from Edinburgh University. *'That was the sort of thing people did with my background. You could always get a secretarial job very quickly and my first job was as a secretary in a publishing house.'* Working as a secretary may have been an acceptable starting position for women from all backgrounds but it was also a foot in the door for those with more serious ambitions. Judith is now Publishing Director of *Rider List*.

Helen Gurley Brown, founder of *Cosmopolitan* magazine, also began as a secretary and worked her way through the ranks. While working for a prominent advertising agency, her employer recognized her writing skills and moved her to the copywriting department where she advanced rapidly to become one of America's highest paid copywriters in the early 1960s. Yet, even when she did not earn a huge salary, her work was always vital to her self-image. '*I didn't have any money and my job made me interesting to other people, so I always found that work brought self esteem.*' This was also a central message in her groundbreaking book, *Sex and the Single Girl*, published in 1962, in which she boldly stated that '*A single woman is known by what she does rather than by whom she belongs to*'.

The golden moment

Lucie Aubrac, French Resistance heroine, was born in 1912 into a family that owned a small vineyard in Macon in France. She reminisced that her generation had fought for many freedoms but the fruits of their battles had passed them by. It was the celebration babies, born straight after the Second World War, who were able to take advantage of the new openings available – a golden moment of opportunity for women in the West.

Lucie's views were confirmed by several other women who also recognized that they had benefited from these historical shifts in the West. Chief Executive of the Prince's Trust, **Martina Milburn**, was quite literally in the right place at the right time to fulfil her ambition of working in Fleet Street. '*The Sex Discrimination Act in Britain had been passed in January 1976 and I left school in July 1976. I planned to go to college to study for a career in journalism. I got a call for an interview from the careers office of the Press Association that took four trainees on. When I went up to Fleet Street they were told to positively discriminate and the story goes that there were seventy young men and two women. The other woman did not want to be a journalist and so I got the job. Instead of going to college, I went straight to Fleet Street at eighteen.*'

Oxfam's Chief Executive **Barbara Stocking** was also fortunate enough to have experienced the 'golden moment' in career terms. '*I went to the US to study after Cambridge and ended up staying there for five years; two years getting a masters degree and then working in Washington DC at the National Academy of Sciences. It was so open in America; young people were allowed to take responsibility. Also the general "can do" attitude in the US really set me off in a very positive way.*'

Lila Poonawalla, Managing Director of Alfa Laval Industries India, also spoke about how she benefited from the 'golden moment' when the novelty of being a woman meant that doors were opened out of curiosity. It also meant that women could be given risky positions as people felt that they had little to lose by appointing them, especially if the men before had made a mess of the job – today called the 'glass cliff'. Lila explained, '*Four Export Managers had left before me and perhaps they felt that I too could go and make a mess of it. When I took over the exports were hardly a million rupees, so the company felt they were not taking a big risk. I really changed that. I started off by breaking through the Sri Lankan market. I went to meet the Agricultural Minister and, because I was a woman, the Minister was interested to see me*'. 'For Lila, being a woman was a distinct advantage, a positive door-opener.

Frances Cairncross, Rector of Exeter College, Oxford, made a perceptive analysis of the advantages for her own generation of working women in Britain. '*I have had the benefit of rarity and my daughters won't have that benefit. They will be judged much more against a whole lot of other women, who are every bit as good, energetic, well educated and ambitious as they are. The older generation of women had huge prejudices to cope with, the younger generation of women has genuine competition to cope with. We are in between, without too much competition and without too much prejudice, the golden generation. The pill came along not very long before I married, so we were the first generation who could judge family size with reliability. We are also a generation that has promised itself enormous pensions, so will be quite well off in old age.*'

The golden girls

While the golden moment may have passed in Britain and the US, it is arguably still open in India. For Indian women there was a real sense of potential. They spoke about how enabling it was for them to enter small companies and work through the company. In the working context they enjoyed the freedom of mobility that Western women had benefited from in the 1960s and 1970s. They knew they were more free to take on a whole range of jobs and create their own niche. Again possibility and passion combined to make extraordinary careers possible.

Editor of *Indian Express*, and former President of the Indian Women's Press Association, **Coomi Kapoor** felt her first job in journalism was very useful to her future career. She started in a newspaper where she had responsibility for many areas of work and was able to gain confidence in every area of newspaper life. NDTV anchorwoman and TV personality **Barkha Dutt** was able to create her own job profile, researching, presenting and making news, when she joined the newly formed NDTV channel in Delhi. She recognized that being a woman war reporter gave her a certain cachet as well as a new perspective. '*I did wonder whether I became the story instead of covering the story. When I report I'm reporting people, other journalists report guns. I did stories of young soldiers in their twenties, discussing their dilemma of going into war, while colleagues were sending stories about technologies and the guns.*'

India is also a positive working environment for women for other reasons, as **Naina Lal Kidwai**, the Head of HSBC India, explained. '*There is no doubt that it is easier to be a young career woman in India. You have the support of an extended family and domestic help is more affordable. India is having its golden moment.*' Naina drew on her own experience to make the point even clearer. '*From the 1988 graduates of Harvard Management School, only three out of eighteen women who qualified now have a career.*'

Christina Lamb   Kiran Bedi

'We allowed "the art of living" courses to be used in the prison. I believed I was a custodian of the prisoners' time, not a custodian of human beings. A miracle happened and so many of the prisoners' characters changed. They started to learn to respect themselves.'

Kiran Bedi

Uta Frith   Angela King

Sharon Choa   Vivienne Faull

A man's world?

It is not just women living through a golden moment who have made a real contribution to the workplace. Many of the women had succeeded, sometimes against the odds, in what is conventionally considered to be a man's world. Interestingly, nearly all of them felt that being a woman had been an advantage in one way or another.

Christina Lamb is internationally known as one of the most daring and astute war correspondents. At just 21 she was sneaking in and out of Afghanistan with the mujaheddin who were fighting against the Soviet occupiers. She has travelled into the remotest parts of the Amazon in search of uncontacted tribes known as the Headbashers. After the fall of the Taliban, she was the first journalist to find and interview some of the Taliban ministers in Pakistan. During the war in Iraq, she sneaked into Basra while it was still under Saddam. She has been in and out of Mugabe's Zimbabwe some thirteen times despite the ban on British journalists and risk of imprisonment. Recently she was caught in a Taliban ambush with British troops in Helmand from which they were lucky to get out alive.

Her reporting has won her a series of awards, most recently being named Foreign Correspondent of the Year in the British Press Awards and BBC What the Papers Say Awards in both 2002 and 2006. Even though being a war correspondent is traditionally seen as a man's job, she is renowned for her cutting-edge reporting. Having been shot at, deprived of food and light for days, and witness to dead and mutilated bodies, adjusting to a normal life was difficult. However, Christina did admit that going from war to war was very addictive, just living on the edge. She was also clear though that there were specific advantages of being a woman war correspondent. '*It's easier to disguise yourself, especially in a Muslim country where you can cover your head and face. We're better listeners than men and also, because men don't take you so seriously and are not threatened by you, they tell you things they wouldn't tell a man. This is especially true of politicians who are so full of themselves.*' Christina has experienced the ignorance of sexism but is also aware that she can carry a different story not accessible to men. '*I remember being* in the American club for journalists and being looked over as a twenty-one-year-old and being asked, "How many conflicts have you covered?" Women are not so blasé. We get under a story, we care more about the people we cover. We understand what it's like to be a woman in those horrific situations.'

UN Civilian Police Adviser **Kiran Bedi's** approach to the tough job of running the prison service in India was both unconventional and genuinely transformative. 'I knew I had over ten thousand people in the prison; 9,500 were men, and they were in my safe keeping, not just as bodies but as people. How was I going to do justice, not just to them, but to the millions of hours that they would spend in prison? I wanted to see a total change in their behaviour. I wanted them to enter prison and then exit as different people. What I did was I cashed in all my good will in twenty-two years of the police service. I asked so many people to come and help and give their time and expertise. Retired teachers were given permission to teach in the prisons, I got yoga specialists to come in and teach yoga and meditation. We started vocational training. We allowed "the art of living" courses to be used in the prison. I believed I was a custodian of the prisoners' time, not a custodian of human beings. A miracle happened and so many of the prisoner's characters changed. They started to learn to respect themselves.' Although Kiran was working in a field that is often defined by crime and punishment, she was able to look beyond the system as it operated and envision a more holistic approach to reform. She saw her own position of leadership as a chance to empower other people and to think and work in original ways. For her job, Kiran has travelled to many challenging environments such as East Timor, Sierra Leone and Kosovo. In contexts of embedded violence and hostility, she *'spoke the language of peace, sharing, contributing and mutual learning'*.

The Reverend Canon **Vivienne Faull** has been one of the pioneers for women in the Church of England. After a degree in Modern History at Oxford, and teaching in India, Vivienne returned to England and campaigned with a group of women to question why women couldn't train alongside men. This caused a great debate in the Church of England.

Eventually she became the first woman to be sponsored by the Church and did train alongside men. She has been at the forefront of the changes in the role of women in the church. Today she is one of only two women deans and is a member of the Church of England's General Synod. Vivienne is a living example of her words, *'We know from experience that women have far more to offer than they have been able to offer'*.

The ability to overcome others' doubts strengthened Former Deputy Secretary-General to the UN, **Angela King**. She was sent by the Secretary-General of the UN to act as Chief of Mission in South Africa where she played a central role in 'Living History', witnessing and being a crucial part of the birth of a new South Africa after years of apartheid. For nearly two years her task was to try to bring all the parties in South Africa back to the table for talks. Angela was under particular pressure as she knew that her presence was unwelcome. *'We started with a staff of about thirty and nobody in South Africa wanted us. The whites didn't want us and said they could do it themselves. The blacks didn't want us because they said why are you sending us a woman and from Jamaica.'* The job was fiercely demanding but Angela saw it through and although she acknowledged that it may have been her most dangerous job, she was also keen to point out that it was *'what made me happiest'*.

Professor **Uta Frith** studied experimental psychology and subsequently trained in clinical psychology at the University of London's Institute of Psychiatry. As Professor in Cognitive Development at the University of London and Deputy Director of the UCL Institute of Cognitive Neuroscience, she has worked in a man's world of science. Her particular genius enabled her to understand childhood disorders such as autism and dyslexia by applying the methods of cognitive neuroscience. She demonstrated that autism is associated with 'mind blindness' and, using brain imaging, identified those systems critical for successful social interactions. She is one of only a handful of UK academics to have been elected both a fellow of the British Academy and the Royal Society for her groundbreaking work.

Managing Director of BSkyB TV, **Dawn Airey** has a huge sense of responsibility as well as a strong sense of having been fortunate to land a top job in what is often regarded as a man's world. She enjoys her work and feels that, as a woman, she has particular qualities to bring.

Sharon Choa, Artistic Director of Chamber Orchestra Anglia, which she founded in 2001, has worked in the very male world of conducting. She has been challenged by this and lives by Pablo Casal's assertion, *'I was determined not to be hampered by any of the restrictions of the past – to learn from the past but not be shackled by it'*. It was easy to see how Sharon had adopted this approach in her own work which seeks to challenge established histories whether they relate to the male world of work, the discreetness of cultural forms or the entrenched conflict in the Middle East. Born in Hong Kong of mixed ancestry, Sharon has developed her own understanding of the value and strength of cross-cultural ties through her work. The meeting point between communities and the crossing of boundaries through music inspired her 'East meets West' project which offers an exploration of the influence of Chinese culture on Western music. She was also involved in the Israeli-Palestinian orchestra established by Daniel Barenboim and the late Edward Said, which sought to promote music as an arena for humanistic exchange in the face of bitter historical conflicts. Sharon's pioneering work has managed to build on music as a cultural form that cements harmony through difference.

Singer not the song

Margaret Lobo, Director and founder of the Otakar Kraus Music Trust, was born in Vancouver, British Columbia. After a promising career as an opera singer came to an abrupt end – when a case of bulbar poliomyelitis temporarily paralyzed one of her vocal cords – she pursued a successful business career with Esso for 20 years. She then trained as a mature student, qualifying as a music therapist at the London Guildhall School of Music and Drama. The Otakar Kraus Music Trust, a music therapy charity with fifteen outreach centres now provides more than 2,000 individual music therapy sessions annually. For the past seventeen years Margaret has devoted her life to providing music therapy for people of all ages who have physical, psychological, behavioural or learning difficulties. *'I came from a large family of seven children and grew up in poverty, inflicted mainly by Father's alcoholism and frequent unemployment. From the age of nine, I was sent to work, looking after neighbourhood children, with the money earned helping to feed my family. Being the second oldest girl, I recognized from a very early age that my duty was to care for, and protect, my five younger brothers. When in Junior School a teacher (I still remember her name and the day very clearly) heard me singing with the other children. She told my mother that I had a special voice and it should be trained. Money for music lessons was impossible and being sympathetic to the family situation, she began to train me privately after school. When I went to Secondary School I auditioned for the operetta group and began my first step towards performing in public. I was the first person in our family to graduate from school and was fortunate to go straight into a job in the accounts department of Sears, a large American retail store. I became the family breadwinner and was also able to pay for singing lessons. I began studying with a teacher who, knowing of the family situation, charged me very little and saved my life. For this I have always remained truly grateful.'*

Sexist still?

Individual women's achievements in areas that are traditionally known to be a 'man's world' are to be admired and emulated. But pervasive sexism still operates in most societies. Chief Executive of Project Parity **Lesley Abdela** experienced the power of sexism in a very direct way when she was an accounts executive in a large advertising agency. *'I was invited by my immediate boss to accompany him on a trip to Germany, to work on an account that we were doing together. He tried to get me to bed and I refused. Very shortly after that the department had to lay off staff. I guess that's how I got laid off. He didn't lay me – he laid me off.'*

Lesley Abdela

Kazue Hatano

'I was extremely young, in my twenties, when I advised the Russian government on their privatization programme. Every time I went into my hotel I had to show my passport because they thought I might be a hooker. Sadly that was one of the few opportunities for young blondes at that time.'

Noreena Hertz

Noreena Hertz

Rosa Maria Juárez

Shami Chakrabarti

Nafis Sadik

Noreena Hertz, an expert on economic globalization and CIBAM Distinguished Fellow at Cambridge University, remembers experiencing sexual discrimination. '*I was extremely young, in my twenties, when I advised the Russian government on their privatization programme. Every time I went into my hotel I had to show my passport because they thought I might be a hooker. Sadly that was one of the few opportunities for young blondes at that time.*'

Japan's foremost stage designer **Kazue Hatano** spoke about the residual sexism in Japanese society as a ceiling that may appear transparent like glass and yet it is really opaque concrete.

Nafis Sadik, Director of the United Nations Population Fund, and with the rank of Under Secretary-General of the United Nations, was full of stories of how badly women were treated in the workplace. I marvelled at her coolness and determination to take the system on, not just for herself, but for other women. She narrated her story about a dogged fight for gender equality. '*I was encouraged to apply for a job at the United Nations and was offered a P4 post, and I asked whether a P4 was higher than P5, thinking it would be better than a colleague of mine. The man said "No, P5 is higher". I said "Why are you offering me a P4 then, when my colleague is a P5?" He was just about to say "You're a woman" but instead he said "You're so young". I asked what my age had got to do with it. "You are interviewing me for my experience, background and the positions I have held. And I have the same responsibilities as the two other directors with the same job who are P5?", to which he answered, "Well, if you come into the organization as P5, what do you expect to become, head of the organization?" I looked at him and I said, "It's none of your business what I want to become. We're talking about my rights here". I came back and told my husband that I was never going to work for this organization. They kept sending this offer of P4. I said "I don't want your offer, I never applied for it, I just want P5!" After six months they reluctantly offered me a P5 post. I accepted it and went on to become the head of the organization!*'

Rosa Maria Juárez, founder and President of the Mexican Franchise and Networking Institute, found no problems succeeding in the Mexican world of work. *'I never felt any obstacle because of my gender, on the contrary it has given me an outstanding position among men's activities. At twenty-four I was the first marketing manager in a Swedish pharmaceutical firm, responsible for ninety salesmen, older than me.'* Nevertheless, she did relate that the legislature and women's groups in Mexico were infuriated when Vicente Fox, the country's President, described women as *'washing machines with legs'* and went on to joke that *'75% of the homes in Mexico have washing machines, and not the kind with two hands and two legs'*. However, the outcry that followed showed that not even a President can now get away with such demeaning humour and he had to admit that *'Mexican society still has a long way to go in eradicating prejudice and changing habits'*.

Director of the civil rights organization Liberty, **Shami Chakrabarti**, spoke about a different form of prejudice against women that is also directed at eroding their position and confidence. *'Some women are called honorary men. Notwithstanding their success, they are diminished in their workplace and are demonized by stories about what hard women they are, tougher than any man. It may be true that a woman has to be incredibly tough to get to her position but it may also be true that she has actually done it in a perfectly natural and sensible way that is good for the workplace.'*

Indian Minister of State **Renuka Chowdhury** argued that institutions have not changed because they have wanted to embrace women but rather because they have finally acknowledged that women are an important power base today. To her mind, women should use their political capital to insist that they be accepted on their own terms. *'In the 21st century we are going to be seeing women in primary decision-making roles. Governments have to realize that women are now a voting bank. Earlier women didn't have that identity. Today political parties look and say "never mind. Bring the women out of the woodwork if necessary!" because it is politically correct to show them, even if they are just shadows, puppets, extensions of our masters. Women do not have level playing fields, legislative support or social acknowledgements. Politicians* want working women to remain stereotyped because the rest of the world is comfortable with that. I am baffled when I read some magazines that tell women how to power dress for the boardroom. Why should I power dress for a boardroom? I don't see a world where men, who are outnumbered by women, wanting to wear frills to belong to us. I do not want acceptance. I do not want me to be homogenized into a male world. I want acknowledgement that I am different and that my differences matter.'

Trail-blazers

A significant number of the women I met were trail-blazers who had pioneered the entry of women into their fields. **Diane Abbott** was the first black woman to go to the House of Commons, **Lila Poonawalla** the first woman in India to run a multi-national corporation, and **Kiran Bedi** the first United Nations Civilian Police Adviser. Director of Creative Innovation at the South Bank Centre **Venu Dhupa** expressed the thrill and significance of blazing a trail. *'I was the first Asian woman to run a theatre company in Britain and that makes me feel great, because people know now that it can be done and there's no secret club.'*

Air Marshal **Padma Bandhopadya** has a whole string of firsts to her name and to her credit. As a Wing Commander she became the first Indian woman at the North Pole, where she stayed for six months to conclude research on the effects of extreme cold on soldiers. On her return, she was the first woman in uniform awarded the Indira Priyadarshini Award. On 26 June 2000 she made history again by becoming the first woman Air Commodore of the Indian Air Force and took over the command of the prestigious Air Force Central Medical Establishment. Once again she made history when she was awarded the Ait Vishisth Seva Medal and was promoted to become the first woman Air Vice-Marshal of the Indian Air Force and the first woman Director General Medical Services of the forces. She is also the first woman Honorary Surgeon to the President of India!

Pera Wells

Padma Bandhopadya

'I remember being accosted by a handsome First Secretary from the Soviet Union who was appalled to meet me, and declared that his government would never send female diplomats to Africa!'

Pera Wells

Katherine Whitehorn

Ann Jellicoe

Wendy Savage

Anando Heffley

Secretary-General of the World Federation of UN Associations, **Pera Wells**, recalls what a profound experience it was to be the first woman sent to black Africa as an Australian diplomat. She spoke with such complete understanding about her situation and her experiences in the diplomatic service as a woman that I was enthralled by her eloquence. *'My first posting was to Ghana in the mid-1970s and it changed my life. I remember being accosted by a handsome First Secretary from the Soviet Union who was appalled to meet me, and declared that his government would never send female diplomats to Africa! However, I settled in very happily and enjoyed wonderful friendships with Ghanaians. I was aware that I was often the only "white person" in social situations, and gradually became skilled at recognizing differences between African people. It astonished me, shortly after I left Ghana and went to a rock concert in London, that white people all looked the same to me. My spectrum of human beings had completely shifted in Africa.'*

Daring

Of equal significance are the many others who were not necessarily the first in any profession or field, but who have collectively made the phrase 'a man's world' sound like a sad adage from a bygone age. They have been part of the growing global portfolio of women's working lives that testify to both excellence and courage. They dared to open new horizons for themselves and other women.

Katherine Whitehorn was one of the pioneers in persuading national newspapers in Britain to focus on subjects that would interest women readers. She was the forerunner of self-help books, and wrote the bestseller, *Cooking in a Bed-sitter*, which became a cult book for young women, like **Helen Gurley Brown's** more sensationally titled *Sex and the Single Girl* was in America. Katherine also turned her hand to all sorts of writing, including being the fashion editor at *The Observer*, where she wrote about clothes for ordinary people, and more recently Agony Aunt for *Saga* magazine.

Directing

In many different fields women have cleared important paths. Theatre director **Ann Jellicoe** was one of the first women to direct plays at the Royal Court. She had talent but also a lucky break: *'I went in for the Observer Newspaper Playwriting Competition and decided to use my experience of teaching at the Central School of Drama. I was extraordinarily lucky. The Royal Court bought my play and it was the Writers Theatre in those days. I wanted to direct, as I had directed plays at the Central School of Drama. Women rarely directed in those days. I was really fortunate that the director allowed me to direct it with him. When he saw that I could handle actors, he simply stepped aside and let me get on with it'.*

Delivering

For most of the women, being a pioneer was challenging and rewarding too. But some were clearly resented. Surprisingly in a field that throughout history had relied on women helping women to deliver their babies, Professor **Wendy Savage**, the first woman consultant to be appointed in Obstetrics and Gynaecology in London, experienced male prejudice that openly tried to hold her back. After working abroad Wendy returned to England in 1969 and went to see the Senior Consultant to discuss her career options. *'I explained that I had spent seven years out of the country and done this kind of work, and the other work, and I would like his advice on how to proceed. He said, "There's no place in O & G for married women". I think they found it difficult to deal with an independent woman. There I am with four children, no visible husband, and when I did have one he was black.'*

From sex to superconsciousness

Anando Heffley's life could have gone in any direction as she was a child prodigy. Born and raised in Australia, her gifts led her to become a child actress and later a star pupil at Melbourne Law School. She travelled to Britain to join the London School of Contemporary Dance, which then led to a scholarship in Krakow, Poland, to study mime. Returning to London she married a struggling artist, John. *'It was like living with Monty Python.'* She then joined Haymarket Publishing and became a successful businesswoman, but life at home was not as successful. Her husband resented her making more money than him and subtly put her down. During a low period she walked out on her husband and job. This led Anando to work in the evenings as a volunteer for St Mungo's charity for the homeless where she felt needed and relaxed. Her next challenge was to live in Norfolk, where she discovered knitting and was able to conjure up jumpers that the likes of Elton John fell in love with. She set up a thriving business with 'little old ladies' throughout Britain who knitted high fashion for celebrities of the day. But once again she decided to abandon this and travel overland to India. Fearless and ready to learn, she took off via Istanbul and Afghanistan on a magical mystery tour. It was in the seventies and the sexual revolution was in full swing. Her 'turning point' was when she arrived in Pune at the Osho ashram; she went *'from sex to super-consciousness'*. She realized that up till then, like all women, she had been living the life that was expected of her. Meeting Osho allowed her to explore herself and that was the beginning of her enlightenment. She believes Osho was one of the first men to empower women. *'He gave the most important positions to women, he believed that women were very intelligent and they had been abused. He believed that their power had been taken away over the years and he wanted to readdress the balance and empower women again.'* Anando herself is both empowered and centred and, although her travels continue, her quest is fulfilled. Today her diverse talents and captivating charm have led her to become one of the most sought-after human development trainers throughout the world.

Joan Davies

Patricia Daver

'I then used my research and writing skills to expose three urgent women's issues of that time: how men in Britain used organizations to block women, the position of women in the third world and how women related to political issues.'

Barbara Rogers

Barbara Rogers

Marian Rivman

Jeroo Roy

Judith Chomsky

Patchwork, portfolio, chequered career

One of the qualities of greatness that clearly emerged was the ability to change direction and find a new path when necessary. So many people are unhappy with what they're doing and yet feel stuck in a rut because they haven't got the courage to move.

The first woman to teach at Sandhurst Military Academy, **Joan Davies**, made an important point about the way in which historical circumstances can also dictate the confidence to take risks. '*I was young at the height of the economic depression, maximum unemployment, businesses crashing, the year after the great slump. It affected me and my parents' view was, if you got a safe job with a pension then you clung to it like anything. By the time my children came along their feeling was that they could go into the world and do all sorts of things before they settled down.*'

Staying put was never an option for aesthetician **Patricia Daver** who went to work for her uncle. She was happy and loved working in the Empire State Building, and '*did very well*'. It came as a tremendous shock when, after two years, her uncle told her that he was firing her! '*I said "Why? I haven't done anything wrong". He said, "Come with me" and he showed me all his employees. He said, "See that women over there? She has been there twenty-five years". Then he took me to another floor, "See that woman who's been there fifteen years. I don't want that to happen to you"*.' Patricia was devastated because she idolized her uncle. Only nineteen, it felt like a difficult lesson, but she now values her uncle's advice: '*There is a whole world out there but people are too scared sometimes to do anything. They get very comfortable and they are afraid to move. That is not going to happen to you*'. When I asked Patricia what she thought the secret of success was, she replied, '*It is having confidence in yourself*' and, of course, it was that very lesson that her uncle had managed to teach her.

After studying at Sussex University, editor and founder of *Everywoman* magazine **Barbara Rogers** was also given some good advice when her tutor told her that she should do what she believed in. It may be that her tutor didn't quite appreciate the range of Barbara's strongly-held beliefs on equality, but her advice gave Barbara the confidence to move from cause to cause with energy. *'I started at the Foreign Office, where I was able to show how governments were subsidizing apartheid in Africa. I then used my research and writing skills to expose three urgent women's issues of that time: how men in Britain used organizations to block women, the position of women in the third world and how women related to political issues. But my best work was setting up and editing the pioneering magazine,* Everywoman.'

Marian Rivman has enjoyed a successful career in PR, but her working pattern also took several different turns. *'I was a school teacher, manpower development specialist, advertising executive, rock band manager, and consumer researcher, before I settled into being a consultant strategist, specializing in public relations. My clients have ranged from the United Nations agencies, programmes and world conferences, to celebrities, and from the scuba diving industry, to retail giants and world renowned scientists.'*

It is hard to think of two such contrasting pieces of a professional patchwork as the world of building contractors and that of fine art and yet **Jeroo Roy** managed a successful career in both. She recalls the sheer determination and conviction that she had to muster in order to be taken seriously as a contractor. *'I had to work five times harder than a man to be on top. I had to convince my partner to be proud of me as a builder, as he was quietly ashamed. He wanted me to return to my painting. I wanted to be independent and not dependent on anybody else for my finances.'* Despite the energy she had to expend to stay ahead in the building world, Jeroo the artist always found her place. *'I've always carried on sketching throughout my life, everywhere I've travelled I've kept a sketch book.'*

Mothers in law

It is probably true that women are socialized to consider caring professions and the spheres of hospitality and administration as typically female, and the 'hard' professions of medicine, law and academia as conventionally male. Although clearly capable of excelling in both, some women may avoid the 'male' professions because their demands appear incompatible with family life. It was surprising how many women had taken up law as a career that best suited the demands of their lives.

Judith Chomsky was a suburban mother of two and a graduate student in anthropology when she answered the call of Martin Luther King Jr to join in a project to organize grassroots opposition to the Vietnam war. The choice to participate was life-transforming. She left graduate school and spent the next several years as an organizer with the Philadelphia Resistance, primarily with anti-war GIs and with Vietnam veterans. As the US participation in the war wound down, Judith decided that her family circumstances did not permit her to work as an organizer and she opted for law school. She was rewarded by a wonderful surprise, the fact that she loved the practice of law. The legal profession enabled her to pursue her commitment to human rights and, with friends from law school, she co-founded the Juvenile Law Center of Philadelphia. After a few years she began the Workers Rights Law Project to serve workers who were trying to organize to create more democratic and active unions. She was then contacted by the Center for Constitutional Rights (CCR), which was looking for a lawyer who could go to Gaza and the Occupied West Bank to help prepare a case involving civilian deaths from the Israeli occupation. Today Judith is an international voice on human rights.

Leila Seth was the first woman to top the Bar examinations in London, the first woman Judge of the Delhi High Court, and the first woman Chief Justice to the High Court in India. Given that her law career has been so distinguished, it was fascinating to hear how and why she took up law. '*I went to England with my husband as he was posted there. I did a Montessori course and I thought I would open a school when I got back to India and teach children. My husband felt I could do more than that.*

Maja Daruwala

Leila Seth

'when I did the Bar finals, I came first. It was the first time a woman had come first in England and it was in all the newspapers. I was pregnant then and the headlines read "A Mother in Law".'

Leila Seth

Shami Chakrabarti

'I was pregnant on 9/11, hormones raging. I thought, "Is this the time to be getting into the civil liberties market?" And of course it was.'

Shami Chakrabarti

Helena Kennedy

I said how could I when I have one child? Then I bought a book called Career Encyclopaedia *and found out which of the courses needed the least attendance. I found that to become a barrister you only needed to eat the dinners and they weren't too strict on attendance. You could study from home. You know, when I did the Bar finals, I came first. It was the first time a woman had come first in England and it was in all the newspapers. I was pregnant then and the headlines read "A Mother in Law". After that I had no choice and I had to go into the legal profession.'* Her initial motivation of flexible working hours and for free suppers may provoke a smile but her professional commitment to justice has endured over thirty years and she has made a very senior and serious contribution to India's justice system. Although she retired as Chief Justice of Himachal Pradesh in 1992 she continues to do arbitration work and is involved in human rights activities.

Maja Daruwala did not come into the law in order to combine a career with her family; in fact she only took her final Bar exams after ten years of marriage and two children, while her husband was working in Sri Lanka. Like **Leila Seth**, she looked up what career she could pursue from a book on career guidance. Maja knew that she had found her vocation the first time she opened a law book and discovered that it echoed her deeply-held beliefs in equity and justice. She wasted no opportunity to make up for lost time and, after a short time practising in the Supreme Court in India, Maja took up a post at the Ford Foundation as a programme officer for South Asia. Since 1996 she has headed up the Commonwealth Human Rights Initiative and is known as a champion for women's rights and advocacy.

The people's Portia

Within the context of British law, Baroness **Helena Kennedy** QC is fondly known as Britain's favourite Portia, an allusion to Shakespeare's gifted advocate. This is an especially fitting title, given that Helena admitted that when she was young *'it didn't occur to me to be a barrister because my big passion was English literature. Reading books excited me about the possibilities of a different kind of world'*. Yet it is as a barrister that she has been instrumental in creating a different kind of world, through her work on prominent cases, including the Guildford Four appeal, the bombing of the Israeli embassy, and her outstanding work on civil liberties. As a life peer, she has become known as one of the most engaging politicians, who will challenge and speak against her own political masters. She articulates the present disgust with shabby political expediency and is campaigning for a new kind of politics that encourages participation and is less about control and dogma.

Life, liberty and the pursuit of human rights

From a younger generation, **Shami Chakrabarti**, who similarly took law as a route to human rights campaigning, has occupied the high profile position, Director of Liberty, the human rights organization. A barrister by background, Shami started her working career as a lawyer in the Home Office where she learnt how the Civil Service worked and what politicians demanded of it. She arrived at Liberty the day before the Twin Towers were bombed. *'I was pregnant on 9/11, hormones raging. I thought, "Is this the time to be getting into the civil liberties market?" And of course it was.'* Since then she has been preoccupied with campaigning against the erosion of civil liberties and what she regards as the divisive and counterproductive anti-terror measures adopted in the wake of the 9/11 attacks in the US.

Saints in politics?

Why people go into politics is still a mystery. Often it is to change the world for the better, yet there are few saints in politics. Most people enter the system as colossal idealists and leave diminished and disillusioned. Politics is certain sorrow and uncertain joy. Nearly every successful politician, wherever they are in the world, leaves office to be forgotten and often reviled. Those who escape ridicule are usually assassinated, and even then history is harsh and exacting as to their true contribution to the betterment of society. I had met nearly all the key political players throughout the world. I spoke their language. I understood their disappointments and had a sneaking admiration for their perseverance. Those who had put themselves forward for public adoration and ridicule, and had suffered at the hands of the electorate, were a strong and valiant breed. Those who were selected for high office or public appointments, without having suffered the rigours of political campaigning and the fickleness of the electorate, were fortunate. Most women who have thrived in politics had it in their blood; they were daughters of political dynasties or politicians' wives. It was my pleasure to know the exceptions to this rule, those who had carved a political identity by themselves. Wherever I travelled I found that political women had certain attributes in common. They mainly had their family support and the encouragement of their party and organization. Their names were recognizable because of their past work or famous family. But, most evidently, they had strong personalities and a confident determination that what they were engaged with was worth while and would hopefully endure.

Baroness **Doreen Miller** was not born for politics, not from a political family, not from the Oxbridge network, and she did not have a background as a local councillor. Yet she was determined to get into the House of Commons and went to great lengths to see her ambition fulfilled. '*I mortgaged the family home to raise the cash for my own business and then built a multi-million-pound business for one reason only, to give myself a CV for politics. For fifteen years I worked tirelessly. I had sleepless nights building up my business so that I would be a different sort of parliamentary candidate; so many of them were lawyers, academics,* *and so few were women or from a business background. Then I said to the Conservative Party, OK here I am! By the time I offered my services I was a fifty-year-old wife, mother and businesswoman, as well as a magistrate, and I knew what it was like to go out and earn a living. I really thought I would be God's gift to the Conservative Party. I couldn't believe they would take one look at me and say "Don't you think you're too mature my dear?"'* Undaunted, Doreen applied to over 140 parliamentary seats throughout Britain. She believes *'if you're not interested in politics, you're not interested in life'* because nothing happens that is not political somewhere along the line. In 1993 she was made a Life Peer to the joy of many in the women's movement, her husband Henry and her three sons.

Born in Kenya, Baroness **Usha Prashar** has all the qualities essential for a high achiever, articulate, analytical in her approach and focused on her goals. Without doubt her career has been a phenomenal success story. Her work in public policy began with the former Race Relations Board and continued when she became the Director of the Runnymede Trust. This gave her a solid foundation for effective mainstream public sector work and her many roles have included leading organizations like the National Council for Voluntary Organizations and the chairmanship of the Parole Board.

Usha has been involved in promoting equality and combating discrimination since the early 1970s. She did this by placing the issues at the heart of policy development. In her various roles she also made a contribution to the criminal justice system, the arts and cultural diversity. A career in the public sector has enabled Usha to make a real difference. She says, *'to bring about change in policies and practices you need data, evidence, strategy, tactics and an ability to persuade people and shift perceptions'.*

She was made a Life Peer in 1999 and in 2000 became the First Civil Service Commissioner, with responsibility for ensuring that the British Civil Service remains impartial. In 2005 she was appointed inaugural chairman of the Judicial Appointments Commission – another significant constitutional change – where she is responsible for selecting judges for appointment.

Clearly her achievement as a immigrant and an Asian woman at the very heart of the British establishment is an important part of how others see her. She, however, sees her own achievements as rooted in her approach and the values that she attempts to live by. *'The values that I live by were a big part of my upbringing. When I left Kenya my mother gave me a* Bhagavad-Gita *which I still read. The meaning of the* Bhagavad-Gita *is simple but powerful. It basically says whatever you have to do, do it to the best of your ability without expectation. This has determined how I have approached my life and various jobs I have done. It enables me to keep an equilibrium, a clear mind and enhances my ability to make a difference.'*

Diane Abbott, another high-achiever, made history by being the first black woman to be elected to the British Parliament and enjoys a distinguished career as a parliamentarian and broadcaster. She always wanted to be a Member of Parliament. Born in London, Diane is seen by her Jamaican family as a 'very special English lady'. When her parents divorced she lived with her father and younger brother in Harrow and was the only black girl to go to the local grammar school. Throughout her life she has continued to be a pioneer for her community. After reading history at Newnham College, Cambridge, she joined the Home Office as a Civil Servant. She explained: '*Anyone in politics needs to understand how the Civil Service works; it taught me how to write a memo, it taught me how to put anything of significance on paper. It taught me how the system worked'.*

Although Diane and Usha have made positive political contributions for women from minority communities, many still saw British politics as a lonely, self-promoting masculine business. Political author **Jo-Anne Nadler** remarked that *'politics is show business for ugly people'*. Other political women spoke about having been in a system in which they have felt unacknowledged. They were among the most disappointed women I met, even though they also had the highest expectation of changing society.

Doreen Miller

Usha Prashar

'Why have you come here, you're already famous?'
'I was expected to fall flat on my face at the first opportunity or to want special treatment ... Parliament has not changed its traditions – countless meetings which are so slow. It's frustrating, as I went into politics to make a difference to people's lives.'

Glenda Jackson

Glenda Jackson

Jo-Anne Nadler

Diane Abbott

Clare Short

All the world's a stage

When the Oscar-winning actress **Glenda Jackson** entered the House of Commons as the Member of Parliament for Hampstead and Highgate, she felt she was not taken seriously by some male MPs who questioned her validity. 'Why have you come here, you're already famous?' 'I was expected to fall flat on my face at the first opportunity or to want special treatment. There was this in-built attitude that I was too big for my boots and that I was not to be given any jobs. Parliament has not changed its traditions – countless meetings which are so slow. It's frustrating, as I went into politics to make a difference to people's lives.'

Why a woman of Glenda Jackson's enormous presence remained in the political arena may be understood in her background. She grew up in a working class family before the 1945 Labour Party landslide. Then there were no free medical services, life was hard and girls were expected to marry. If, as Glenda recalled, *'you were not blond or beautiful then you had better be employable'*. Earning her first pay-packet at the local chemist and the joy of her first acting job was still imprinted on her memory. She also recalled the day she heard the results of her eleven-plus exams, which determined whether she went to a grammar school and had a chance in life, or was abandoned educationally by the system. *'It was the day my exam results were declared. On my way to school, being a small town and everyone knowing each other, people asked me whether I had cleared my exams. I said that my letter had not come. There was a sudden change in attitude. When I came back home for lunch the letter had arrived stating that I had passed and would go to grammar school. At once the behaviour of these same people changed. In one afternoon I discovered how people's attitude fluctuated, which is disgraceful. I still remember the incident very clearly.'*

At the height of her illustrious acting career, Glenda announced that she had decided to dedicate her life to working for others' rights. Although she has remained principled in her political work and has opposed her government on several important policies, including university tuition fees and military action against Iraq and Afghanistan, she still has never been given a Cabinet position worthy of her extraordinary talents. Whenever I think of Glenda the Latin words *'suaviter in modo, fortiter in re'*, which translated means 'stylish in appearance and strong in substance', come to mind.

Passionate politics

Clare Short is one of Britain's most famous woman politicians. Working as Private Secretary to the Conservative minister Mark Carlisle gave her the idea that she *'could do better'* than many of the MPs she dealt with. In the 1983 UK general election she became MP for Ladywood, Birmingham, the area where she grew up and attended a Roman Catholic grammar school. From the start of her career she was on the left wing of the Labour Party and successfully gained attention for campaigning against 'Page 3' photographs of topless models in British tabloid newspapers. Admired for her grit, Clare attributes her political success to her fervent and energetic approach: *'I passionately cared that I was making the world more just. But I wasn't so driven and I never calculated, which I think is very female – I just got stuck in and did it. Then people would promote me. I didn't calculate my way up, I just worked hard and did the work convincingly'.*

However, if Clare's ardent and engaged way of working proved her success, it also led her to her refusals and resignations. She resigned twice from the Labour Front Bench, over the Prevention of Terrorism Act in 1988, and over the Gulf War in 1990. She went on to become Shadow Minister for Women, and then Shadow Transport Secretary, and in 1996 she was moved to the Overseas Development portfolio. Although this move was widely seen as a demotion, or even a punishment for her outspokenness, it gave Clare a new brief for equality. She was appointed Secretary of State for International Development in 1997 and resigned in May 2003. Clare believes politics has been the secular religion into which she invested all the moral passion of her Catholic upbringing. *'I think I applied* my belief in justice or truth and morality into my politics. It sort of became my church – I knew its imperfections but working for a more just world was the meaning of my life.' No one can doubt the conviction that has underpinned Clare's political career and her unshakeable will to make a difference. However, like other women who have entered politics with high humanitarian ideals, her disappointment is palpable.

Interestingly, the women who have entered Indian politics were equally independent spirits but they felt much more optimistic about the possibility of seeing change happen.

Political warriors

Selja Kumari, India's Minister for Urban Employment and Poverty Alleviation, explained how she *'was born into a political family, a ministerial house. My father was a remarkable judge of character and taught me that politics is about being single-minded and fighting for justice. I am single-minded about empowering women and the underclass'*. Although she has chosen to focus her political energies on women's issues this is not the result of personal discrimination. *'In India when you come into a political position you are respected and they forget you're a woman. I've never had a problem because I'm a woman, even though it's a man's world and women in politics must have the grit and the fight, or politics isn't for them.'*

Renuka Chowdhury, India's Minister of State for Women and Child Development, is known as one of India's most outspoken politicians and describes herself as being *'off the radar screen'*. She is a firebrand who was motivated to go into politics by her sheer indignation at being a member of a democracy that she felt was failing her. *'I was this pregnant housewife with certainly no recommended qualifications for entering politics; with no political godfather within three generations. I marched into this public forum, took decisions, drove into the deposed Chief Minister's camp, sat with him and asked him what was his POA and he looked at*

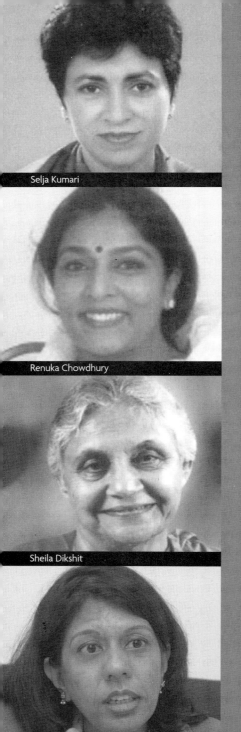

'... women in politics must have the grit and the fight, or politics isn't for them.'

Selja Kumari

'I fight for what I believe in. It doesn't matter if the rest of the world and their mother tell me I am wrong.'

Renuka Chowdhury

'In a democratic sector, you need a very large heart. Not only to help people, but to understand people, because there will be different kinds of people, different aspirations, different demands.'

Sheila Dikshit

'I am a woman who loves her country and is able to recognize the bigger picture that inevitably impacts on to everyday Mauritian life.'

Nita Deerpalsing

me blankly – that's Plan of Action – but he didn't know!' Renuka's lack of regard for the 'recommended' pathways to power meant that she could act as a fireball, bringing heat and light to the political scene. Her intent on burning off the impurities that dogged the political system was rooted in a rare and absolute confidence in her own conviction: *'I fight for what I believe in. It doesn't matter if the rest of the world and their mother tell me I am wrong; it doesn't matter. I have to believe that'.* What is rarer still perhaps is that she was not at all complacent about her own success: *'It is really no big deal because I have educated parents, I had money, I had education – that is why I could reach where I did'.*

Sheila Dikshit, who, as Chief Minister of Delhi, is immensely powerful in anybody's terms, sees it as her *dharma* (duty) to use that power responsibly. She is respected by the people and understands that her power is a gift from the people to whose needs she remains attentive and emotionally open: *'In a democratic sector, you need a very large heart. Not only to help people, but to understand people, because there will be different kinds of people, different aspirations, different demands. I would like to be remembered as somebody who was committed to, and loved, Delhi. Respect is something which you cannot demand, it has to come naturally, it is something you earn and not demand'.*

Selja, Renuka and Sheila have all thrived in the political environment and it has energized them, rather than brought disappointment. Selja is an independent and confident representative of India's youth. Renuka is a dynamo and represents twenty-first century India with a sense of its own direction and power. Sheila is the dignified face of Indian womanhood, a strong personality who stands for the traditional values of family, community and nation. Together they show the lively face of Indian democracy.

Global politician

Nita Deerpalsing, a Member of Parliament in Mauritius is a new breed of 'globalized' politician, dynamic, very clever, an insider, and yet an outsider. As she says, *'I am a woman who loves her country and is able to recognize the bigger picture that inevitably impacts on to everyday Mauritian life'*. Educated in Mauritius and Canada, she went on to study business in London and Paris. Upon her return to Mauritius from Canada in 2003, she was approached by the Labour Party to participate in policy reflection and formulation, within the Policy Unit of the Party. Much encouraged by the Leader of the Labour Party, The Honourable Dr Navin Ramgoolam, who is respected internationally for his active support of women's participation in public life, Nita courageously took the plunge into the political arena and was successfully elected in the 2005 general election. Since then she has represented her party in the European Union and sits on numerous important committees. She has also been entrusted, by the Prime Minister, with responding to the Mauritian opposition on the Budget, because of his confidence in her economic acumen. Nita was a star graduate in actuarial mathematics and statistics in Canada and later, while working in the capital Port Louis, was recognized as a high-flyer in the business and economic arena. She now represents the young, vibrant and cosmopolitan Mauritius, at ease with its own success and with a more inter-connected world of Europe, Africa. America and Asia.

Mediawallas

As **Bachi Karkaria** recalled, *'My career was decided before I was'*. Bachi was simply born a 'third-generation' journalist. In 1917 her grandfather founded Eastern India's first Gujarati journal, *The Navroz*, by plunging his life savings into the paper in the heady days of the freedom struggle from colonial rule. This same paper was later edited by her parents. Bachi did not continue with the family paper, because her education and skills were in English, not Gujarati. But she takes some consolation in the fact that she has contributed one of her sons, Urvaksh, to the media world in the US. It is perhaps the fiercely principled nature of Bachi's work that has made the biggest impact in what is an illustrious career. She is among India's most-read columnists and respected journalists. Her weekly satirical column Erratica, is read by everyone. It has a sign-off character called Alec Smart who makes a cheeky one-liner comment, and who has acquired a persona of his own. The column's popularity is helped by the fact that it appears in the Sunday edition of the *Times of India*, which is the world's largest selling English language broadsheet. *'Sometimes I think Alec Smart actually competes with my own by-line. I need to put him in his place,'* says Bachi, in her usual feisty way. I felt sorry for poor smart Alec. Did he really think he could compete with Bachi's singular signature style?

She is the professional's professional, with the ability to see the big picture, as well as connect with the detail. I have seen Bachi be briefed on the plight of street children and then sit and type out a brilliant article that demands action. She can distil the essence from a vast pool of data, extract facts from the hype and yet remain humane. She also knows how to tell a story with both style and substance. Bachi has pioneered serious AIDS reporting in India, determinedly piercing through prejudice, exploitation and hypocrisy. Her pieces influenced the milestones in the Indian epidemic and helped to sensitize public understanding of the illness. Her awareness of media power is matched by her determination not to be corrupted by that power. *'Your biggest armour is your integrity.'* Like so many of the women that I admire she gives back to others in very practical ways. Recently she has diversified to training the next generation of media leaders world-wide. As the first Indian on the board of the Paris-based World Editors Forum, she is part of the core team conducting master classes for editors in emerging economies. It would seem, that along with an ease of writing and a strong sense of purpose, she has inherited the adherence to personal beliefs and integrity that also informed her father's life. He used to say that *'it was better to eat one less chapati than lose one's principles'.*

Bachi Karkaria

Coomi Kapoor

'When the newspaper started, sustainability was a fringe interest. Now there are millions of people seeking to create a positive and sustainable future … As new technologies like the Internet become available, people can interconnect with like-minds around the globe, sharing their stories and their hopes.'

Shauna Crockett-Burrows

Christina Lamb

Shauna Crockett-Burrows

Helen Gurley Brown

Sue Douglas

Late nights

Coomi Kapoor is also one of the pioneers of women in Indian journalism — former President of the Indian Women's Press Association, and Editor of the *Indian Express*. When she started in journalism she was one of the few women who would do 'late nights and crime', not seen as a woman's area. If women were writing it was mostly features. '*In those days there was a lot of prejudice against hiring women; if you came into the profession you came in with special contacts. They were usually good writers and did the features, but they were not considered hard news journalists, nor did they go on to edit newspapers. The late night work made all the difference, it was then that the men realized that women could do all the duties of a man.*' Coomi has two distinct qualities that make her an outstanding journalist and editor. The first is that she has news sense; she knows the tiny things that will attract the reader, as she explained: '*Politicians always want to project their own point of view and many people will write the things the politician want said. There is something called the water cooler idea which people will discuss and give prominence to. It might just be a little thing. Not the routine, not the hackneyed. Take Nepal, there was a shoot-out. People took the story at face value and, surprisingly, even the British press wrote the story that the Crown Prince killed everybody including himself. Nobody with any sense would believe that story. It was our probing that is enabling the real story to come out*'. Coomi's second strength is her ability to channel her energies appropriately. Her reflections on her own career are considered and to the point and modest, considering her special place in Indian journalism. '*I was brought up in a generation where you put yourself down. I'm not seen as a threat because I'm less ambitious than most people. I have refused jobs as an editor as I didn't feel I needed the job at the time. I'm steady and security conscious and have never had any difficulty finding a job. The younger generation are far more convinced of their self-worth and their ambition can lead them into conflict.*'

On the front line

The role of the media as a public information and opinion-forming service clearly excited many of the women who have chosen it as their career. Foreign correspondent for the *Sunday Times* **Christina Lamb** was very modest about her ground-breaking reporting of the human cost of conflict. *'It's nice to think that what you write actually makes people realize, open their eyes to things and change the way they behave. I've written books and I hope, indirectly, it will change some policies.'*

On the wire

The media is not only in the hands of reporters, writers and presenters. Much of the real power of the media world is wielded by editors who make the decisions about which stories make the headlines. In many ways editors are the opinion brokers, with the power to change how we perceive issues. This fact was brought home in 1986 by **Sue Douglas**, the then editor of *The Mail on Sunday*. Against the grain of her established conservative readership, Sue took the bold step to put the mindless racial attacks that I had suffered during my parliamentary campaign on the front page, and thereby brought racism to the fore of the paper's agenda and the public's awareness. The subject of racial violence was then picked up by the British media and became an issue for politicians, police and the public. Sue took the courageous initiative to set a new agenda and used her media power to just and responsible ends. There is a Hebrew saying that captures Sue's being. It is *'hazak ve'amatz'*, which translates as 'strong and has courage'.

Positive news

The founder of the newspaper *Positive News* and the magazine *Living Lightly*, **Shauna Crockett-Burrows** is one of the older wise women I met, a beautiful and ancient soul. In traditional societies grandmothers like Shauna would have been revered as the holders of wisdom. Today, they are told to learn to retire gracefully.

When she was asked how she kept momentum over such a long period of time, she replied that she was here for a purpose and wanted to fulfil it. She felt sustained by a deep inner connection. '*I feel I have to be thoroughly grounded in the outer world, although my real world is an inner one. I remember someone once saying to me that it's no use being so heavenly that you are no earthly good.*'

'*There is much more good news in the world than bad, but the mainstream media tends to focus on the negative. If people don't know about the news that is positive, how can they be expected to support and celebrate it?*' *Positive News* has always been at the forefront of reporting the things that have been working in the world.

'*When the newspaper started, sustainability was a fringe interest. Now there are millions of people seeking to create a positive and sustainable future. It is a deeply exciting time to be alive. As new technologies like the Internet become available, people can interconnect with likeminds around the globe, sharing their stories and their hopes. Young people are going to inherit a very different world from the one we live in now. They will have to learn many new skills, but will also need to remember the old ones and reconnect with past wisdom.*'

Bronwen Astor

'even late into life, some women have a magical life-force.'

Bronwen Astor

Helen Gurley Brown

'I missed the boat in terms of retirement and so I just kept on going.'

Helen Gurley Brown

Mary Marsh

'I have no wish to retire … I still want to do other things, even though I don't know what they are as yet.'

Mary Marsh

Phyllis Krystal

'We have all failed at retirement.'

Phyllis Krystal

Magical life-force

I was not surprised to read an article in *Time* magazine discussing how middle-aged women are twice as likely to be hopeful about the future as middle-aged men. For many women, middle-age may be the time in their life when they have most freedom from intensive childcare or parental care commitments, and from the fear of failure or others' disapproval. Therefore, it is a time when they can reflect on, and follow, their own ambitions. If there is one quality that unites all the women I met it is that whatever freedoms they have, they use them purposefully and to the full. If *Time* magazine had researched women's lives beyond middle-age, they would have discovered that age is never a barrier. Now in her seventies **Bronwen Viscountess Astor**, a renowned beauty, is determined not to waste a moment. A psychotherapist, her Christian faith has been integral to her work as a therapist as she brings together the spiritual and the psychological. She has also explored alternative therapies including Rebirthing and is becoming a Spiritual Director when most people have given up on life and are happy to be retired. Bronwen is still using her spiritual gifts to serve others. As she says, *'even late into life, some women have a magical life-force'*.

Carrying on regardless

It was fascinating to find that the women who viewed work as a landscape became more and more interesting and never wanted to reach the horizon. Dame **Mary Marsh** was very clear about this. *'I have no wish to retire. I will know when it's the right time to leave the NSPCC and I still want to do other things, even though I don't know what they are as yet.'* **Helen Gurley Brown** made me laugh *'I missed the boat in terms of retirement and so just kept on going'*. She still goes into her New York office in her eighties and looks like a movie star. Similarly **Phyllis Krystal** is still active in her field of spiritual development in her nineties and looks sensational. All these women love their work and see its benefit to others. As Phyllis amusingly said, *'We have all failed at retirement'*.

Das F-wort Das F-wort Das F
اللفظة النابية اللفظة النابية
La parola che comincia con F
也谈女权 也谈女权 也谈女权
Das F-wort Das F-wort Das
اللفظة النابية اللفظة النابية
La parola che comincia con F
也谈女权 也谈女权 也谈女权
Das F-wort Das F-wort Das
اللفظة النابية اللفظة النابية
La parola che comincia con F
也谈女权 也谈女权 也谈女权
Das F-wort Das F-wort Das F
اللفظة النابية اللفظة النابية
La parola che comincia con F
也谈女权 也谈女权 也谈女权
Das F-wort Das F-wort Das F
اللفظة النابية اللفظة النابية
La parola che comincia con F

The f-word

Feminism – the good fight

Intensive womanising can produce strange and unexpected side-effects. In my case, it has transformed me into a fully fledged feminist, ready to fight for the cause. Listening to so many stories about the disadvantages, narrow mindedness and discrimination women still experience has made me dedicate my life to ensuring that wherever women live and work, life's opportunities will be open to them, including meeting me!

Feminism has demanded and won many rights for women: the right to determine their lives, the right to expect freedom and justice and the right to be recognized as different but equal. All the same, today the term 'feminist' is one of the most contentious 'f' words in the dictionary. It has been misunderstood, misrepresented and demonized. It has been mistaken for 'man-hating'; accused of denying the differences between women around the world and dismissed as irrelevant and outdated. Like all big social movements, feminism has run into problems, yet its campaign for the rights of women must go on.

As someone who admires women and marvels at their talents, I am outraged that throughout the world women still do not enjoy equal status with men. Interestingly they are participating in the economy and excelling in the classroom; becoming more politically empowered and starting to have better access to healthcare, but they are still subjected to violence, poorer resources, lower wages and deeply embedded prejudices.

Many thoughtful women recognized that their sisters remained at the bottom of the heap, and that the goals of money literacy, body literacy, civil literacy and word literacy, were yet to be achieved.

Meher Heroyce Moos, who has journeyed extensively for her work as a travel journalist, explained the gender picture in the developing world. *'The major issues facing women are still the same as centuries ago. There is no emancipation of women amongst the under-privileged. Jobs and education are still not accessible to all. There is no financial security for them. Rape is not given the severest of penalties. Women are molested by close family members. Divorced women are thrown out of the house. There is great need to banish superstitions and harsh primitive religious rituals where widows are concerned.'*

Lisette Talate, Vice-President of the Chagos Refugee Group and Nobel Prize nominee, spoke directly from her experience of the deprivation that many women still experienced. *'It is the woman who cooks and has to make sure that the family is fed, that the children and husband have clothes to wear and takes care of the house. There's a Creole saying "It is the hand that holds the pan that knows how hot it is". The woman is the one that has the task of budgeting money and making sure that everyone is looked after. My own suffering and that of my family motivated me to fight against this situation.'*

Although many Western women did not have to bear the kinds of acute oppression that Lisette endured, they were motivated to change the historically sanctioned privileges of male power in their own fields. The feisty arts animateur **Margaret Sheehy** spoke about her work empowering women in British theatre in the early eighties: *'We initiated a survey of women working in British theatre. We concentrated on writers, directors and administrators; it was these roles that decided the profile of what you saw on stage. We created a stink. We started to lobby, agitate; we deliberately attacked the Royal Shakespeare Company for their dismal lack of representation. They were getting all these subsidies and they were not representing the other half of the population. It was important for women to see other women achieving. You can imagine that the men in positions of power panicked and the word went around "Quick, quick, somebody find us a woman!"'*

Meher Heroyce Moos

Lisette Talate

'Young people today don't realize how static and status quo things were, nor how far women have progressed through direct action for better representation and involvement.'

Lesley Abdela

Margaret Sheehy

Lesley Abdela

Barkha Dutt

Barbara Rogers

Margaret's experience reflected that of other women's campaigns in the eighties. In politics the 300 Group, founded by **Lesley Abdela**, called for better representation of women in the political sphere. The political response was also *'Quick, quick, find us a woman!'* As a result women are now represented on the theatrical and political stages. What was seen as transgression and tokenism has become inclusion and involvement. Many radical activists echoed Lesley's thought that *'Young people today don't realize how static and status quo things were, nor how far women have progressed through direct action for better representation and involvement'.*

Although some young women cannot understand the continued relevance of feminist struggle, several were passionately committed to the cause. **Barkha Dutt** is known to champion women's causes. When reporting from Kashmir on the campaign to enforce the veil, a fatwa was issued against her. Barkha grew up calling herself a feminist and she still does. *'I am extremely alarmed at the fact that it's a term women feel defensive about. I'm uncomfortable with the "but" in "I'm not a feminist but ..."* On the other hand, I also recognize that my notion of feminism in India is borrowed from the West and may not always apply to a country where a woman will walk eight kilometres to fetch a pot of water, bring up children without money, and deal with an alcoholic husband at home who does not believe in reproductive health or equality. Gender politics have become such a splintered debate. Women need to reclaim the space.'

Barbara Rogers spoke about how feminism, which she had helped to articulate as a cause in the eighties through her magazine *Everywoman*, had broken down because of internal divisions between women of different political, ethnic and sexual orientations. *'Feminism had won some important victories, such as an independent credit rating for women who previously could not have a mortgage in their names. Equally, it has failed to take young people with it.'* Like Barkha, Barbara was very clear that feminism needed to make a comeback in one shape or form, because *'young women need to confront the vogue for the obnoxious laddish approach to women as sex objects'.*

Raunch culture

Barbara's particular concern about the way in which young Western women were being sexualized in a very aggressive way was also shared by others. Throughout history women have been exploited as sex objects but sexual innuendoes are now prominent in youth and popular culture. Parliamentarian **Diane Abbott** cannot stand the parade of breasts and G-strings that greet her whenever she walks into her local newsagent. As she stated in an article for London's *Evening Standard*, *'I am a feminist. But I feel uncomfortable that we have gone, in one generation, from fighting for the right to read* Lady Chatterley's Lover *to a popular culture saturated with sex. Somehow, some feminists seem to have bought into a raunch culture in the name of freedom of expression, which really means the right to get 'em out for the lads. Thus girls learn that the way to fame and fortune is to pump breasts up to the size of small puppies'*.

Other women were also seriously concerned about a generation who were collaborating in their own sexual exploitation. Many questioned how liberating was it to be represented as sex object or to indirectly support pornography? Charity consultant **Ruth Powys** may be of the generation supposedly liberated to follow all their desires, but she is very alert to the trap such freedom can represent. *'What really gets to me are advertising campaigns, rappers on MTV and magazines like* Nuts *and* Loaded *which put a jokey spin on the darker side of women's sexual objectification; opening upper class airport lounges under the slogan of 'Pimp My Lounge'; producing TV shows called 'Pimp my Ride' and giving out free Christmas guides to London's "best" prostitutes. We are bombarded with advertisements that tell you you are not sexy, not attractive, unless you look like a porn star. Raunch culture is a backlash against feminism.'* For Ruth, feminism is needed now more than ever and there needs to be an urgent reassessment of the idea that we live in a post-feminist world. *'"Post-feminism" seems to be all about choice, regardless of who presents the choices in the first place. It is okay if I want to be a stripper, that's my choice and it even makes me a feminist. Well, no it doesn't, it makes you a sex object.'*

Perhaps of equal concern is the fact that often young women have not really considered what it means to be liberated and what kind of freedoms they want to achieve. Playwright and founder of the global movement V-Day, **Eve Ensler**, ventured to say that if you investigate most young women and their lives, you see that they have the same dependencies on men. *'I don't think they've completely shifted in the way they think and behave. It doesn't matter how much you encourage women, if you do not also encourage men to take responsibility, you are not going to stop male violence towards women.'*

In the extreme situation of exploitation, where women are forced into the sex trade, there are some courageous women challenging the status quo. Spirited campaigner, Indian Minister **Renuka Chowdhury** believes that prostitution needs regulation, and that sex workers need to be legitimized. *'You have to eliminate the pimp, the politician and the policeman. These three Ps contribute to the fourth P – "prostitution". Sex workers provide a valuable service. If they didn't exist, you'd have a lot more incest, a lot more problems at home. It is fine to have a vent, but it must be legitimized so that women enter the profession voluntarily. When they get the status of sex workers, they have access to healthcare and it is easier for governments to care for them and to rehabilitate them after they decide to retire. It should be just another job as long as women are not manipulated, and coerced and kidnapped, raped and forced into it.'*

Anonymous was woman

Virginia Woolf's *A Room of One's Own* is perhaps the most brilliant thesis on women's betrayal and belittling at the hands of male institutions of power and learning. Yet the 1928 edition of the book described Virginia as the wife of Leonard Woolf and the daughter of the esteemed man of letters, Leslie Stephen. Her work was reduced to a piece of writing by

Ruth Powys

'Post-feminism seems to be all about choice, regardless of who presents the choices in the first place. It is okay if I want to be a stripper, that's my choice and it even makes me a feminist. Well, no it doesn't, it makes you a sex object.'

Ruth Powys

Eve Ensler

'It doesn't matter how much you encourage women, if you do not also encourage men to take responsibility, you are not going to stop male violence towards women.'

Eve Ensler

'I gathered together a group of modern-day revolutoinaries, women who had leap-frogged obstacles to hurry history.'

Holly Sargent

Holly Sargent

a woman with a famous husband and father. Nothing could have been more ironic and nothing could have made Woolf's point more clearly! As Woolf poignantly reminded women, *'For most of history, Anonymous was a woman'.* Woolf's work aimed to provoke women to bring themselves forward and challenge the idea that history is only the story of powerful men and their achievements.

For many of the women throughout the world their personal and ancestral memories of a culture, in which women were routinely regarded as less capable and less important than men, remained a vital spur in their quest to achieve self-fulfilment. They were impatient and wanted to hurry history towards a more just record of women's achievements and potential. They also recognized that a dearth of women in policy-making positions sent a silent message that power still belonged to men.

Modern-day revolutionaries

Holly Sargent, of Harvard University, felt that the most effective way to advance women and achieve global goals was to nurture women leaders. She had led by example and had helped to found the Council of Women World Leaders. Holly explained *'I gathered together a group of modern-day revolutionaries, women who had leap-frogged obstacles to hurry history'.*

The Very Reverend **Vivienne Faull** identified the unequal status of women that exists within the Church of England. She was also aware that often people felt that equality has already been achieved and so are blind to the huge injustices that still limited women's empowerment. *'Most people assume that women can be bishops; that it is just a question of timing before we have women bishops. They do not realize it is illegal. When you say there has got to be a change in the law before we have women bishops ordained, people are horrified. As they stand, the rules are contrary to equal opportunities legislation and the Sex Discrimination Act in Britain. The Church of England is exempt from this. All faith communities have an exemption.'*

Aliki Roussin

Frances Cairncross

Alison Donnell

Clare Short

'Nobody explains to boys that they may have to learn to work the washing machine and support their successful partners.'

Frances Cairncross

'Young men do not know what society expects from them any longer. They are also at an historical crossroads and receive mixed social messages. Masculinity is in crisis, which might be a huge asset for feminism, if we can help men to come to new understandings about power and empowerment in all dimensions of their lives.'

Alison Donnell

Economist **Devaki Jain** also wants to hurry history and yet looks to the past for inspiration. The recognition of deep inequalities in the thriving democracy of India continues to motivate her. *'It seems unfair and unnecessary for so many people in India to be living in such horrific conditions of deprivation, when the nation had the opportunity to have levelled itself off with its extraordinary civilization and intellectual resources. The Gandhian approach to our development could have really healed the inequality. We have not only lost it, but we continue to worsen it. Therefore there is a motivation to fight for a more just kind of development.'*

Men – the new allies?

Interestingly, for many women, it was men and their attitudes that were the most important focus to help transform the lives of women worldwide. The majority wanted to work harmoniously with men. The first woman President of the Jersey Cattle Association, **Anne Perchard**, summed it up for many women of her generation: *'I loathe women who belittle men and want them to be effeminate. They are men and we are women and long may the distinction last'*. This same sense of needing to work on common ground for all was also echoed by others. The feisty Greek award-winning photojournalist **Aliki Roussin** also articulated the view of many. *'The greatest success will be for women and men to collectively co-operate.'*

If discrimination and prejudice against women is to be genuinely overcome then men must also be allies in the cause. **Frances Cairncross**, Rector of Exeter College, Oxford, felt that too much time was spent inspiring women and not nearly enough helping men come to terms with the consequences. *'Nobody explains to boys that they may have to learn to work the washing machine and support their successful partners.'* **Lesley Abdela** agreed with Frances and thought that the most important thing was to keep working on changing the system so that men and women could thrive together. *'We need to create the space* for both to do things in their own styles. I invented the word "shevolution" because it's got both "she" and "he" in it. Organizations need to be revolutionized in a peaceful way to get things done. At the moment there needs to be work on men to change, whereas there is huge concentration on women to change.'

Masculinity in crisis

As someone who teaches young men at university, Dr **Alison Donnell** also believed that masculinity was an important focus for feminists in the twenty-first century.' *Lots of young men do not know what society expects from them any longer. They are also at an historical crossroads and receive mixed social messages about success and fulfilment. Masculinity is in crisis, which might be a huge asset for feminism if we can help men to come to new understandings about power and empowerment in all dimensions of their lives.'*

Collective femininity

Clearly feminism must continue to respond to changing circumstances if it is to remain relevant to people's aspirations for equality. Former British Cabinet Minister **Clare Short** put forward a strong argument for feminism as an inclusive movement that worked for equality and social justice. *'Feminism isn't about a middle-class women's obsession, a few women being organized. It's about a collective group transforming the world we live in. Many people think it's right that at least one-third of the world's parliament should be women, and that women should be given equality because the majority of people in the world are women and children.'* There is still a long way to travel before such goals can be achieved, but a determined focus on women's worth remains much alive.

Tzedakah (justice and charity)

Many of the women I couldn't help admiring were in the business of 'giving it away', which only made them more attractive in my eyes. They were charismatic, generous with their time, affections and vision. Many of the women felt poverty was not inevitable, that three-quarters of the world did not have to go to bed hungry every night and one hundred million children did not have to be in bonded labour. They stressed that we just needed new ways of looking at, and approaching, problems – and as ever the answer was to be kind.

Hilary Blume is someone who has helped to transform the way we give to charities and in turn she has raised millions for good causes through Good Gifts, Card Aid and the Charities Advisory Trust, which she set up from her kitchen table. However, she is not averse to criticizing her peers who lose sight of the beneficiaries that they are paid to work for. *'Many people use charities these days as a career move, I'm not saying that everyone should be self-sacrificing, but they've not got the values you'd hope they have.'* Religion is central to Hilary's life; her notions of charity are derived from *tzedakah*, a Hebrew word meaning both justice and charity. *'I have very distinctive views on the role of charity, mostly derived from the Talmud. The rule says that we should give 10% of our income. I give 10% and I'm happier.'*

The Jewish religion is also central to **Sallie Gratch's** philosophy. Today, Project Kesher, another kitchen-table venture, engages people of all faiths and ethnic backgrounds to build issue-orientated, multi-ethnic coalitions that strengthen the fabric of individual communities. It is one of the largest women's advocacy and human rights organizations in the Independent States of the Former Soviet Union (FSU), with grassroots women's groups across eight time zones. Their leadership programme offers women in local communities the opportunity to do the extraordinary, by developing their understanding of how to leverage existing resources to create an activist network.

Esther Rantzen

Jane Grant

'Children are all too often neglected, abused or exploited. Women should understand that, until recently, they suffered the same fate. The rewards society has gained from the emancipation of women have been huge; protecting and enabling children to fulfil their potential will mean a far brighter future for all humanity.' Esther Rantzen

Mahabanoo Mody-Kotwal

Bam Bjorling

Meher Banaji

Lily Thapa

Gender agenda

Dr **Jane Grant**, former Director of the National Alliance of Women's Organizations, is also the British adviser to the 'Global Fund for Women' which distributes funding to groups who are catalysts for change at a local level. *'We want to support not just the poorest of the poor, who are nearly always women, but the bravest of the brave: the women who are challenging the status quo around the world – and it is extremely dangerous for them to be doing so. Just a small grant for them at the right time can be very strategic.'*

Having worked with traditional NGOs like the Swedish Red Cross and the Ministry of Social Affairs, in the business sector **Bam Bjorling** founded the Swedish charity 'Kvinnoforum', which has projects in seventy countries around the world. It aims to increase girls' and women's influence in their own lives and in society. Like the 'Global Fund for Women', it has a gender and empowerment perspective which works on a small-scale level, with the aim of translating positive change on to a macro-level. *'When you are doing things that have never been done before, it is necessary to prove that they are possible and successful.'*

In her work empowering widows, Nepalese **Lily Thapa** offers single women (a term Lily uses to replace the heavily symbolic 'widow') encouragement to build a new future. Her work allows isolated women who have been considered unlucky and unwanted to become a force for change in their communities. *'When I first reached out to Lakshmi, a widow who was ill-treated by her family members, her mother-in-law refused me entry into her home, fearing that I would corrupt her daughter-in-law's mind. I was undeterred and I finally convinced Lakshmi's family to allow her to take a four-month sewing course. Now Lakshmi has her own tailoring shop and has opened a branch in another village. She is now financially independent.'*

Fundamental to all of these dynamic women is their strong sense that they can best serve others by enabling women to serve themselves.

Little warriors

Charity is not about sympathy but about empowering others. Principal of the Happy Home and School for the Blind, **Meher Banaji** runs her school according to these principles. *'Blind people are not objects of pity; they are capable of being productive; what they need is an opportunity. Because they are deprived of their vision, charity will open doors for them, but if they have a sound education they can be independent. I aim to give my pupils a way of life that is meaningful, so that they can go out in the world and not depend on friends, family or charitable organizations.'*

A hundred million children around the world are child labourers, deprived of education and love. Many are subjected to sexual and physical abuse, denied any childhood – an indictment on us all. Brazilian model **Ana Lucia** explained that she had called her charity for sexually abused children 'Little Warriors', because a force as strong as an army was needed to fight the problem of paedophiles and sexual predators. *'So many children are crippled for life by sexual abuse and they deserve proper care.'*

Until recently many children literally suffered in silence. It was the vision of **Esther Rantzen** that enabled them to voice their concerns to 'Childline', a telephone helpline for children in trouble or danger. In the seventies Esther was appointed producer and presenter of *That's Life!*, a television series that drew audiences of more than eighteen million and was on the air for twenty-one years, making her a household name in Britain. She also created *The Big Time*, a documentary series tackling subjects such as mental health, drugs and child abuse. From this platform Esther launched 'Childline', as she believed that it was important to protect children from avoidable pain. *'Children are all too often neglected, abused or exploited. Women should understand that, until recently they suffered the same fate. The rewards society has gained from the emancipation of women have been huge; protecting and enabling children to fulfil their potential will mean a far brighter future for all humanity.'*

Eco-warriors

Increasingly people recognize that we need global awareness to survive but we also need planetary awareness. Caring for each other has to be put into the larger context of caring for a planet that must sustain our collective needs.

Aban Marker Kabraji, the regional director of the World Conservation Union (IUCN) in Bangkok, is helping to integrate ecological principles into development work in Asia. Through the IUCN, Aban encourages and assists societies to conserve the integrity and diversity of nature and helps them to ensure that any use of natural resources is ecologically sustainable. She explained that over 15,589 species of animals and plants are threatened with extinction and many eco-systems, including wetlands and forests, are being degraded and destroyed. Action was needed now. In the future it might be too late. Today Aban is at the forefront of a wake-up call to save our planet which is central to the agenda of many enlightened thinkers and doers. The urgency to action is unavoidable if we are to have clean air to breathe, fresh water to drink and unpolluted land to cultivate.

This wake-up call echoed the work on a smaller scale by German **Petra Dobmeier**, President of the Agropark Climate Association, which promotes renewable energies and has started a 'village' concept where children can be taught about conservation and living an eco-friendly lifestyle. Her project, 'Petra House', is on the lines of a Wendy house, but is solar-powered and designed to teach the young about being eco-friendly, and the awareness of preserving resources. She explained that: *'In Europe there is this "rottweiler mentality", whereas what is needed is "Labrador thinking" to help integrate new ideas. A softer approach to new thinking is needed if we are to save our planet.'*

Aban Marker Kabraji

Petra Dobmeier

'I think that poetry is a potent tool for change in that it promotes greater awareness about the world around you and gives you a language that militates against following the crowd. This often means reminding people about painful truths they don't want to hear, but it is also a record of joy, which is highly infectious and a force for freedom.' Gwyneth Lewis

Gwyneth Lewis

Ann Jellicoe

Eve Ensler

Diana England

Community warriors

It is remarkable the number of women who had felt inspired to take their personal passions into communities to act as catalysts for groups to recognize their common concerns and shared future.

Diana England, who initiated 'Stitches in Time, Tapestry for the Millennium', treated art as a process through which to community-build. *'We worked in mixed media with musicians, thespians and other artists. This became a People's Arts Trust. We went around Britain by van and people came out on the street and took part. Lots of artists gave their time freely. It was a real mixture of artists doing their bit and the community doing their bit.'* When she started 'Stitches in Time' Diana used her vibrant personality to engage all the various communities in the East End of London to come and participate in a huge tapestry to represent their lives for future generations. Whereas the Bayeux tapestry, a historical record of William the Conqueror's Battle of Hastings in 1066, was embroidered by a few Norman aristocratic women, Diana's millennium tapestry was a collective endeavour by ordinary Londoners who came together to stitch their identity as a legacy of their lives.

Playwright, theatre producer and creator of modern community theatre, **Ann Jellicoe**, explained how she too used her art to bring communities together. *'When I started the community theatre I realized the whole process had to breathe an atmosphere of trust and friendliness. When you involve individuals and they become communities then it becomes theirs. You just facilitate them. One of the first community plays I did was about the Vikings. It brought two communities, Denmark and Dorchester in England, together. We took the Danes to Dorchester to do the play and the people from Dorchester to Denmark. It takes time to do the plays, two years minimum. You talk to small groups of people and gradually bring them together. You spend the first year building the structure, building the play, deciding on key positions and people. Who is going to research the play, to write it, where is the money coming from? You need self control, diplomacy, energy, vision, and extraordinary sensitivity to other people. In Denmark there was a 16-year-old* *boy who had a slight speech impediment. I knew that the best way to make your enunciation better was by putting a thumb between your teeth and say "Jack and Jill went up the hill to fetch a pail of water". If you do that three times you feel your speech is infinitely better. I didn't single out the boy to put his thumb in his mouth. I got everyone in the room to do it. Anyway, it did a hell of a lot of good for everyone. When the boy did it and did it well, everyone was absolutely delighted.'*

For **Gwyneth Lewis**, Poet Laureate of Wales, the Poetry for Wales project was much like community theatre. It created groups of people who had not worked together before and gave a momentum to the whole community so that spontaneous networks evolved. *'I think that poetry is a potent tool for change in that it promotes greater awareness about the world around you and gives you a language that militates against following the crowd. This often means reminding people about painful truths they don't want to hear, but it is also a record of joy, which is highly infectious and a force for freedom.'*

Vagina warriors

Playwright **Eve Ensler** did not go into communities directly, but her groundbreaking play, *The Vagina Monologues* has become a highly networked community 'franchise', with people throughout the world encouraged to perform the play and make it their own. As Eve explained: *'There are certain guidelines but you can produce it, you can direct it, you can perform it, you can own it. It becomes culturally connected to your community and you can use the money for work with violence against women in your area. What excites me is that women are all connecting through the play. It is the complete opposite to how imperialism works, where you go in and tell people how you think, what to do, how to do it and then you do it for them'.* It is this very sense of handing power down the line to others that makes community ventures so empowering.

If the good fight is about empowering victims to end cycles of abuse and educate others then 'vagina warriors', who had witnessed and experienced sexual violence themselves, were model fighters. *'They were great women who held the pain. They grieved quietly and that helped transform their bodies. It compelled them to devote their lives to ensure that it would never happen to anybody else. No one recognizes them because the media hates women who do good. Their work is invisible and yet it is central to the fabric of life. Slowly it dawned on me that nothing was more important than stopping violence toward women. The desecration of women indicated the failure of human beings to honour and protect life.'*

It was fortunate to meet several women now connecting with each other to confront the barbarity that so many women still endure. Actress **Mahabanoo Mody-Kotwal**, who acted in *The Vagina Monologues* in India, became part of the chain of women inspired to stop the violence. Mahabanoo not only helped to pass on the stories of these women, but she also donated all the profits from the play for shelters for abused women. She spoke about another remarkable woman, Dr Fernandes, who narrated the story of an 8-month-old baby girl who had been raped and left at her surgery. *'Her vagina was slashed up to her umbilicus because the sexual parts were so small. That day changed my life.'*

Through her travelling exhibition of paintings centred on the theme of violence against women, international artist **Jeroo Roy** has also raised awareness about atrocities against women. Like Eve and Mahabanoo, Jeroo empathized with the trauma and vulnerability experienced by women. *'Their sufferings have penetrated my very being. I have been able to depict those sufferings very strongly without any "sugar coating". Both women and men have viewed my paintings with tears in their eyes. I hope my paintings will create awareness and be instrumental in averting yet more atrocities against women and the girl child.'*

ter Framgångens hemlighet
Τά Μυστικά της Επιτυχίας Τά Μυσ
Los secretos del Êxito Los Secre
از موفقیت راز موف

ter Framgångens hemlighet
Τά Μυστικά της Επιτυχίας Τά Μυσ
Los secretos del Êxito Los Secre
از موفقیت راز موف

ter Framgångens hemlighet
Τά Μυστικά της Επιτυχίας Τά Μυσ
Los secretos del Êxito Los Secre
از موفقیت راز موف

ter Framgångens hemlighet
Τά Μυστικά της Επιτυχίας Τά Μυσ
Los secretos del Êxito Los Secre
از موفقیت راز موف

ter Framgångens hemlighet
Τά Μυστικά της Επιτυχίας Τά Μυσ

The secrets of success

'Success is doing the best you can with what you've got.'
Helen Gurley Brown

'… success is something quite personal, when you have broken your own barrier and done something quite different.'
Rifat Wahhab

'Oscars and awards are prizes for people who voted for you.'
Glenda Jackson

'Many young people are turning their backs on lucrative work in order to take on jobs that involve working with people and making a difference in others lives.'
Dorothy Dalton

Surprising secrets

All the women who held special interest for me had broken old traditions and taboos to find fulfilment. They were independent in their thought had intellectual integrity and did not know what mediocrity meant. They were adventurous, had an extraordinary drive and an irresistible sense of fun. They were on top of life and were loved for it. And yet their own ideas of success were often surprising in that they had little to do with power, influence or money.

For most, success was not something that could be measured by others. The founder of *Cosmopolitan* magazine, and voted one of the most influential American women in history, **Helen Gurley Brown**, defined it in very pragmatic but profound terms: *'Success is doing the best you can with what you've got'*.

Rifat Wahhab maintained that, *'success is something quite personal, when you have broken your own barrier and done something quite different'*. Rifat's words echoed **Glenda Jackson's** idea of success. Of her two Oscars for acting, Glenda made me laugh by saying that *'Oscars and awards are prizes for people who voted for you'*. She went on to explain that: *'As life goes on, personal fulfilment becomes attached to much smaller things. My son was in my house during the summer and had no shoes on his feet. He has the most beautiful feet and I looked at them and thought, "That is my greatest achievement"'*.

Dorothy Dalton explained that the idea of success was changing. *'There are still people who want to be famous and make money and measure success in those terms. But amongst the young there are a growing number of people who measure success differently. They are disillusioned with politicians and politics, and are looking for different ways to change the world. Many young people are turning their backs on lucrative work in order to take on jobs that involve working with people and making a difference in others' lives. Today they are more likely to get involved in campaigning on single issues such as the environment and world poverty and are more inclined to get involved as volunteers*

'To be remembered with pleasure is success.'

Esther Rantzen

'Success is actually being able to relate to others.'

Jennifer Gretton

'to be satisfied with one's own achievements and in society's terms it should be about serving others.'

Sukey Cameron

'There is nothing softer, sweeter or gentler than water, but water has the power to move mountains.'

Claire Bertschinger

in community action. Often they also show a much greater willingness to take the initiative and set up local projects of their own to help their community,'

Television personality **Esther Rantzen's** notion that *'to be remembered with pleasure is success'* was repeated time and again. Being successful was about showing kindness, honesty, fidelity to your ideals and service to others. The women understood that real fulfilment only came when you were relaxed and confident enough to follow your own goals. If one was always striving for success, or happiness, it remained elusive.

For **Tricia Sibbons**, success was a lightness of being, a gentle touch to push and guide ideas to fruition. In an official South African language, Tswana, this would be *Lesedi* (Light/ness). Successful women had the ability to connect to other people at different levels and discernment, to work with those who do good, and to pull away from those who use others for selfish gain.

Interestingly, the Lord Lieutenant of Leicestershire, Lady **Jennifer Gretton**, commented that the most important quality of a successful person is getting on with others. *'Success is actually being able to relate to others.'*

Representative for the Falkland Islands **Sukey Cameron** felt that success was *'to be satisfied with one's own achievements and in society's terms it should be about serving others'*.

As ever, my mother had the answer. *'The key to a successful relationship with other people is not to crush their egos or impose your own. It comes with integrity and being comfortable with your strengths and weaknesses and never pretending to be anything but what you are.'*

Mother's advice reminded me of **Claire Bertschinger's** comment. *'There is nothing softer, sweeter or gentler than water, but water has the power to move mountains.'*

'Successful people don't let opportunities pass them by, no matter how busy they are.'

Mahabanoo Mody-Kotwal

'Successful people have the confidence to seize opportunities when they come and to learn from them when things go wrong.'

Mary Marsh

'If the rest of the world sees you as successful, but you do not feel it in your heart – success is a sham.'

Shernaz Vakil

'A great deal of success often comes down to being friendly, and treating people on a one-to-one basis.'

Jan Morgan

Some secrets – take opportunities

One of the least hidden secrets of success is to take the opportunities that come your way without fear or hesitation. As actress **Mahabanoo Mody-Kotwal** declared, *'Successful people don't let opportunities pass them by, no matter how busy they are'.* Being hungry for life and fully engaged will increase your chances of success, or as **Clare Beckwith** put it, *'Success is people who give life a go, in contrast to those who can't be bothered'.* Of course, the real secret is to find out what takes away the fear and hesitation and enables us to embrace our chances with open arms.

Dame **Mary Marsh**, identified one of the true secrets of success when she said, *'Successful people have the confidence to seize opportunities when they come and to learn from them when things go wrong'.*

Industrialist **Shernaz Vakil** felt successful women took opportunities, but they worked very hard and had the stamina to get ahead. Yet she explained in her gentle philosophical way, *'If the rest of the world sees you as successful, but you do not feel it in your heart – success is a sham'.*

Be confident and have fun

Many, like **Jan Morgan**, identified confidence as the main asset. *'The secret is confidence in yourself. Success is how you feel about yourself and what you do with the opportunities that are there for you.'* For several women success was measured by the ability to resist social expectations and rules or what Jan Morgan called 'independence of spirit'. Jan is the founding Chair of Grosvenor International, a boutique London-based property consultancy, and Chair of the British section of the International Women's Forum, which has over four thousand women members world wide and is a powerful network of successful dynamic women who support each other.

An entrepreneur by nature and motivated by opportunity and optimism, Jan also spends much of her spare time on charity work. Nearly all the women I met were directly or indirectly engaged in some form of charitable work, often as a positive response to their own misfortunes, which they had turned round and used for the benefits of others. Jan had cancer at a relatively early age, but she has learnt great lessons from the experience. *'I woke up and realized that life was for living and I had better get on with trying to realize my dreams sooner rather than later, in case later never came. Cancer also taught me that when times are really tough there is no need to be afraid, things can only get better or one will die. Somehow this has enabled me to be incapable of real depression and adopt an optimistic and philosophical approach to life. I believe fun is much undervalued, as everyone, including a successful woman, is entitled to and needs some every day! Finally a great deal of success often comes down to being friendly, and treating people on a one-to-one basis.'* Jan explained that she aimed to be able to get up every morning unashamed of the day before.

I am, therefore I can

Of course, such confidence is hard to learn but sometimes just acting with confidence is enough to provoke a sense of real purpose. Widows champion **Margaret Owen** shared her secret. *'I think that many people who show great confidence in public are like me. Sometimes I fear I cannot do something and then suddenly I am overtaken by determination and I can.'*

Positive thinking

For **Meher Banaji**, Principal of a School for the Blind, confidence is also about training the brain to take a positive outlook. *'I am optimistic and never pessimistic. I believe things will happen if you think and work hard to make them happen.'*

Celebrity chef **Karen Anand** shared this view. *'Successful people never sit back and wait. They use the power of positive thinking which always triumphs. If you wish for good things hard enough, they will happen. You have to focus on what you want and then nothing can bring you down.'*

Karen Anand　　　　　　　　　　　Jo-Ann Nadler

'Even people that appear to be in positions of power or influence are not necessarily any cleverer or any better than the rest of us. Perhaps, they have been clear about what they wanted to do and have set themselves certain goals and have achieved those positions; very often through extremely hard work.'

Vanessa Hall-Smith

Vanessa Hall-Smith　　　　　　　　Zeba Kohli

Ruth Uglow　　　　　　　　　　　Patsy Robertson

Set your own goals

One of the interesting secrets of success was not to be over-ambitious but to set goals that were worth while, significant to one self and achievable. **Vanessa Hall-Smith**, Director of the British Institute in Florence, exploded the myth of success as being something that happens to people who are somehow better than us. *'It is important to recognize that even people that appear to be in positions of power or influence are not necessarily any cleverer or any better than the rest of us. Perhaps, they have been clear about what they wanted to do and have set themselves certain goals and have achieved those positions; very often through extremely hard work.'* An equally grounded view was given by the political biographer **Jo-Anne Nadler**. *'The majority of people who succeed are not the most brilliant, they are the ones who are just about good enough at their job, they are efficient, good at self-publicity and good at putting themselves at the right place at the right time.'*

Artist **Ruth Uglow** spoke great sense in her simple pronouncement that *'success comes from the happiness and confidence of work being well done'*. As women's campaigner **Parvin Ali** recognized, success comes from a sense of accomplishment but only when the achievements are meaningful. *'Success should be how a woman measures her own achievements. Has she been able to satisfy her needs and attain the goals she set herself?'* Chief Minister of Delhi **Sheila Dikshit** was in agreement with Parvin, *'to me success is the satisfaction that you have done what you thought you should have done'*.

The secret is to measure your own success and not follow society's conventions as the Chocolate Queen, **Zeba Kohli**, appreciated. *'Success is my feeling at this moment, a feeling of elation, a feeling of having achieved a couple of dreams and goals which I set for myself.'* For **Marian Rivman**, this ability to hold steadfastly to one's own goals is central to success. *'A woman, who has achieved what she herself wants to achieve as opposed to what the society tells her she ought to achieve, is successful. These women have a passion about what they want to do, realize that failures along the way are part of learning, are not afraid to get out of their comfort zone, and have innate personal integrity.'*

Rebel with a cause

As editor **Sarida Brown** told me, *'The people who succeed are the people who disregard the norms, so they have to rebel. They have to be slightly obsessed'.* Sarida works as a 'cultural creative' at the leading edge of 'soft revolutions', in arenas where consciousness is expanding, and people are sensing a greater depth to their potential and giving it expression. Her particular interest is in healing on all levels, physical, emotional and spiritual, and in giving expression both to the human ideals of our time and to the actual projects which are making these ideals a reality.

One unusual step she took in her 20s, having completed a history degree in England, was to be a car mechanic in San Francisco. Later she became one of the first wave of Europeans to train in acupuncture in the early 1970s, when 'energy medicine' was generally unknown. With the vision of opening this tool for self-empowerment and self-health for the whole community, in 1976 she organized the ground-breaking Health Festival of holistic therapies in Britain. Sarida recalls that: *'During this period there was a complete barrier between holistic and conventional biomedicine; biomedicine branded all alternative approaches (even diet for constipation!) as worse than useless'.* In 1987 Sarida founded and edited *Caduceus Journal*, to bridge all modes of healing: holistic and biomedical, traditional and modern, scientific, psychological and spiritual. Central to Sarida's work, through *Caduceus Journal*, her teaching, and organizing conferences, is the task of melting perceived identity barriers which obstruct the vision of our common humanity. Underlying all her work is the exploration of our true human nature as beings of body, mind, soul and spirit.

Pride in one's own heritage

For Chair of the Commonwealth Society **Patsy Robertson**, asserting her right to succeed as a black Jamaican woman meant refusing to play by the rules of racist societies. *'I never accepted racism, so it never had any effect on me. I always felt that I could do whatever I wanted to do.'* Patsy's distinguished work in the international public sphere in key positions in both the Commonwealth Secretariat and the United Nations has had a transforming impact on millions of lives throughout the world. Her distinguished life has been at the centre of world politics, where she has been able to play an instrumental role in social justice and struggle for equality. As she said: *'Knowledge of the history of my country and of my ancestors imbued in me a strong determination to oppose the use of power to deny any people their rights as human beings. I grew up knowing about the horrors of slavery and the hypocrisy which surrounded the entire abolition question and the century-old struggle of the freed slaves to carve out a living under the rampant racism of those days. This revulsion against racism was strengthened by my days at university in the US, before the end of segregation and the overt racism which characterized life in the "Land of the free and the home of the brave". It is this background which empowered me to support wholeheartedly the efforts of those, including the Commonwealth, working to end apartheid in Southern Africa, aptly described as "the modern face of slavery", by the then Commonwealth Secretary-General, Shridath Ramphal. This background still propels me to be involved in issues where power is used to diminish and deny the powerless their rights'.*

As Patsy says, *'you can't get anywhere in life unless you know who you are, have an idea of where you want to go and have the brains and daring to do it'.*

Nita Deerpalsing

Divya Mathur

'You're only successful when you never end the quest.'
Nita Deerpalsing

'through honesty and perseverance, you can achieve anything in this world. Success achieved any other way does not survive.'
Divya Mathur

Anu Aga

Sharon Choa

Wendy Luers

Shernaaz Engineer

Fidelity to your ideals

There was also a shared focus on the importance of how you achieve success. Human rights lawyer **Judith Chomsky's** definition of success as a 'kind of fidelity of your ideals' was echoed by others who insisted that methods were as important as results. **Shernaaz Engineer** spoke for many in her observation that: 'At the end of the day, success is meaningless if you have cheated, manipulated, clawed and mauled your way to the top'. **Divya Mathur** put a more positive spin on the same idea with her belief that 'through honesty and perseverance, you can achieve anything in this world. Success achieved any other way does not survive'.

Mauritian Member of Parliament **Nita Deerpalsing** offered the most daunting but also inspiring words on the subject, 'You're only successful when you never end the quest'. Thinking about the sad figures of the discarded celebrities, I could only agree with Nita and theatre director **Sanjna Kapoor** who explained, 'You think success and you are finished. I think you always have to have a challenge ahead of you and if you don't, then you are sunk'. All the same, I was relieved to hear **Anu Aga's** wise caution, 'I am a great believer that success at work should not take a toll on our life. Then success is a failure'.

Share your success

For many, success was not measured by the ability to improve one's own status alone but by the positive influence that could be shared with others. As Hong Kong-born conductor **Sharon Choa** explained: 'Success is making good use of your talents and sharing them with others'. For **Dorothy Dalton**, who works at the forefront of the charitable sector, 'Success is for people to think that the world is a tiny, tiny bit better because you had lived'.

Kate Parminter

'Women look at issues from a different perspective. ... Maybe that's one of the reasons that women in the peace movement are incredibly invigorating.'

Kate Parminter

Kirsten Rausing

'It's a fact. Women are stronger than men. Gutsy women don't have to play by the rules.'

Kirsten Rausing

Ann Jellicoe

'Women are receptive people – that is one of the most powerful weapons of a woman. It is like martial arts; there is an appearance of giving way but actually gaining what you want.'

Ann Jellicoe

Beverly Payeff-Masey

'Women's whole brain structure is different from men and this enables women to offer new insights. They produce more fertile solutions, and have the ability to see the complexity of the issues.'

Beverly Payeff-Masey

Serving and sharing

The lawyer **Shireen Irani** explained that the ultimate success was a place in heaven. There was a story of a woman who was having a conversation with God. She wanted to know the secrets of success. He took her to Hell where he showed her a room with a large table, in the middle of which was a large pot of stew. Sitting around the table were thin sickly people who were holding spoons with very long handles. Although they could reach the pot of stew and take a spoonful, they could not get the spoons back into their mouths because the handles were longer than their arms. They were miserable and hungry. God then took her to Heaven and showed her another large table with a pot of stew in the middle and the same long handled spoons. But here the people were nourished and laughing. The woman said *'I don't understand'* and God replied, *'It's simple, it just requires one skill. You have to learn to think of the other person. Here each person feeds the person across the table with their long spoon'.* Serving and sharing is the answer to real happiness.

Make friends

Many inspirational women were great networkers. As American PR consultant **Marian Rivman** explains, *'The key to networking is viewing people as elements. When you see them singly you have no clue what will happen. When you put them together think of hydrogen and oxygen. Together they are water, something that neither element could be alone. People are the same'.*

Wendy Luers, President of the Foundation for a Civil Society, has the gift of networking and making friends wherever she goes. In Czechoslovakia with her American Ambassador husband Bill, she used her extraordinary ability to bring people together. She invited writers, painters, intellectuals from America, to come and stay with them and make contacts with their Eastern European counterparts who were often dissidents and whose only opportunity to meet and exchange ideas was through Wendy's vision. *'Everybody ended up making friends.'*

Power and empowerment

How do women use their power? Campaigner and actress **Tamsin Larby** commented amusingly that *'power lies in my pelvic floor muscles'*. Many womanisers would agree! But there are other kinds of female power that are also intriguing.

There is no doubt that in the twentieth century, women like Maragret Thatcher, Indira Gandhi and Golda Meir, were celebrated as having made it against all odds. It was also undeniable that women were systematically denied power and had to grab it if they could. The small group of women who made it were strategic and worked with the system. They did not see their main role as questioning or breaking down the system. They did earn respect in a predominantly male world but had to sacrifice a great deal for that. They dressed in a male code, lowered their voices, and often sacrificed family life. Their public and private lives were given over to combating a masculine monopoly of power and privilege. When they accomplished what they set out to do, they felt that the power that they had wrestled from men made them powerful too but often at a cost to themselves and their loved ones.

The inspirational women I spoke with gave neither conventional nor conservative views on the subject of power. They saw power as interpersonal and its effects extending through all structures of human life. Many of their aims were not just about equality, but more radical and challenging of the status quo. Many got their strength from the grassroots; still others from having a balanced personal life and a supportive partner. Some saw themselves as powerful through their faith in God and in other people. Their power was not selfish but enabling.

Shevolution

Some had built their success by helping to open up the political arena for other women. Labour MP **Barbara Follett** used her energy and resources to bring the American idea of 'Emily's List' to England, to offer training and funds to aspiring Labour Party women in search of winnable Parliamentary seats.

Lesley Abdela's dedication and vision of a better-run world of politics started from her kitchen table when she lived at The Mill House, Burford, in Oxfordshire. The result of her thinking was the formation of a brand-new campaign and training organization titled The 300 Group, whose aim was to help get 300 women into the UK House of Commons, up from 19 female MPs at that time. As Lesley put it, *'Most of the women leaders I see around the world are in the informal sector – NGOs, consultancies, and community groups. By contrast, the majority part of the power, money and resources remains in the formal sector. Most senior positions in that parallel world, whether on the boards of corporations, in diplomatic services, or heads of military or politicians, are held by men. Added to this, around the many conflicts since the end of the Cold War more sinister circles are developing. The type of men who are included at the negotiating table after these conflicts, as I saw myself in Kosovo, Iraq and Afghanistan, are the warlords, mafia and men who see a chance to grab money on whichever side is most profitable. Women are equally scarce on this international side and the result is that their peacebuilding skills are absent, and the seeds are too often sown for future conflict. If you have a different paradigm, with women in large numbers at the top table, I believe peacebuilding would be far more effective for the simple reason that if women were at those important negotiation tables, their priorities and the majority of the population they would particularly represent would be different. That is an example of what I call "shevolution": a revolution for equal participation of men and women'.*

Magic circle

Numerous other women also wanted to connect with others and co-operate. They wanted to reclaim meaningful power, to change things for the better. Many were altruistic and had changed the ethos of the voluntary sector they now lead. They had started to insist that funds and practical help were directed to the poorest, who were inevitably women. They were confidently starting to pass their own ideals and beliefs on to those around them. The climate was now right for radical and creative change. A few, like the Chief Executive Officer of the Pearson Group, Dame **Marjorie Scardino**, seemed reticent to discuss the great economic power they wielded. Yet what was power if not the ability to impact on others' lives? Marjorie Scardino has power. She was able to change lives. I admired her because she used power wisely and courageously by confronting society's crippling prejudice while running the Pulitzer-winning newspaper, *The Georgia Gazette*, with her husband, Albert.

Another heroine, human rights advocate Baroness **Helena Kennedy**, pointed out that you can access power when you are outside the magical circle, *'because then you see with a clearer eye and you don't have to conform and please'.*

Knocked down but not out!

Often our instincts in life are to protect ourselves and especially our children from failures and set-backs. But, surprisingly, many of the exceptional people that I met had grown in self-confidence through being knocked down and coming back. The ability to accept and even embrace failure and disappointment was life-affirming. Those who have had to endure a level of public disappointment had often regarded this experience as strengthening. Once they have lived through the experience, fear of the situation no longer held them back from risking pathways that seemed unusual in society's eyes.

A blessing in disguise

Sooni Taraporevala, the Oscar-winning screen writer of *Salaam Bombay* and *Mississippi Masala*, only decided to concentrate on film when she faced rejection as a photographer. When the well-known photographer Raghubir Singh advised her to approach *National Geographic* magazine, she took along a hundred rolls of film but they did not want her work. Sooni withdrew from photography after this rejection, but luckily this gave her the clear time and space to write the script for the film that brought her great acclaim. *'I was very disappointed. I felt inadequate. I stopped photography for some time and that was when I actually got down to writing the script for* Salaam Bombay.' All the same Sooni returned to photography later and her compelling photographs have since been exhibited world-wide.

When the principled and courageous **Jackie Ballard** started her political career she was the star of the Liberal Councillors' Association, the power base of the Liberal Party. She won her seat as the Member of Parliament for Taunton in 1997 and went on to stand as the only woman for the leadership of the Liberal Democrats. Her political career was cut short when she was brought down by the hunting lobby who hounded her for her stance against foxhunting and Jackie lost her parliamentary seat. Most telling about this event was the treatment she received from the male hierarchy of her own party. On the night of the General Election they insisted on three recounts so that the Liberal Democrats would not be shown as having lost a seat during the television coverage. Jackie knew she had been rejected by the electorate and naturally wanted to go home and rest. Instead she was exposed to the harsh methods of party politics, as she had to wait all night for a result she already knew.

At the moment of disappointment, the powerful men had withdrawn their support and protected their political interests over hers. The experience gave Jackie the time to reassess her life and take the bold step of learning Persian and going to live in Iran, a life change she never regretted. After her year in the Middle East she was head-hunted for the top position at the Royal Society for the Prevention of Cruelty to Animals, becoming its much admired and respected Director-General.

Rekha Mody, founder of Divya Chaya Trust, had been made aware from a early age that, as a girl, it was her destiny to follow male authority. *'I had been denied higher education in a prestigious institution. It was frustrating as I had the resources and not the opportunity. I wanted to study law, but my father did not want a lawyer in his family.'* Despite this Rekha always resisted the conventional pathways set before her. *'I always wanted my own identity.'* She asserted this most openly when she was only seventeen. *'I decided to break my engagement with a rich man. It was the first critical moment. Making such a bold decision was a tough task, yet I had faith in myself.'* Later she married the industrialist Padam Mody and continued to transform obstacles into opportunities. *'My husband would not have me in his business so I had to create my own work, which has been a blessing in disguise.'* Her successful ventures in the world of art and publishing gave her resources to start her charitable work and help empower the vulnerable in Indian society.

Meeting hundreds of inspirational women was rewarding but the stories and faces that remain as a daily inspiration were those who had overcome serious physical and mental adversity. **Liz Jackson**, the founder and Managing Director of Great Guns Marketing, is extraordinary. With no advanced educational background, Liz launched her multi-million pound telemarketing company in the late 1990s with the modest but vital help of The Prince's Trust. This phenomenal success story is even more remarkable given the fact that within a year of starting the business Liz lost her sight as a result of the progressive eye disorder, retinitis pigmentosa. Her determination to start her own company was only fuelled by adversity. In a working environment that consistently underestimates the potential of workers with disabilities, she simply had to create a workplace that was challenging enough for her needs. As she told me, *'I crave responsibility. I like to have things I can do and drive forward and people I can lead and inspire. It's the thing that gets my heart thumping'.* Both Liz and her business have won numerous awards and accolades, including the 'Women Mean Business Award'. She is a beacon of strength for others. She lives by a simple commitment: *'I choose to look on the brighter side. I do not concentrate on the negatives, but on the positive things in my life and am thankful for the gifts that I have.'*

Liz Jackson

Dhun Adenwalla

'... when you suffer and are at the lowest of the low and feel you have a layer of skin too thin, it does give you a huge understanding of other people's vulnerability.'

Jane Grant

Jane Grant

Gwyneth Lewis

Rhona MacDonald

Dinah Radtke

Sans frontières

The realization that her eldest daughter, Dinaz, had been born deaf was an experience that turned **Dhun Adenwalla's** life around. *'Our reactions were expectedly confused and painful, as we knew nothing about deafness. However, there was one thing we were absolutely sure about – we wanted Dinaz to be a happy well-adjusted child, no matter what problems we may have to face with regard to her development.'* At the time Dhun was a librarian for the British Council but she immediately decided to focus on Dinaz's needs and took a place on the first postgraduate course for educators of the deaf at the EAR Centre in Mumbai. After qualifying, Dhun returned to Kolkata, where her husband was working, to find that the only school for the deaf did not admit children under the age of eight years; Dinaz was just three. *'There was only one course open to us – to start a school for deaf children ourselves!'* The Oral School for Deaf Children was started in August 1964. When it began there were only two children, but within weeks the numbers increased to twenty lively children between the ages of three and nine years. *'The aim of the school is to provide a stimulating learning environment, to help deaf children acquire language through modes of communication best suited to their needs, involving the use of amplified sound, speech reading, sign language, reading, writing, finger spelling, mime and drama. The ultimate aim is to preserve and build up the resources of normalcy which have not been impaired by deafness.'* Indeed, her daughter Dinaz is living proof of this claim; she has a Masters Degree in Education and is Director of the Rhode Island School for the Deaf in the USA.

This same direct and practical outlook on life is shared by **Rhona MacDonald**, a doctor with Médecins Sans Frontières who, like Liz and Dhun, is always looking for ways to inspire and lead other people towards positive change, despite her own disability. Rhona has dedicated her life to ease the pain others suffer, although in constant pain herself. She suffered the loss of her fingers but is still able to use her medical skills. Rhona occupies every minute of her precious life to bring health and dignity to people around the world. She is the living testimony to the triumph of will and the love of her profession over adversity.

The gift of transcendence

Gwyneth Lewis, the renowned national poet of Wales, brought her own struggle to overcome depression into public circulation with her candid book *Singing in the Rain: A Cheerful Book about Depression*. Her memoir of over a year of catatonic depression details mental pain in a way that is vivid, uplifting, remarkably lacking in self-indulgence and humorous. It details the harrowing but astonishing lessons that depression can teach. *'Depression's gifts are dark but very precious… After months of being ill and of thinking of my depression as a sign of utter failure on my part, it suddenly occurred to me that the opposite was true. My illness was, in fact, a sign of my success. My body and mind had delivered me a breathing space.'* All the same, as Gwyneth warns *'Recovery can be heavy on the credit card. I went into town on my own "just for a look". The only thing I needed was a pint of milk. I came home four hours later with a furry hat and a sparkling black evening dress split to the hip. Of course, I forgot the milk'.* Her capacity to transform the dark side of life into something illuminating is also a feature of her poetry, a collection of beautiful narratives, coy rhymes and simplicity. Tackling themes like the Welsh language, life in Cardiff and an alcoholic past, her verse is astoundingly accessible and, at times, breathtaking.

Dr **Jane Grant**, former Director of the National Alliance of Women's Organizations, also suffered depression and felt that, despite its extreme negative effects, in many ways it brought her the rare gifts of humility and a huge empathy for others' sufferings. *'When one is young and arrogant, you think everybody with those sorts of problems are sort of hopeless. But when you suffer and are at the lowest of the low and feel you have a layer of skin too thin, it does give you a huge understanding of other people's vulnerability.'*

For **Dinah Radtke**, born in Germany just after the war with spinal muscular atrophy, the process of accepting her disability was far more prolonged and painful because of others' attitudes towards her. As a young child her parents did not send Dinah to secondary school because both her mother and her father, a neurosurgeon, felt that it was not worthwhile. The consequences for Dinah were grim. *'As an adolescent I was very isolated and unhappy as I had no friends and nothing to do. We lived on the first floor of an apartment house. I couldn't leave the house very often as I had to crawl up and down the stairs myself, a fact of which I was very much ashamed. I only had a wheelchair at the age of fourteen.'* However, when she was eighteen, secondary school was introduced on television in Germany and Dinah was able to persuade her father to allow her to finish her studies. She later went to a boarding school to learn languages and managed to live independently as an interpreter. Although Dinah's life had been bleak, she was not at all self-pitying. *'All these restrictions and limitations during my childhood and adolescence have given me the power to fight and find my way as a woman with a disability.'* More than finding her own way, Dinah's involvement in the disability movement as the Vice-Chair of Disabled People International, and Chair of the Women's Committee, has empowered many other disabled people and brought forward a whole range of issues such as sexual violence against disabled people, bioethics, euthanasia, and professional training and work. As she says with her usual vitality and determination: *'There is still a lot to fight for, and for us to change. We can do it because we are powerful, we have courage and we are beautiful!'* Dinah's story just goes to prove that people really are more disabled by others' attitudes towards them than by their own body's limitations.

Beyond colour-coding

It is well known that Europe exported the attitudes of white supremacy as part of its centuries-long colonial enterprise and that this racial arrogance and blindness lived on most cruelly and visibly in the apartheid system. What is often not spoken about is the much more insidious and everyday racism that colonialism promoted around the world, that continues to divide people and carry mutual distrust and hostility into present day communities. Many women I met had experienced overt and subtle forms of racism that sought to block their paths.

Angela King, former Deputy Secretary-General of the UN, explained how racism lives on in her post-colonial homeland of Jamaica. The island's most powerful colonial legacy is the preoccupation with different body shades and shapes that continues to create internal hierarchies and divisions. *'There was Jamaica white and a whole mix of intermingling colours. You could also have somebody who was quite dark but had straight hair who would consider themselves better than somebody who was two shades fairer but who had curly hair. It went according to your nose, your hair, your face, your skin. Even in our boarding school the dormitories were colour-coded!'*

It is usually a personal experience that triggers a wish to change the way we behave towards others.

I will never forget a particular scene I witnessed when young that provoked my strong desire to campaign against all forms of discrimination. I was in a Greyhound bus with my grandmother, mother and Aunty Map. We were travelling round the Southern States of America in the 1950s. I still remember the shock at seeing black people, openly called 'niggers', having to drink from a different fountain, use a different toilet, and to sit at the back of the bus. I remember the unconscious repulsion I felt at seeing such repressed hatred to those with darker skins. I felt their hurt and have spent much of my adult life trying to find a way of representing and righting the profound injustices that racism has embedded.

Human rights lawyer **Maja Daruwala** also recalled a particular incident that triggered her repulsion to racism and apartheid when her family's ship to London docked for a day at Cape Town, South Africa. Her eminent father, India's first Field Marshal, Sam Manekshaw, refused to go ashore but Maja, her sister and mother were curious. *'Everything was fine until the shopping break. There was this gleaming shop with an escalator which I had never ever seen before and glass doors at the entrance. Near the handle it said "only whites". My sister and mother went in nevertheless. They are very fair and Italian looking. I sat on a bench outside looking at the people and thinking they could see I was not white. My arms and legs looked berry brown and I kept thinking "This is why I can't go in". My sister and mother must have come out in a few minutes but the interlude had a huge effect on me. It made me realize my worth, the value of equality and the meaning of discrimination. I told my father about it that night. He said that these people would pay a terrible price for their regime and that I was entirely right in liking myself and my colour.'*

Connie Jackson, a financial expert, was also fortunate to have both enlightened parents and a teacher to inspire her against the grain of racist wrongs. Her parents experienced segregated schooling in the Deep South of America and recognized that their education was impoverished by this. *'The books were twenty years old because the white schools would get them first and they would discard the old books to the black schools.'* After they married, Connie's parents moved north to Chicago where she went to an integrated school, but the expectations of black students were still low and even within the black community she was made to feel as though she was *'trying to be white'* because she was smart and enjoyed reading. One teacher in particular made a difference. *'Mrs Harrison who was six foot tall and had graduated as the only black woman out of a class of six thousand, with the third highest grade in applied mathematics, wound up teaching little kids. Had she been a six*

Julia Neuberger

Connie Jackson

'As a black woman, no matter how old you are and how much you have done, you have to get up every morning and you have to do it yourself and you have to prove it again and again.'

Diane Abbott

Diane Abbott

Maja Daruwala

Shami Chakrabarti

Françoise Vergès

foot tall white woman she would probably have been in NASA.' The institutionalized racism of America had undervalued Mrs Harrison but she did not overlook Connie and was able to pass her love of learning across the generations without bitterness. *'She really made me love maths and love being smart.'* Connie beautifully defined Mrs Harrison's triumph, *'You are great when you are not in any way overcome by your circumstances but rather are fuelled by them'.* Without knowing it Connie had, of course, defined her own greatness as well.

While some felt that they had managed to overcome the barriers of racism, for others the daily realities of living in a racist society were always visible and tangible. I understood all too clearly when pioneering parliamentarian **Diane Abbott** explained, *'As a black woman, no matter how old you are and how much you have done, you have to get up every morning and you have to do it yourself and you have to prove it again and again'.*

Like all forms of discrimination, racism is always reinventing its targets. In the West, the most potent targets for hate speech are now Muslims and asylum-seekers. As a Muslim woman **Rifat Wahhab**, who was born in Bangladesh, came as a young girl to Britain where she witnessed and experienced open discrimination. *'England is being driven by an unspoken dictum which says that top positions can only be filled by people who look a certain way, behave in a certain way.'*

Like **Diane Abbott** she has turned her own experience of feeling disempowered towards the empowerment of others. *'My schooling years in England were very difficult. Being racially harassed and even attacked and called a Paki, has taken its toll, the experience never leaves you. My reaction has been to make sure it does not repeat itself in my life and in the lives of others. I have participated in campaigns against injustice all my life. I feel proud that Asians are doing so well wherever they go. Everyone is enriched by their contributions.'*

Voices against intolerance

One of the most significant campaigns against injustice in the twenty-first century will centre on the rights of asylum seekers. **Shami Chakrabarti**, Director of the human rights organization Liberty, felt that British government policies contributed to a dehumanization of asylum seekers, which could not always be blamed on the tabloid press. Baroness Rabbi **Julia Neuberger** also supported this view: *'The tone of present political debate in Britain is disgraceful – "bogus asylum seeker" is a term of abuse. You may come from the most terrible circumstances and your claim may be turned down, but that does not mean you are bogus, it doesn't necessarily mean that it isn't true'.* Julia's passion for this subject is rooted in the fact that her mother was a refugee who came to England as a domestic servant in the 1930s to escape Nazi Germany. *'With all the rows that there are now about refugees, asylum seekers and economic migrants, people need to distinguish what actually motivates people, why people want to come to this country. My mother wanted to come to this country because she was terrified for her life in Germany.'*

Maeve Sherlock, the Director of the Refugee Council, explained how important it was to put an end to the centuries-long cycle of racism and victimization that poisons people's hearts and limits their human capacity for sharing neighbourhoods, and nations. Although each individual stand against racism is a valuable act, she also understood that discriminatory attitudes were mimicked by children and strong guidance needed to be given to the young if we are to end the West's most damaging inheritance. *'It seems to go unmentioned that young children can abuse vulnerable asylum seekers and call them "rubbish". It often goes unchallenged. We need a leadership that speaks out against intolerance.'*

A world shaped by slaves

Françoise Vergès was born into a family of leaders that challenged intolerance. She grew up in Réunion Island, a former French colony in the Indian Ocean, now a French overseas department. She learned early to understand and fight against the consequences of racism and colonialism as her family were involved in these struggles: her paternal grandfather, an important advocate for anti-colonialism, her father a political leader in Réunion and her mother a feminist.

As a child, Françoise witnessed the brutality and violence of the remnants of colonialism and as an adult she has devoted her career to recovering the memories and voices of resistance, including that of the poet and anti-colonial leader Aimé Césaire. *'I want us to remember colonial slavery. First, because it was a crime against humanity and we must honour the memories of those who were deported, exiled, separated from everything they knew, family, friends, language, rituals... Second, because the world in which we live is a world shaped by the slaves. Their contributions in music, philosophy, the law, food, poetry, art are inestimable. Brazil, the United States, the Caribbean, Europe, the Indian Ocean, would not be what they are today without the slaves' contribution. I refuse the marginalization of this contribution. We will no longer accept to be kept at the backdoor; we will enter the house of humanity through the front door.'*

Aban Marker Kabraji

'I always find challenging people a pleasure to work with ... It's like running a stable of high spirited stallions; you have to be able to give them the space, a lot of indulgence, careful handling, and then watch them win. So much of my work is nurturing this kind of high maintenance leadership.'

Aban Marker Kabraji

Rennie Fritchie

'... listen to the people who don't want the change. If you listen and try to understand you usually end up with better changes.'

Rennie Fritchie

Elaine Attias

'The need to co-operate, not simply to compete, is going to be essential for a modern successful life.'

Elaine Attias

Women leaders

For many, the most important qualities of leadership are those of being inclusive, empowering others, and being a source of continuous inspiration. When leaders are an inspiration, everyone is motivated.

Aban Marker Kabraji is a modern global leader in the field of conservation – incisive, clear-thinking and proactive. She understands how to motivate the unconventional leaders of tomorrow. *'I look for leaders and potential leaders; usually these are the rebels, who are intellectually challenging, and difficult. I always find challenging people a pleasure to work with, but I have recognized over the years that the majority find such people very difficult and in many cases they end up being disaffected and marginalized. It is important to help tomorrows leaders keep the fire in their belly and still be able to channel it into an organization and productive work. It's like running a stable of high spirited stallions; you have to be able to give them the space, a lot of indulgence, careful handling, and then watch them win. So much of my work is nurturing this kind of high maintenance leadership. Leadership works on two levels; the part which can be taught or trained involves an ability to set goals, bringing teams along with you, taking responsibility, leading by example. The other quality, which has to do with real pioneering vision, has to come from within. It can be identified, it can be nurtured, but it cannot be taught.'*

Baroness **Rennie Fritchie,** former Commissioner for Public Appointments and consultant on strategic management, had a very well-measured three-part solution to the question of contemporary leadership. *'The first is to surround the goal, come at it from different angles. The second is to be steadfastly determined and implacable; that is very hard for people to deal with! The third is to listen to the people who don't want the change. If you listen and try to understand you usually end up with better changes.'*

The Dean of Leicester Cathedral and a leading woman in the Church of England, **Vivienne Faull**, saw one of her roles as working with the diverse local community, not just in terms of justice and opportunity, but celebration, peace and right relationships. She regarded leadership as a privilege and not a power and understood the crucial link between power and empowering. She uses her position to work in partnership with other faiths and to engage them in creative inter-faith dialogue. *'I think we need people from every faith and community who know their own faith but know that there is a bigger picture too. Working together in partnership can help transform a whole culture. At the moment British society is still fearful of differences and those who approach life from an unfamiliar angle. They find it an enormous threat despite the fact that throughout history, thousands of people of difference have arrived on this island and transformed the way we live for the better. We seem to forget this lesson from one generation to another. As a faith community leader, my responsibility to the next generation is to keep listening, and keep talking to all sorts of people.'*

Nurturing power

Arguably, the day of the charismatic masculine leader is over. It is the feminine qualities of leadership that are now in demand. Alongside the claim that women should become leaders because they are equal to men, there is a mounting case that women make good leaders precisely because they are different in attitude and behaviour to men. As film producer **Elaine Attias** explained *'Many men are beginning to realize that women's intuitive and empathetic abilities are highly useful to leadership in this new age. Women have skills which they have learnt from childhood. Their nurturing qualities are developed very early. If a woman doesn't nurture and understand her baby, her child is not going to survive. The ability to help other people is going to be increasingly in demand. The need to co-operate, not simply to compete, is going to be essential for a modern successful life'.*

Power house

Her Excellency **Maleeha Lodhi** believes the main indicator of success is to be of value to society. She can correctly be called a woman of substance. She has notched up so many firsts and been the beautiful face of Pakistan in every world arena, from heading the Pakistani embassy in Washington DC to sitting on the United Nations Advisory Board on Disarmament Affairs, to editing *The News*, Pakistan's leading English daily, to being a Professor of Political Science. She has strength of character, and strength of purpose. She is a powerhouse. Maleeha added to Elaine's argument with her view of women's particular strengths for leadership. *'I think women are much more flexible, adaptable, and less rigid than men. We find it much easier to move between cultures, between continents, between classes, because we have multiple roles. For us multitasking is the easiest thing in the world.'*

Feminine power

In her work with SEED, the training programme and network for women entrepreneurs, author and PR guru **Lynne Franks** believes *'that by empowering women and unleashing the feminine energy they possess, we can lift many out of economic as well as societal oppression. Wherever we have conducted our courses around the world — from the poor townships of South Africa, to the war-torn villages in Bosnia, to the localities in the United Kingdom — we have given hope, along with real solutions, to a vast number of women'*. More than just stressing the sense of possibility and the potential for new forms of feminine power that women can facilitate for each other, Lynne puts emphasis on the particular kind of qualities that these working styles can develop. *'I believe that there is a new way of working and living that is based on values and ethics. The world has an urgent need for these feminine principles: connection, nurturing, compassion, communicating and, most importantly, love.'*

Maleeha Lodhi

'I think women are much more flexible, adaptable, and less rigid than men. We find it much easier to move between cultures, continents, classes, because we have multiple roles. For women multi-tasking is the easiest thing in the world.'

Maleeha Lodhi

Lynne Franks

'The world has an urgent need for feminine principles: connection, nurturing, compassion, communicating and, most importantly, love.'

Lynne Franks

'Soft power is the way forward.'

Claire Bertschinger

Claire Bertschinger

Soft power

Claire Bertschinger was confident in her prediction that *'The twenty-first century is of and for women. Soft power is the way forward'.*

Qualities which mark out such soft power are a willingness to listen and adapt as necessary, a creative and open approach to situations and a strong sense of vision. For the Reverend **Miranda Macpherson**, *'a good leader needs to be doing everything possible to stay true to the vision and to remain open to new ways in which that vision can be implemented and deepened'.*

This belief, that women have particular qualities to offer that can transform both huge global inequalities, as well as create a balance between work and family, and masculine and feminine styles of being, is a very alluring idea and one advocated by Miranda. She believed that women now had the confidence to follow a new style of feminine behaviour that had been down-graded historically. *'The women's movement in the late sixties and early seventies had to be quite masculine; they had to break through and be heard but there is a new wave coming that is about bringing in other feminine qualities that are very much about grace and love in an overt sense. Not just hidden away in homes, not just in traditional roles. Those qualities are now being valued and utilized in absolutely every department of life: politics, medicine, education, and the challenge for men is to embrace those qualities.'*

Miranda was eager to stress that feminine power was not weak, although it takes a less oppressive and confrontational form. *'The highest attributes of the feminine are an absolute clarity that is not harsh. There is a sword-like quality about it. It is strong but it is graceful. It isn't just about beauty. I define grace as the direct experience of love. So if you think of a really evolved woman, of a really evolved feminine nature, it is just pure love coming off them. Those feminine qualities exist both in men and in women, but I think that if you are a female then you are majoring in those qualities. The world has been a bit too devoid of those qualities, but there is re-emergence of the feminine soul. It isn't just about women; but women need to bring it forward.'*

Schwestern machen es füreinander
Сёстры работают ради друг друга
siskot pitävät yhtä
姐妹一条心

sisters are doing it for each other

Parvin Ali

'You feel right when you have achieved your dream. You get a wonderful thrill when something happens successfully … When you come together with your destiny and recognize it as such, you feel that same thrill.'

Parvin Ali

Shusha Guppy

'The heart desires to endure.'

Shusha Guppy

Gillian Beer

'I hope I will be remembered with affection for a while.'

Gillian Beer

SISTERS ARE DOING IT FOR EACH OTHER

Coming together with destiny

'You feel right when you have achieved your dream. You get a wonderful thrill when something happens successfully. It is not unlike the coming together of a man and a woman having an orgasm. Orgasms are never just physical. It is being able to focus mentally and spiritually on what you are doing and enjoying it. Then you achieve that orgasmic sensation – peace. When you come together with your destiny and recognize it as such, you feel that same thrill.'

How could I disagree with **Parvin Ali**, founder of the Fatima Women's Network? I was slowly learning that my womanising days were numbered, as sisters were not only doing it for themselves but, more importantly, for each other. Where did this leave me, a serial womaniser? What was it all about and what had all these extraordinary women from all over the world taught me?

My life had been transformed by the women I met. I hardly begin or end a conversation without remembering a story or a face that has inspired me. I wanted the legacy of the women to live on but wasn't sure whether a book was enough. The beautiful Iranian singer and author **Shusha Guppy** enlightened me. *'The heart desires to endure'* she whispered in French. This was what it was all about. We believed our legacies were our children, our books, our monuments, our great fortunes we have amassed and given away. But at the end of it all, the love people have in their hearts and others' memories of us are the only things that really endure.

Professor Dame **Gillian Beer** mused on this subject. *'I don't think you can hope to be remembered personally for a very long time. Possibly your children and grandchildren will remember you for a while, and it will be dispersed, and that's all right. There will be a sense of all the things you've done and all the people you've been in contact with, but you can't measure it. I love it when people say "Oh I remember your mother" and I hope I will be remembered with affection for a while.'*

Seeds of success

I must confess I cannot offer the perfect answer to what is an inspirational woman, as every woman I met was unique. Yet there were some characteristics they shared with each other. They had nobility of spirit, integrity, discernment, morality, manners and endurance, all qualities which seem old-fashioned today and yet are timeless. They energized me, entertained me and finally exhausted me with their intuitive understanding of the *Zeitgeist* and its demands for adaptability, brilliance, daring and vitality. They taught me that no knowledge is ever wasted, that kindness is the most precious gift and life is to be lived magnanimously.

Thinking back through my odyssey, there were thirteen attributes that shone most clearly.

Strong sense of self

A strong sense of self has always drawn me; a self confidence, charisma and authentic knowledge that you are the right person to do the job.

War correspondent and NDTV anchor woman **Barkha Dutt** is a household name in India, although still in her thirties. The devoted millions who regularly watch her present *We, the People* and *Sixty Minutes* know that when she delivers the news they will understand the human dimension of political conflicts. Her famous coverage of the Kargil War sensitized the viewers to Kashmir politics. Genuinely concerned with the plights of others, Barkha also has an amazing awareness of her own strengths which is focused on maximizing her opportunities. It was her extraordinary ingenuity when she concealed herself in a catering trolley in order to gain access to a hijacked plane and report on the event, that marked her out as one of the world's most self-assured, dynamic and popular television journalists.

Samaritan generosity

Throughout my life I have loved big-hearted people who had a 'Samaritan generosity'. Those great souls who were kind, with no anticipation of reward and had an innate sense of doing the right thing, which made a difference in the world. What seemed to matter most wasn't so much their individual belief systems, be it religious or philosophical, but how they behaved towards others, their generosity of spirit. They were conscious to extend their benevolence beyond their own community to the entire world. They were not parochial. Like the generosity of the original 'Samaritan', they gave to those not of their own group. They were global in their giving and outlook.

Claire Bertschinger, heroine and the inspiration for Live Aid, had helped to transform the lives of millions by her selfless gift of nursing care. While in Ethiopia, four months before the BBC crew arrived to sensitize the world to the horrors of the famine, she took an anaemic baby to hospital for a blood transfusion. *'They had no blood so I gave him one unit of mine and I was able to say "Today I have done something".'*

Sense of social justice

A commitment to something greater than oneself has always been compelling to me. In today's world, still too few people believe they can make a difference, but great women know that they have to make a difference. Many of the women spoke to me about their wish to be part of a 'collective noble endeavour' and their need to right history's cruel wrongs.

Barbara Stocking, Director of Oxfam, is one of the most respected and admired international voices working to alleviate poverty and suffering. She has dedicated her life to making sure that every human being deserves the right to be 'secure, healthy, skilled, safe, heard, and equal'. Although a leading woman in the international voluntary sector, Barbara never

Barkha Dutt

Claire Bertschinger

Barbara Stocking

Marjorie Scardino

'They had no blood so I gave him one unit of mine and I was able to say "Today I have done something".'

Claire Bertschinger

shies away from hands-on help and direct action to help others. As well as meetings with world politicians and directing policy initiatives she has dug latrines in refugee camps supported by Oxfam. Social Justice is action and not just kind wishes.

Success through failure

Every woman admitted to disappointments and mistakes but they saw these as opportunities to learn, rather than failures. They were not held back by the fear of failure, mockery, losing face, or disappointing others. They knew mistakes were lessons in the making.

Dame **Marjorie Scardino**, the first woman to head a top 100 FTSE company in the London Stock Exchange, and described by *Forbes* magazine as one of the most powerful women in the world, understood this. She and her husband, Albert, founded the *Georgia Gazette*, which went on to win the Pulitzer Prize for the paper's campaigning journalism. Yet circumstances had it that the paper folded. When Marjorie went for an interview in New York for head of *The Economist*, she was challenged as to how she could run such as prestigious paper, having failed in her last venture. She had the honesty and courage to admit that she had made mistakes but she had learnt by them. Marjorie not only took the job with *The Economist*, but went on to successfully run the whole media conglomerate that includes Pearson Education, the Financial Times Group and the Penguin Group. Few would dispute that Marjorie has carved her name into our shared history.

Angela Lennox

Dadi Janki

'I have given up my life to do this, I am driven to do it, I don't have a life … many women would not want to do what I do.'

Angela Lennox

Lila Poonawalla

Shahnaz Husain

Carole Stone

Daphne Minihane

Sunday always

I am an obsessive hard worker and laziness is not on my agenda. The women I met worked hard and played hard. They did not take their positions or success for granted and were never completely satisfied with their accomplishments.

'I have given up my life to do this, I am driven to do it, I don't have a life … many women would not want to do what I do' was how Dr **Angela Lennox** described her struggles to tackle the disadvantages and inequalities of health and social care. I completely understood. Many believed that they had to work twice as hard as men and be twice as good to succeed, because that was the way of the world. **Shahnaz Husain**, admitted she worked every Sunday to build her empire and one should *'Never say die!'* **Lila Poonawalla's** life at the forefront of the engineering world, and through her Foundation – that has transformed the lives of hundreds of young aspiring women graduates – was underpinned by hard work. They were three magnificent women who never stopped, as life's potential was there to be harnessed for themselves and others.

Sharing their success

Those who were really successful were not scared of sharing their success, recognizing that the wider the circle becomes the more lives were touched. They empowered others by sharing their contacts, passing on opportunities and giving honest and practical advice. They understood that success was a chain reaction and that a kindness shared would be returned in kind.

The success of broadcaster and author of *Networking: the Art of Making Friends*, **Carole Stone**, lies in her big-hearted kindness. Carole is not jealous or protective of her friends. She thrives on seeing her network grow and watching her extraordinary number of friends become even more successful. Her weekly soirées and annual Christmas Party are the 'talk of the town.' Carole is not just the undisputed Queen of Networking but also the Queen of Hearts.

Spiritually curious

If you are looking for your heartbeat to quicken and for women who can take your breath away, those who had experienced enlightenment and were spiritually curious fitted the bill. They are explorers who were looking for new ways to experience God and 'the other'.

Amma, the hugging saint, held me in her arms and an electric shock went through me. I meditated with **Dadi Janki**, head of the Brahma Kumaris World Spiritual University and was awakened to my own goodness. For days I read the Bible every morning with **Sister Cecily**. I learnt that the answers to a good life are there if you look for them. I stayed in the Himalayan foothills with **Sadhvi Bhagwati Saraswati**, who has taken *sanyas diksha* (vows of renunciation), and learnt the art of breathing. I was spiritually aroused. I learnt that life is not measured by the breaths we take but by the moments that take our breath away.

Sensitive good manners

I just love courtesy and charm: qualities that are now considered out of fashion. **Daphne Minihane**, who was chosen by the people of Jersey to have her portrait painted for the National Jersey Museum, was a modern-day heroine; she had the sensitive good manners that I craved to find. I had heard about all her charitable works with the homeless, destitute and elderly but it was her kindness in preparing a buffet lunch that first struck me. She knew I had a tight schedule and she did everything in the most gracious way to make life easy for me. Thoughtfulness and generosity are never forgotten; in recognition of her services to the community and the Catholic Church Daphne has just been created, by Pope Benedict XVI, a Dame of the Order of St Gregory the Great – one of the Catholic Church's highest honours and rarely awarded to a woman.

Sense of humour

I adore politically incorrect people, but their humour must be gentle and not vicious.

There is a lovely story that the wonderful Reverend **Rosemary Perry** told me. 'A Hindu shopkeeper, knowing that it is important to die with the name of God on your lips in order to go to heaven, named his four sons after the Hindu gods, Ganesha, Krishna, Shiva and Rama. He knew he would be bound to call for them at the end. When his time to die was upon him he called for his sons, "Ganesha! Krishna! Shiva! Rama!" The four sons assembled round their father's bed. With his very last dying breath the shopkeeper looked round his bed and gasped in anxiety, "But who's looking after the shop?"'

Sweetness of being

In an age when more and more people are well-educated and well-resourced, often what most strikes one is not a person's qualifications or their achievements but a 'sweetness of being'. So often, one is asked 'What makes a great woman?' It is a mixture of qualities but just as, without sugar, yeast cannot make bread rise, so, without sweetness, greatness can never be magical.

Three women **Pheroza Godrej**, **Shakira Caine** and **Arnaz Marker,** possessed no pomposity and took pleasure in making others feel good about themselves. They exuded a special charm and beauty, 'a sweetness of being'.

Pheroza Godrej

Arnaz Marker

Shakira Caine

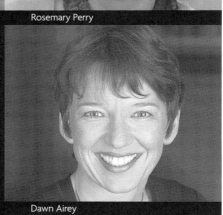
Rosemary Perry

Meera Gandhi

Dawn Airey

Mother

Shattered womaniser

Special

I have always admired those who know they are special without being overpowered by their own ego. From an early age, many women admitted to feeling different, knowing they were destined to do something important. **Meera Gandhi**, goodwill ambassador to the UN, remarked that many people *'see life as a dress rehearsal, instead of the opening night'*. The women I met weren't understudies, they weren't the chorus line. They were the stars who knew every night was the opening night.

Dawn Airey, managing director of BSKYB TV was one of those sparkling stars. She had the confidence to laugh about failing her eleven plus school exams as she hadn't been *'taught to do quizzes'*. This had not dented her confidence. She explained that she had seized every opportunity and always believed that anything was possible. She now has 400 channels at her command and is undoubtedly a star in the SKY. Her vitality was captivating. Sometimes one cannot explain a person's charisma; all one can say is they are 'special', maybe even 'very special'.

The final confession

I confided in my darling mother that I had learnt so much from all the women and I hoped I had given something back in return. But the time was now right for me to press the pause button, if only for a short while. Besides, womanising had become an exhausting business. I started to imagine that there was a woman around every corner waiting for me, and I would not be able to resist the temptation of meeting her. I had to learn to turn a blind eye and let them walk on by. I gave mother my mobile phone, she confiscated my little black book, and I planned my escape far from the madding crowd. Mother thought my retreat would be short-lived. Maybe just a weekend before being summoned to another adventure. As ever, Mother had the last word. *'Sweetheart'* she laughed *'Don't ever think it's a man's world'*.

Un esemble d'étoiles
سیتاروں کا جھرمٹ
La galaxia de estrellas
d'étoiles Un esemble d'étoiles
سیتاروں کا جھرمٹ
La galaxia de estrellas
d'étoiles Un esemble d'étoiles
سیتاروں کا جھرمٹ
La galaxia de estrellas
d'étoiles Un esemble d'étoiles
سیتاروں کا جھرمٹ
La galaxia de estrellas
d'étoiles Un esemble d'étoiles
سیتاروں کا جھرمٹ
La galaxia de estrellas
d'étoiles Un esemble d'étoiles
سیتاروں کا جھرمٹ
La galaxia de estrellas

A galaxy of stars

Aban Marker Kabraji
(Regional Director, World Conservation Union, Asia)
162, 165, 333, **334**, **372**, 373

Anando Heffley
(Author; Life Trainer)
190, **208**, 210, **288**, 291

Antonia Byatt
(Director, The Women's Library)
16, 18, 53

Aliki Roussin
(Photo-journalist; holder of the Royal TV Award for International Journalism)
249, **250**, **326**, 327

The late Angela King
(Former Deputy Secretary-General, UN)
278, 281, 366

Anu Aga
(CEO Thermax Industries; Chair, Western Region CII)
58, 59, 173, 195, **230**, 231, **352**, 353

Alison Donnell
(Academic, Writer and Researcher)
212, 215, **326**, 328

Angela Lennox
(Director, Community Health Care Studies, University of Leicester)
162, 165, **194**, 195, 265, **386**, 387

Arnaz Marker
(Pres. All Pakistani Women's Assoc. N. America)
102, 161, 389, **390**

Alpana Kirloskar
(Architect)
50, 51

Angela Morris
(Lecturer in Political History)
162, 166

Ashminder Kaur Dhadialla
(Founder, Sikh Scholarship Foundation) 131, **132**, 133, 207, **232**, 233

Amisha Patel
(Bollywood Actress)
97, **168**, 170

Anna-Liisa Fazer
(Finnish linguist)
84, **86**, 195

Audrey Kitagawa
(Advisor, UN Secretary-General for Children in Armed Conflict; Divine Mother)
208, 209, **224**, 225, 227

Amma
(The Hugging Saint; recipient of Gandhi-King Award)
224, 225, 241, **388**

Ann Jellicoe
(Theatre Director and originator of community plays)
288, 290, **334**, 335, **354**

Bachi Karkaria
(*National Metro* Editor; Board member, World Editors Forum)
308, **310**

Ana Lucia
(International Model; founding Director, Little Warriors Charity)
101, 139, **140**, 250, 253, 332

Anne Perchard
(President, World Jersey Cattle Bureau);
98, 99, **112**, 114, 135, **136**, 327

Bam Björling
(Founder President, Kvinnoforum, Swedish Women's Charity)
330, 331

A GALAXY OF STARS

Bani Dugal
(Dir. UN Office for Advancement of Women; Principal Rep. of Baha'i Community to the UN) **168**, 171

Carole Stone
(Author, Broadcaster and former BBC Producer)
40, 42, 167, 257, 274, **386**, 387

Coomi Kapoor
(Former President, Indian Women's Press Corps; Contrib. Editor *Indian Express*;) **22**, 24, 116, **118**, 160, 277, **310**, 311

Barbara Follett
(Labour MP for Stevenage)
82, 83, **154**, 160, 357, **358**

Caroline Casey
(Founder, Aisling Foundation; a 'Mahout')
145, **146**

Dadi Janki
(Joint Head, Brahma Kumaris World Spiritual University)
222, **224**, 226, 241, **386**, 388

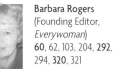
Barbara Rogers
(Founding Editor, *Everywoman*)
60, 62, 103, 204, **292**, 294, **320**, 321

Christina Lamb
(*Sunday Times* Foreign Correspondent; award-winning War Journalist)
127, **132**, 134, 135, **278**, 279, **310**, 312

Dana Gillespie
(International Blues Singer, Actress)
66, 67, 192, 199, 218, 253

Barbara Stocking
(Chief Executive, Oxfam)
100, 109, **110**, 121, **154**, 276, 383, 384

Claire Bertschinger
(Red Cross Nurse; Lecturer; Muse, Live Aid) 69, 135, **136**, **190**, 207, **272**, 273, **342**, 343, **376**, 377, **383**, **384**

Daphne Minihane
(Dame, Order of St Gregory the Great; Chair, Help the Aged, Jersey)
112, 114, **386**, 388

Barkha Dutt
(NDTV anchorwoman; War Correspondent)
127, **254**, 256, 277, **320**, 321, 382, 384

Clare Beckwith
(TV-presenter)
34, 35, 345

Dawn Airey
(Managing Director, BSkyB TV)
100, 131, 265, **266**, 282, **390**, 391

Beverly Payeff-Masey
(Neuro-design pioneer)
22, 23, 116, 197, **200**, 229, 230, **354**

Clare Short
(Labour MP, Ladywood; former Minister for Overseas Development)
70, 71, **302**, 304, **326**, 328

Devaki Jain
(Economist)
56, 57, 327

Bronwen Viscountess Astor
(Psychotherapist; former BBC Newsreader)
78, 79, 174, **176**, **314**, 315

Connie Jackson
(Financial and Strategy Consultant for non-profit organizations)
24, **28**, 261, **266**, 267, 367, **368**

Dhun Adenwalla
(Founder, Oral Home for the Deaf)
362, 363

395

Diana Cooper
(Broadcaster; Author; Founder World Angel Day)
182, 183, **212**, 213

Divya Mathur
(Author)
352, 353

The late Elizabeth Diggory
(High Mistress, St Paul's Girl's School)
56, 57, 119

Diana England
(Textile Artist; Co-ordinator, the Millennium Tapestry)
334, 335

Doreen Miller
(Baroness; Women's Campaigner; Entrepreneur)
157, **158**, 299, **302**

Emily Payne
(International Market Consultant)
196

Diane Abbott
(Labour MP, Hackney & Stoke Newington; Broadcaster) 53, **54**, 100, 204, **206**, 287, 301, **302**, 322, **368**, 369

Dorothy Boux
(Author; Calligrapher)
64, 65, **212**, 215, 226, **232**, 233

Esther Rantzen
(Broadcaster; Founder of Childline)
24, **28**, 85, **86**, 172, **214**, 241, **242**, **330**, 332, **342**, 343

Diane Burton
(Artist & Illustrator)
152, 153

Dorothy Dalton
(Founder, Journey of A Lifetime Trust; former CEO, ACENVO)
60, 61, 80, **200**, 201, **340**, 341, 353

Eve Ensler
(Award-winning Playwright; Founder of V-day)
104, 323, **324**, **334**, 336

Dina Glouberman
(Psychotherapist; Author; Founder Skyros Holistic Holidays)
136, 137

Eirwen Harbottle
(Founder, Centre for International Peace Building) 121, **122**, **136**, 138, 160, 169

Eve Pollard
(Former Editor, *Sunday Mirror* & *Sunday Express*; Broadcaster)
36, 37, **82**, 83, 155, 160, **268**, 269

Dina Vakil
(Editor, *Times of India*)
130, **132**, 167

Elaine Attias
(Film Producer; Journalist) 21, **22**, 36, 37, **76**, 77, 100, 202, **372**, 374

Farzana Contractor
(CEO, *Afternoon Newspaper* and *Upper Crust* magazine)
22, 21, **234**

Dinah Radtke
(Chair, Disabled People International Women's Committee; Vice-Chair, DPI) 25, **28**, 167, 237, **362**, 365

Elena Ragozhina
(Founder, Russian Media House)
190

Frances Alexander
(Founder, Women Welcome Women)
271, **272**

A GALAXY OF STARS

Frances Cairncross
(Rector, Exeter College, Oxford; President, British Association)
60, 61, 157, 211, **212**, **248**, 276, **326**, 327

Harriet Crabtree
Director, Interfaith
94, 95

Isabel Morgan
(Executive Producer, Christian Aid TV; former Producer *Roving Report*)
101, **122**, 126

Françoise Vergès
(Academic; holder, Francoise Seligmann Foundation Prize against Racism)
368, 371

Helen Alexander
(Chief Executive, *The Economist*)
119, 157, **158**

Jackie Ballard
(Director-General, RSPCA; former Liberal MP) **168**, 171, **224**, 226, **358**, 360

Gillian Beer
(Dame; Emeritus Prof. of English; President of Clare Hall, Cambridge)
45, **46**, 55, 237, **380**, 381

Helen Gurley Brown
(Founder President, *Cosmopolitan* magazine) 68, **70**, 169, 274, 289, **310**, **314**, 315, **340**, 341

Jan Morgan
(Former President, International Women's Forum, UK; MD, Grosvenor International)
103, **344**, 346

Gillian Clarke
(Oxfam Trustee)
33, **34**

Helena Kennedy
(Baroness; QC; former Chair, British Council; President, SOAS)
101, **154**, **214**, **296**, 298, **358**, 359

Jane Grant
(former Director, National Alliance of Women's Organizations)
204, **206**, **330**, 331, **362**, 364

Glenda Jackson
(Labour MP, Hampstead & Highgate; Oscar-winning Actress) **16**, 24, **198**, **302**, 303, **340**, 341

Hilary Blume
(Founder Director, Charities Advisories Trust);
101, 245, **246**, 329

Jennifer Gretton
(Lady; Lord Lieutenant of Leicestershire)
158, 159, **342**, 343

Gwyneth Lewis
(Poet Laureate, Wales)
69, **70**, **334**, 336, **362**, 364

Holly Sargent
(Senior Associate Dean, University of Harvard)
33, **34**, 155, **324**, 325

Jeroo Roy
(Artist and Children's Book Illustrator)
16, 15, **98**, 99, **292**, 294, 337

Han Feng
(International Designer)
45, **46**, 47

Indu Jain
(Chair, *Times of India* Group)
100, 125, 193, **194**

Jo Williams
(Dame; Chief Executive, MENCAP)
85, **86**, 95

397

Joan Davies
(First Woman Lecturer, Sandhurst Academy; First woman Chair, Electoral Reform Soc.)
64, 65, **110**, **111**, **292**, 293

Karen Anand
(Celebrity Chef; Broadcaster; Author; Entrepreneur)
140, 142, 347, 348

Kiran Bedi
(First woman UN Civilian Police Advisor; former Prison Governor)
168, 170, **278**, 280, 287

Jo-Anne Nadler
(Political Author and BBC Journalist)
76, 79, 301, **302**, 348, 349

Karen Cox
(Professor, Head of School of Nursing, Nottingham University)
272, 273

Kirsten Rausing
(Board member, Tetra Laval Group; International Horse-breeder) 24, **28**, **70**, 71, 96, 100, **268**, 269, **354**

Judith Chomsky
(Human Rights Attorney, Center for Constitutional Rights)
78, 80, 111, **292**, 295, 353

Karen King-Aribisala
(Lecturer and Commonwealth prize-winning Author)
156, **158**

Kusoom Vadgama
(Doctor of optometry; Author & Historian)
36, 37, 124, **128**, 189, 204

Judith Kendra
(Publishing Director)
115, **118**, 274

Kate Harcourt
(Dame, New Zealand; Actress)
81, **82**, **152**, 153

Kusum Haider
(Actress)
121, **122**, 161

Julia Middleton
(CEO, Common Purpose)
78, 79, 192,

Kate Parminter
(Former CEO CPRE; Trustee, Institute of Public Policy and Research)
132, 133, **354**

Lakshmi Shankar
(Renowned Indian Classical Vocalist)
64, 65, 91, 205, 241, **242**

Julia Neuberger
(Baroness; Rabbi; Broadcaster; former Chief Executive, Kings Fund)
193, **194**, **234**, **368**, 370

Katherine Whitehorn
(Award-winning Journalist; Author; Agony Aunt)
85, **86**, 119, 157, 172, **288**, 289

Leila Seth
(First Woman Chief Justice to the High Court of India)
54, 55, 120, **122**, **188**, 189, 199, 295, **296**, 297

Julie Mellor
(Partner, PriceWater-houseCoopers; former Chair, Equal Opportunities Comm.)
138, **140**, 156

Kazue Hatano
(Japan's foremost Stage Designer)
144, **146**, 187, **284**, 285

Leonora van Gils
(The Reverend; Founder, Human Dolphin Institute)
48, **196**, **208**, 210

A GALAXY OF STARS

Lesley Abdela
(Founder, 300 Group;
Chief Executive,
Project Parity)
93, **94**, 283, **284**, 320,
321, 327, 357, **358**

The late Lucie Aubrac
(French Resistance
Heroine)
26, **28**, **112**, 113, 201, 275

Maggie Bellis
(Director, Transport for
London)
68, 115, **118**, 269, 273

Lila Poonawalla
(Chair, Tetra Laval
Group, India)
122, 123, **158**, 160, 265,
266, 276, 287, **386**
387

Lynn Jones Parry
(Co-President,
Women's International
Forum; Biologist)
161, **188**, 191

Mahabanoo Mody-
Kotwal
(Actress)
330, 337, **344**, 345

Lily Thapa
(Founder, Nepalese
Women for Human
Rights)
175, **176**, **330**, 331

Lynne Franks
(PR consultant;
Founder, SEED, women's
empowerment
programmes) **58**, 59,
208, 209, 274, 375, **376**

Maharani Bibhu
Kumari Devi of
Tripura
(Politician)
16, 27, 160, 163, 192

Lindiwe Mabuza
(HE, High Comm of the
Republic of South
Africa to Britain)
91, **92**, 120, **122**

Lyutha Al-Mughairy
(Head of UN Communi-
cations; formerly a
pioneering broadcaster
in the Middle East)
91, **92**, 245, **246**

Maja Daruwala
(Dir, Commonwealth
Human Rights Initiative)
38, **39**, 85, 115, 200, 203,
213, 296, 297, 367, **368**

Lindsay Rosenhead
(Assoc Head, School of
Design and Media,
Westminster
University)
254, 255, **268**, 270

Madhuri Dixit
(Bollywood Icon)
24, **200**, 202, **254**, 255

Maleeha Lodhi
(Pakistani High Comm
to Britain; Member, UN
Board on Disarmament;
former Editor of *The
News*) 117, **118**, 375, **376**

Lisette Talate
(Vice-Pres, Chagossian
Refugee Council;
nominated for Nobel
Peace Prize in 2005)
60, 63, 189, 319, **320**

Maeve Sherlock
(Chief Executive,
Refugee Council;
former President,
National Student's
Union) **22**, 24, 370

Margaret Lobo
(Director, Otakar Kraus
Music Trust)
40, 43, 282

Liz Jackson
(MD, Great Guns
Marketing; former
Business Woman of
the Year)
228, 361, **362**

Mae-Wan Ho
(Director, Institute of
Science in Society)
21, **22**, **94**, 95, 117, **118**,
139, 232, 235, 243

Margaret Owen
(Founder, Widows for
Peace and Democracy)
38, **39**, 48, **176**, 177, 347

399

Margaret Sheehy
(Cultural Animateur)
258, 261, 319, **320**

Meera Gandhi
(UN Goodwill
Ambassador; Author
and Humanitarian)
390, 391

Nadya
(Fashion Designer)
82, 83, 139, **140**, 167

Marian Rivman
(New York PR
Consultant)
81, **82**, **140**, 141, 171, **292**, 294, 349, 355

Meher Banaji
(Principal, Happy
Home and School for
the Blind)
330, 332, 347

Nafis Sadik
(Exec Dir, UN
Population Fund)
58, 59, 80, 193, **258**, 261, **284**, 285

Marigold Verity
(Harpist and Singer)
198, **214**, **250**, 253

Meher Master Moos
(Dame; Professor of
Law; Founder,
Zoroastrian Monastery)
66, 67, 87, 133

Naina Lal Kidwai
(CEO, HSBC Bank,
India)
162, 164, 222, 277

Marjorie Scardino
(Dame; CEO, Pearson
Group Plc)
100, **154**, **358**, 359, **384**, 385

Meher Heroyce Moos
(Traveller and social
commentator)
78, 79, 144, **146**, 319, **320**

Nita Deerpalsing
(Mauritian Member of
Parliament)
253, **254**, **306**, 308, **352**, 353

Martina Milburn
(Chief Executive, The
Prince's Trust)
60, 61, **94**, 95, 101, 116, **118**, 275

Miranda Macpherson
(The Reverend;
Founder, Interfaith
Seminary) 15, **16**, 81, **82**, **208**, 209, 219, 241, **242**, 377

Noreena Hertz
(CIBAM Fellow,
Cambridge University;
Assoc Dir., Centre for
International Business)
205, **206**, **284**, 285

Mary Marsh
(Dame; Chief
Executive, NSPCC)
172, **314**, 315, **344**, 345

Mithali Raj
(Captain, Women's
Indian Cricket Team)
86, 87

Oonagh Shanley-Toffolo
(Former nun; Princess
Diana's Spiritual guide
and healer)
196, **230**, 231

Maureen Mannion
(Interpretative Actress,
Jersey Heritage Trust)
190

Mother
390

Padma Bandhopadya
(First Woman Air
Marshal)
54, 55, 84, 287, **288**

A GALAXY OF STARS

Parvin Ali
(Founding Director, Fatima Women's Network)
184, **188**, 211, **212**, 349, **380**, 381

Petra Dobmeier
(Ecologist)
333, **334**

Rakhi Sarkar
(Founder, International Centre for Modern Art)
78, 80, 101

Patricia Bardon
(Opera Singer)
101, **110**, 113

Pheroza Godrej
(Author; Founder, Cymroza Art Gallery)
64, 65, 253, **254**, 389, 390

Ramma Bans
(Fitness Guru)
192, 202, 257, **258**, **268**, 269

Patricia Daver
(Aesthetician)
256, **258**, 271, **272**, **292**, 293

Phyllis Krystal
(Spiritual Giantess and Author)
16, 26, **46**, 47, **220**, 222, 223, 241, 244, **314**, 315

Rekha Mody
(Founder, Divya Chaya & Stree Shakti Trusts; Publisher)
26, **28**, 104, **358**, 361

Patricia Licuanan
(Pres, Miriam College, Philippines; Chair, UN Beijing Conference for Women)
74, **76**, 77, 95, 261

Pim Baxter
(Director, Communications & Development, National Portrait Gallery)
138, **140**, 274

Rennie Fritchie
(Baroness; Comm. for Public Appointments, Cabinet Office)
188, 191, 211, **212**, **246**, 247, **372**, 373

Patsy Robertson
(Chair, Comm Assoc; former Dir of Information at Commonwealth Secretariat)
200, 202, **348**, 351

Rachel Oliver
(Former Director of Communications, National Farmers' Union)
50, 52, 165

Renuka Chowdhury
(Indian Minister of State for Women & Child Development)
152, 153, 164, 165, 204, 286, 305, **306**, 323

Paula Garton
(Astrologer)
181, **182**, 184

Radha Chandrashekaran
(Mixed Media Artist and Researcher Indigenous Art)
139, **140**

Rhona MacDonald
(Doctor, Médecins Sans Frontières; Asst Editor BMJ)
362, 363

Pera Wells
(Secretary-General, World Federation of UN Associations; former Australian Diplomat)
167, **168**, **288**, 289

Rajmata Gayatri Devi of Jaipur
(Politician)
252, **254**

Rifat Wahhab
(Organizational Consultant for learning, development and health)
51, **54**, 55, 91, 95, 199, 204, **340**, 341, 369

401

Rosa María Juárez
(Founder & President, Mexican Franchise and Networking Institute)
206, 207, **234**, 237, **284**, 286

Sallie Gratch
(Founder, Kesher Project) 166, 195, **266**, 267, 329

Shakira Caine
(Artist)
40, 41, **92**, 93, 155, 191, **250**, 252, 389, **390**

Rosalyn Dexter
(Building design guru)
44, **46**, 84, **86**, 138, 166, 187

Sanjna Kapoor
(Theatre Director, Prithvi Theatre)
44, **46**, **98**, 99, 353

Shami Chakrabarti
(Director of Liberty)
284, 286, **296**, 298, **368**, 370

Rosemary Perry
(The Reverend; Analytical Past life Hypnotherapist & Homeopath) 181, **182**, 212, 213, **248**, 389, **390**

Sarah Miles
(Actress; Author)
33, **34**, 62, 79, 151, **152**, 172, 181, **182**, **248**, 253

Sharon Choa
(Artistic Director and Conductor, Anglia Chamber Orchestra)
198, **278**, 282, **352**, 353

Ruth Powys
(Charity PR consultant and campaigner)
102, 105, 322, **324**

Sarida Brown
(Founder Editor, *Caduceus Journal*, healing for people, community and planet) 33, **34**, 350

Shauna Crockett-Burrows
(Founding Editor, *Positive News & Living Lightly*)
212, 213, **310**, 313

Ruth Uglow
(Holder, Royal Overseas League Scholarship for Visual Arts) 140, 141, **348**, 349

Sathya Saran
(Editor, India's first weekly magazine *ME*; former Editor *Femina*)
78, 79, 163, **182**, 183, **258**, 259

Sheila Dikshit
(Chief Minister of Delhi)
156, **158**, 172, **306**, 307, 349

Sadhvi Bhagwati Saraswati
(Sanyas) 125, **128**, **182**, 183, **208**, 210, 243, 388

Selja Kumari
(Indian Minister of State for Urban Employment & Poverty Alleviation)
305, **306**

Shernaaz Engineer
(Journalist; Editor)
35, **36**, 183, **194**, 195, **352**, 353

Sai Paranjpye
(Film-director; Scriptwriter; Chair, Children's Film Society, India)
205, **206**

Shahnaz Husain
(Founder, Cosmetics Empire)
200, 202, 255, **386**, 387

Shernaz Vakil
(Managing Director, Dai-ichi Karkaria Industries)
344, 345

A GALAXY OF STARS

Shireen Irani
(Lawyer)
198, 355

Shireen Isal
(Impresario; Founding
Director, Sangam
Association)
56, 57

Shusha Guppy
(Author; Singer and
Persian Songwriter)
162, 164, 191, 207, **380**,
381

Shyama Perera
(TV-presenter; Author
and Journalist)
186, **188**

Simone Poonawalla
(Horse-breeder)
76, 79, 103

Simone Tata
(Director, Tata
Industries)
60, 61, **112**, 114

Sister Cecily Pavri
(Singaporean
Educationalist)
220, 221, 388

Sister Cyril
(Pioneering
educationalist;
Headmistress, Loreto
Day School)
128, 129, **220**, 221, 240

Sister Nirmala
(Superior General,
Missionaries of
Charity; Mother
Teresa's successor)
220, 221, 227

Sooni Taraporevala
(Award-winning
Screenwriter;
Photographer)
130, **132**, **358**, 360

Susan Douglas
(Director, Condé Nast
Publishing International;
former Ed. of *Mail on
Sunday* & Dep Ed. *Sunday
Times*) 85, 100, **310**, 312

Sue Stapely
(Director, Quiller
Consultants; former
Head of PR at Law
Society) **50**, 52, **168**,
171, 195, **234**

Sukey Cameron
(Representative,
Falklands Islands; Chair,
BIOT) 90, **92**, 169, 274,
342, 343

Swamini Kaliji
(Founder, TriYoga
International Centres)
25, **28**

Taleya Rehman
(Broadcaster; Director
of Democracy Watch,
Bangladesh)
143, **146**

Tamsin Larby
(Director, V-DAY until
the Violence Stops
Campaign; Actress)
38, 39, 356, **358**

Teresa Hale
(Founder, Hale Clinic
for Complementary
Medicine)
236, **246**, 249

Thelma Holt
(Producer, National
Theatre)
33, **34**, 144, **206**, 207

Tracy Worcester
(Marchioness; Assoc
Dir, International
Society for Ecology
and Culture)
49, **50**

Tricia Sibbons
(Social Entrepreneur;
Founder, South Africa
Memorial) **66**, 69, 117,
188, 189, **232**, 236, 343

Usha Devi Rathore
(Princess of Burdwan;
Yoga Teacher
15, **16**, 51, 185

403

Usha Prashar
(Baroness; CS Com;
Chair of Parole Board &
Judiciary Appointments
Commission) **66**, 67,
93, 100, 269, 300, **302**

Uta Frith
(Professor in Cognitive
Development; FRS,
Fellow, BAMS) **56**, 57,
159, 160, 191, 215, **278**,
281

Vanessa Hall-Smith
(Director; British
Institute, Florence)
348, 349

Venu Dhupa
(Director, Arts &
Creativity, British
Council) 44, **46**, 115,
253, 287

Vivienne Faull
(The Very Reverend;
Dean of Leicester
Cathedral) 68, 163, **278**,
280, 325, 374

**Wendy Fortescue-
Hubbard**
(Maths Agony Aunt)
101, **128**, 129, 150

Wendy Luers
(Founder, Justice in
Times of Transition)
161, **352**, 355

Wendy Savage
(Prof. of Gynaecology;
Champion of Women's
Rights in Childbirth)
58, 59, **132**, 133, **248**,
288, 290

Wendy Somes
(Prima Ballerina, Royal
Ballet) 100, 151, **152**, 241,
242

Yue-Sai Kan
(TV personality; Author;
Founder of a cosmetic
empire; immortalised
on stamps in China)
16, 24, 100, **258**, 260

Zakia Hakki
(Iraqi MP; First Woman
Judge in the Middle
East) 24, **28**, 91, 109,
110, 207, 215

Zandra Rhodes
(International Designer;
Founder of the Fashion
and Textile Museum)
40, 41, **152**, 153, 265

Zeba Kohli
(CEO, Fantasia
Chocolates) **98**, 99,
162, 164, 253, **348**, 349

Zena Sorabjee
(Chair, Baha'i House of
Worship; Chair of
Lotus Charitable Trust)
67, **196**

Zenobia Nadirshaw
(Professor; Head of
Psychology,
Kensington & Chelsea;
Govenor Metropolitan
University) 102, **214**, 253

Zerbanoo Gifford
(Human Rights
Campaigner; Author;
Founder, Asha
Foundation)

Zerbanoo Gifford

Author, human rights campaigner and founder of the ASHA Foundation, Zerbanoo Gifford holds the International Woman of the Year Award 2006 for her humanitarian work, which spans over thirty years of grassroots and global activism. In 1989, Zerbanoo was presented with the Nehru Centenary Award for her work championing the rights of women, children and minorities. Pioneer for Asian Women in British politics, she chaired the Commission 'Looking into ethnic minority involvement in British Life' and was a member of the advisory group to the British Home Secretary. A former director of Anti-Slavery International, she was awarded the Freedom of the City of Lincoln, Nebraska, for her work combating modern slavery and racism.

Zerbanoo has authored *The Golden Thread: Asian Experience in post-Raj Britain*; *Dadabhai Naoroji: Britain's first non-white Member of Parliament*; *Asian Presence in Europe*; *Celebrating India's 50 Year Anniversary*; *Thomas Clarkson and the Campaign Against the Slave Trade*.

As the director of ASHA Foundation and ASHA Centre, Zerbanoo actively promotes philanthropy and peace worldwide.

Zerbanoo means *Golden Lady* in Persian.

For more information on Zerbanoo, see
www.zerbanoogifford.org
www.asha-foundation.org

Thank you

The proceeds from the sale of this book will go to the ASHA Centre, an international retreat for greater peace and understanding amongst diverse communities. Located in the beautiful surroundings of the Forest of Dean, England, the ASHA Centre fosters community participation through a holistic programme of performing and visual arts, conservation projects and personal transformation.

The ASHA Centre embodies the inclusive vision of the remarkable women featured in this book. As a collective noble endeavour, I invite you to contribute to the ASHA Foundation's marvellous work with communities around the globe. The Centre seeks to harness the skills, ideas and participation of all people working towards positive change. The work at the Centre will engage and inspire you, as much as it is enriched by your involvement. If you have an interest in making a positive change in the world, we want to hear from you!

'Of course, money is always welcome. Please buy as many copies of this book as possible for your family and friends, as all the money goes directly to the ASHA Foundation's charitable work. Every woman in this book expressed in her own unique way that in life you reap what you sow. Your generosity to the work of the ASHA Centre will also blossom, bear fruit and bring joy to you and many others. From everybody who will benefit, a big thank you!'

Visit ASHA Centre's website and find out how you can do more and how to purchase more copies of this book. **www.asha-foundation.org**

The ASHA Centre, Gunn Mill House, Lower Spout Lane, Mitcheldean Gloucestershire GL17 0EA
E-mail: info@ashacentre.org Website: www.ashacentre.org

ASHA comes from the Sanskrit root meaning '*eternal law*', '*the inherent nature of existence*'. In Avestan Persian ASHA means '*the righteous way*' and '*divine justice*'. In many languages it also means '*hope*'.

MINES001/1762/05.08